Managing as Designing

Managing as Designing

EDITED BY RICHARD J. BOLAND JR.
AND FRED COLLOPY

Stanford Business Books

An imprint of Stanford University Press
Stanford, California   2004

Library of Congress Cataloging-in-Publication Data

Managing as designing / edited by Richard J. Boland, Jr. and
Fred Collopy.
     p. cm.
   Includes bibliographical references and index.
   ISBN 0-8047-4674-5
     1. Production management.   I. Boland, Richard.
II. Collopy, Fred.
TS155.M33215 2004
658.4'01—dc22   2004007558

Typeset by G&S Book Services in 10/12.5 Electra

Original Printing 2004

Last figure below indicates year of this printing:

13   12   11   10   09   08   07   06   05   04

Special discounts for bulk quantities of Stanford Business Books
are available to corporations, professional associations, and
other organizations. For details and discount information, contact the special sales department of Stanford University Press.
Tel: (650) 736-1783, Fax: (650) 736-1784

CONTENTS

Acknowledgments

The Managing as Designing workshop on which this collection is based, as well as the Managing as Designing DVD, available at http://design.case.edu, was funded by the Weatherhead School of Management, the National Science Foundation (SES-0132757), and the S. Rose Company.

Preface

THIS BOOK emerges from an interest in design and design thinking that has been nurtured by the two of us for almost thirty years. It reflects our belief, and that of the many distinguished scholars, artists, and managers who participated in creating the book, that more widespread design thinking among organization leaders is desirable for the creation of a humanly satisfying and sustainable future. Design thinking is crucially important for managers, but remains overlooked in much management practice and education. We believe that if managers approached their problem solving as the best designers do, that organizations, products, services, and processes would be more functional and better able to create lasting value in society. Today, management is in a crisis, but that very fact makes it possible for us to envision wholly new approaches to its practices and responsibilities. Our hope is that *Managing as Designing* opens new horizons for the practice of management and presents guiding images for the future.

For the last fifty years, management education has followed a path of least resistance and embraced formulas for approaching organizational problems that have outlived their usefulness. The possibility that managers could be revered as true leaders in society with a valued set of ideas, skills, and competencies to offer is profoundly threatened. Managers now operate under a cloud of suspicion that self-interest, shortsightedness, and failed morals are their hallmark. The centuries-old dream of rags to riches through the creation of unique products and services that had energized our economic growth has degenerated into the dream of the deal, the belief that some exotic financial transaction or stock market leveraging are the preferred paths to wealth.

For example, in the face of overwhelming evidence that growth through acquisitions does not lead to sustainable, value-creating organizations, CEOs still play that tired hand in an espoused effort to "maximize value" for stockholders (for example, Tyco and AOL Time Warner). More likely, the desire of obtaining personal wealth through the dream of the deal is the prime motivator. But the dream of the deal does not create true value for society. It does not create jobs, does not provide new products or services, does not develop new technologies, does not draw on our highest ideals as human beings, and leads to a famine of ideas in management. No wonder there is a cynical view toward managers in the global economy today.

But that cynical view of "big business" overlooks the managers and companies that do operate with a taste for creating value in society by the old-fashioned way of taking bold initiatives to design products and processes that create growth in the economy. This is especially true of smaller, entrepreneurial firms, which are the only reliable engine for growth in jobs and ideas on the world stage. The above characterization refers to the professional managers who are trained by schools of management and their MBA programs to take a place in the corporations, consulting firms, and financial houses that make up the most visible and powerful bulk of our global economy. Those are the sites of design mediocrity created and sustained by a culture of management education that focuses on training students to make choices among the alternatives presented to them, rather than training them to design new alternatives. This book is an attempt to stimulate change in management practice and education. Its creation was motivated by our good fortune to work on the Peter B. Lewis Building project with the architect Frank Gehry and his associates as described more fully in Chapter 1. We were inspired by the power of his design thinking and the almost universal interest in his creations — especially the Guggenheim Museum in Bilbao, Spain, and the Walt Disney Concert Hall in Los Angeles — to believe that the moment was right for beginning an effort to bring ideas from great designers to bear on management practice and education.

This book grew from an invited workshop held at the Weatherhead School of Management in June 2002 that brought together a stellar collection of scholars, artists, and managers to explore the implications of taking the manager's role and responsibility as a designer more seriously. Attendees represented a wide range of disciplines including, among others, architecture, sociology, design, history, choreography, strategy, economics, music, accounting, and product development, as well as managers of for-profit and not-for-profit organizations. Frank Gehry opened the workshop with a keynote address on his design process and approach to management. Karl Weick, Rensis Likert Professor of Management at the University of Michigan, gave a keynote on the second day of the workshop, using Frank Gehry's design process to recast our concept of organization design. Those two talks are included as Chapters 2 and 3 in Part I. The balance of the book is composed of short contributions on aspects of design that are relevant to understanding and implementing managing as designing.

Before the workshop, each participant wrote an initial statement on design intended to provoke discussion. They provided material to spark large and small group discussions during the workshop; these pieces were rewritten after the workshop in light of the ideas generated. We are very proud to be associated with the many wonderfully insightful papers in this volume and hope the reader shares our enthusiasm for them. Each paper is short and self-contained, intended for reading and reflection in its own right, but the contributions are grouped into book parts by theme, with each part arranged to provide a narrative flow within the theme. The book concludes with an initial vocabulary of design for management, which draws from the keynotes, the contributions, and the workshop discussions.

Part I sets the stage for considering management as a design discipline. Part II explores some intellectual foundations for approaching managing as designing. The chapters in Part II consider the design act from theoretical positions ranging from phenomenology to ethics, touching on the structure of argument, the relation of form and function, and the role of language. Part III presents a number of experiences of design practice and what we can learn from them. The theme of those chapters is to reveal the experience of design thinking and design action to understand better how organizations are shaped through design. They pay special attention to the role of collaboration in design projects and its importance for successful designs. Part IV presents some images for the road forward and an initial vocabulary of design terms raised during the workshop and developed in the book.

Moving management practice and education toward design thinking will take many years, and these papers can serve as anchor points for guiding that long process. Changes in management education, public policy, and management practice will all play a part in making managers better designers. The vocabulary of design is a tangible place to begin transforming management education and practice toward a design attitude. A design vocabulary alone is not going to effect change, but using it in our everyday practice, teaching, and researching about management, in ways that bring the words to life in action settings, will. We hope that readers will add to the vocabulary from their own experience and will adopt a design attitude toward their problem solving, so that in the future more managers think of themselves as designers who contribute to human betterment.

Richard J. Boland Jr.
Fred Collopy
design.case.edu

I   MANAGING AND DESIGNING

THIS SECTION PRESENTS *an overview and introduction to the topic of managing as designing. We begin Part I by recounting the experience of working with Frank Gehry on the design of the Peter B. Lewis Building. It stimulated our thinking about the design attitude — both its power and its promise — and its peculiar absence from most considerations of managing. Next, the keynote speech by Frank Gehry presents reflections on his own process of design and his approach to managing his architectural firm. This is followed by Karl Weick's keynote talk in which he uses Frank Gehry's design process as an inspiration to rethink the familiar topic of organization design. Moving back and forth from the design of VISA and the creation of Gehry's architecture, Weick provides a most compelling vision of how managers can work toward good designs. Finally, Richard Buchanan discusses how designing and managing are inescapably intertwined and as a result, design principles should permeate and inform management practice at all levels and stages of an organization. He describes how he and colleagues at Carnegie Mellon's School of Design have been applying design principles to guide large-scale organizational interventions, using the approach of interaction design.*

1

DESIGN MATTERS FOR MANAGEMENT

Richard J. Boland Jr. and Fred Collopy

RECENTLY, OUR faculty had the good fortune to work with the world-renowned architect Frank O. Gehry and his firm, Gehry Partners, on the design and construction of the Peter B. Lewis Building as a new home for the Weatherhead School of Management. During the four and one-half years of working with Gehry Partners on the planning, design, and construction of the Lewis Building, we experienced an approach to problem solving that is quite different from our own, from that of the managers we study, and from what we teach to our students. We refer to this unique mind-set and approach to problem solving as a *design attitude*.

A DESIGN ATTITUDE

We believe that if managers adopted a design attitude, the world of business would be different and better. Managers would approach problems with a sensibility that swept in the broadest array of influences to shape inspiring and energizing designs for products, services, and processes that are both profitable and humanly satisfying. Gehry's approach to problems reflects the entrepreneurial spirit that was at the heart of the industrial and information revolutions. He approaches each new project with a desire to do something differently and better than he has done before and to experiment with materials, technologies, and methods in his quest. Working with him has led us to see

Richard J. Boland Jr., *Weatherhead School of Management, Case Western Reserve University and University of Cambridge.* Fred Collopy, *Weatherhead School of Management, Case Western Reserve University.*

how both management practice and education have allowed a limited and narrow vocabulary of decision making to drive an expansive and embracing vocabulary of design out of circulation. In our focus on teaching students advanced analytical techniques for choosing among alternatives, our attention to strengthening their design skills for shaping new alternatives has withered. What is needed in management practice and education today is the development of a design attitude, which goes beyond default solutions in creating new possibilities for the future.

A decision attitude toward problem solving is used extensively in management education. It portrays the manager as facing a set of alternative courses of action from which a choice must be made. The decision attitude assumes it is easy to come up with alternatives to consider, but difficult to choose among them. The design attitude toward problem solving, in contrast, assumes that it is difficult to design a good alternative, but once you have developed a truly great one, the decision about which alternative to select becomes trivial. The design attitude appreciates that the cost of not conceiving of a better course of action than those that are already being considered is often much higher than making the "wrong" choice among them.

The decision attitude toward problem solving and the many decision-making tools we have developed for supporting it have strengths that make them suitable for certain situations. In a clearly defined and stable situation, when the feasible alternatives are well known, a decision attitude may be the most efficient and effective way to approach problem solving. But when those conditions do not hold, a design attitude is required. The decision attitude and the analytic tools managers have to support it were developed in a simpler time. They are the product of fifty years of concerted effort to strengthen the mathematical and scientific basis of management education. Today's world is much different from that of the 1950s when the movement to expand analytic techniques in management began to flourish. We are suggesting that now is the time to incorporate a better balance of the two approaches to problem solving in management practice and education.

The premise of this book is that managers are designers as well as decision makers and that although the two are inextricably linked in management action, we have for too long emphasized the decision face of management over the design face.

AN EXAMPLE OF THE DESIGN ATTITUDE

Toward the end of the design process for the Lewis Building, there was a need to reduce the floor space by about 4,500 square feet. One of us traveled to Gehry's Santa Monica offices and worked with the project architect, Matt Fineout, on the problem. We first identified those miscellaneous spaces that had to be squeezed into the smaller footprint (tea kitchens, closets, rest rooms, storage areas, and spaces for copiers, fax machines, and printers). There were many constraints to be met including proximity to classrooms and offices, "ownership" by various departments and research centers, and circulation patterns in each area. We went through the floor plans, beginning with the lower level and working our way up to the fifth floor. The process took two days.

Working with large sheets of onionskin paper laid on top of floor plans, we would sketch possible arrangements until we had something we all agreed was a good solution. Then we would transfer the arrangement in red pencil onto the plans. Each move of one element affected others and often required backtracking and revising previously located elements. Many times during the two days, we would reach a roadblock where things were just not working out, so we would start with a clean sheet of onionskin and try a different approach. At the end of two days, it was a tremendous sense of accomplishment to have succeeded in locating all the required elements into the reduced floor sizes. We were working at a large table and Matt was leaning far onto it, marking the final changes. As he pushed back from the table, we were joking about how tedious the process had been and how glad we were to have it over. As we joked, Matt gathered all the sheets of onionskin and the marked-up floor plans, stacked them, and then grabbed an edge and tore them in half. Then he crumpled the pieces and threw them in the trashcan in the corner of the room. This was a shock! What was he doing? In a matter-of-fact tone, he said, "We proved we could do it, now we can think about how we *want* to do it."

What was going on there? A perfectly good solution had been worked out. It responded to all of our requirements and fulfilled the needs of the program. And it was difficult to accomplish. Why tear it up? A very different mind-set for approaching problems was evident here. Was this approach to problem solving an aberration of no consequence, or was it worth figuring out and considering its implications for management generally? The design approach of Frank Gehry and his associates may not mirror the work practices of the vast majority of architects. But he is one of the most successful and highly regarded architects of our day, and we believe there is something in his approach to problem solving that is an important part of his success. Bringing at least the flavor of his design thinking and design attitude to managers stimulated both the workshop and this book. Like the plans that Matt tore up that day, the ideas in this book are not meant to be the end point of managing as designing. They just show that we can do it—we can rethink managing as designing. The question is, how do we as managers want to do our designing?

6   THE DECISION ATTITUDE

A decision attitude toward problem solving is overwhelmingly dominant in management practice and education today. It solves problems by making rational choices among alternatives and uses tools such as economic analysis, risk assessment, multiple criteria decision making, simulation, and the time value of money. But for all the power of analytic approaches to problem solving, they share a central weakness in that they take as given the alternative courses of action from which the manager is to choose. The decision attitude is concerned with the various techniques, methods, algorithms, and heuristics that a manger can use in making such choices. In other words, it starts with an assumption that the alternative courses of action are ready at hand — that there is a good set of options already available, or at least readily obtainable. This is a decidedly passive view of the decision maker as a problem solver, and one that makes the untenable assumption that the alternatives that are on the table, or the first ones we will think of, include the best ones. The design attitude, in contrast, is concerned with finding the best answer possible, given the skills, time, and resources of the team, and takes for granted that it will require the invention of new alternatives. So, the decision attitude is in the unrealistic position of assuming that good design work has already taken place, even though that is not usually the case. It is, therefore, doomed to mediocrity in its organizational outcomes.

Take the classic inventory control problem as an example. A decision attitude toward that problem has traditionally modeled the inventory process as a buffer between varying demands placed on different sections of the production, distribution, and consumption chain. That image became the default approach for thirty years, while research and teaching on inventory control worked to perfect that model and enable the best possible decision making about the timing, quantity, and location of inventory acquisitions. As a result, we have developed elegant and powerful techniques for calculating reorder points, economic lot sizes, and risks of stock outs, as well as for minimizing holding costs. But we also became more deeply enmeshed in a default model of the inventory process that carried with it its own form of closure. We were blinded for decades to the possibility that inventories could be minimized by different means, such as by rethinking how we design our production processes, our relations with suppliers, our workforce, and our information systems. Only when we broke from the decision attitude in thinking about inventory control and engaged in a design attitude, did we start to see how it was possible to take the elimination of inventory, rather than its management, as our goal in a lean manufacturing approach to production. The design attitude toward problem solving was a higher order approach that allowed us to step back from the decision-making techniques we had developed and ask the more fundamental question "what are we trying to do?"

The decision attitude is too susceptible to early closure of the problem-solving space, just as the design approach is too susceptible to keeping the search going long after it is beneficial. There is a time for openness and a time for closure in our project-based episodes of problem solving, and managers need to develop strength in both the decision and design attitudes.

WHY DESIGN MATTERS FOR MANAGEMENT NOW

It is commonplace today to note that management as a profession is in a difficult situation. The last few years have been a continuing tale of misdeeds, failures, and embarrassments. Both the fantasies of a "new economy" and the exuberance of the dot com bubble are things that the entire managerial establishment participated in creating. From government policy to investment banking to venture capitalists, to auditors, to educators, to stock analysts, the scope of complicity is almost universal. Where do we look for an explanation of failure on such a mass scale? Is it the complexity, uncertainty, and chaos of modern times that brought about the dot com bubble, or Enron, or Global Crossing, or First Capital, or the telecom collapse? Or is it something more fundamental? We argue that our everyday image of what a manager is, along with a specialized language of management education that has been developing for more than fifty years, has very much to do with it. The problem is rooted in the training of managers as decision makers and in the vocabulary of choice that is imbedded in our increasingly monoclonal MBA programs and their Executive Education arms.

The recent failings of management have been attributed to moral lapses or lack of adequate regulatory oversight, but that seems an unlikely or at best only partial cause. Over time, we will no doubt see additional regulation and a call for more ethics courses in management schools, but we do not believe that either of those attempts at remedies will be successful. That is because the failings of management are most directly attributed to a famine of good ideas. To take one highly visible example, Enron's management failed to make the earnings and cash flows it had promised and resorted to creating revenues and hiding debt through complex transactions because they didn't have sufficiently good ideas to make sales and profits in real ways. Off-balance-sheet financial manipulation was the best idea they had, and no matter how bad that idea was, they were not able to generate a better alternative.

Exotic methods of financial analysis do not create value. Only inventing and delivering new products, processes, and services that serve human needs can do that. But managers are not trained for that type of life. Instead, they are

8   trained and rewarded for being decision makers—to have alternatives presented to them from which they make choices by computing net present values, optimizing underassumed constraints, and trading off risks for returns. There is something tragically missing from management practice and education today, and missing even from our managerial icons. That missing element is an image of the manager as an idea generator who gives form to new possibilities with a well-developed vocabulary of design. Managers as form-givers care deeply about the world that is being shaped by a business and refuse to accept the default alternatives. They understand that the design of better products, processes, and services is their core responsibility. The design attitude is the source of those inventions. A decision does not generate inventions, no matter how advanced its analytic capabilities.

Management school faculty members should also consider how our own role as educators has played a part in bringing about the conditions and mindsets underlying recent events. Like it or not, management education is involved in the current problems of the corporate world and will also be involved in any reforms that help lead to a recovery of management's leadership role in society. More of the same does not seem to be a viable formula for the future of management education.

PRECEDENTS FOR A DESIGN ATTITUDE
IN MANAGEMENT THINKING

Herbert Simon, Nobel laureate in economics, wrote *The Sciences of the Artificial*, which is one of the finest examples we have of a well-developed theory of the design attitude for managers. Simon called for a new curriculum for management education based on design. He saw management as a profession whose training should follow that of engineering or architecture as an applied science, not that of the natural sciences. The manager's professional responsibility is not to discover the laws of the universe, but to act responsibly in the world to transform existing situations into more preferred ones. Simon held that, like the engineer or the architect, the manager is a form-giver who shapes organizations and economic processes. As he states in the preface to the second edition:

> Engineering, medicine, business, architecture, and painting are concerned not with the necessary but with the contingent—not how things are but how they might be—in short, with design. (Simon, 1996, p. xii.)

To summarize Simon's argument very briefly, humans have a limited cognitive capacity for reasoning when searching for a solution within a problem space. Given the relatively small size of our brain's working memory, we can only consider a few aspects of any situation and can only analyze them in a few ways. This is also true of computers, although the constraints are less obvious. The problem space that a manager deals with in her mind or in her computer is dependent on the way she represents the situation that she faces. The first step in any problem-solving episode is representing the problem, and to a large extent, that representation has the solution hidden within it. A decision attitude carries with it a default representation of the problem being faced, whereas a design attitude begins by questioning the way the problem is represented. To use Donald Schon's classic example, if we refer to an urban neighborhood as a blight it evokes a particular problem space where certain types of design intervention are seen as most appropriate (cutting out the blight, bringing in a fresh form of life). We have seen the results in town planning that flattened whole sections of a city and replaced them with more "healthy" elements. If we label the same area a folk community, we can marvel at the resilience of its social support networks and approach it with designs for strengthening its existing social infrastructure.

Simon concludes by asking us to strive for a kind of design that has no final goals beyond that of leaving more possibilities open to future generations than we ourselves inherited. He also asks us to avoid designs that create irreversible commitments for future generations and to strive to open ourselves to the largest number of diverse experiences possible, in order to allow us to draw from an ever-wider variety of idea sources in order to make our designs humanly satisfying as well as economically viable.

BASIC ELEMENTS OF A DESIGN ATTITUDE

By *design attitude*, we refer to the expectations and orientations one brings to a design project. A design attitude views each project as an opportunity for invention that includes a questioning of basic assumptions and a resolve to leave the world a better place than we found it. Designers relish the lack of predetermined outcomes. As Frank Gehry said several times during the workshop, "If I knew how a project was going to turn out, I wouldn't do it." Each project is an opportunity to ask oneself anew what is the real problem being faced and what is a best solution?

In the design of the Peter B. Lewis Building, Gehry Partners started with some disarmingly simple questions: "What is teaching?" "What is learning?" "What is an office?" "What is a faculty?" Design is often an opportunity to go back to those assumptions that have become invisible and unnoticed, yet are the real reasons we are working on the project. A designer looks for the real thing we are trying to accomplish, unvarnished by the residue of years of organizational habit.

The single overriding commonality in all design projects, as Simon puts it, is the urge to "change an existing state of affairs into a more preferred one." Each project is an opportunity for betterment over existing products, services, or processes. Obviously, we don't start with a clean slate and must take into account the current state of technology, human skills, environmental forces, and so on. Even given that, each project is a chance to ask what we are really trying to accomplish in our organization and how the piece that we are working on now can help make the experience of our workers, customers, suppliers, and publics a better and more rewarding one. A good design solution is one that is more satisfying in more ways than any available, feasible alternative. A good design solution solves many problems, often ones that were not envisioned in its development.

The importance of the design attitude was attested to by Frank Gehry several times during the workshop, especially when he pointed out that wherever we look in the world, we are surrounded by mediocrity. Why is that? And more importantly, why do we continue to create a mediocre world for ourselves? One often hears the argument that it is "economics" or "costs" or "limited budgets" that are to blame. If only we had more money, more time, more staff, more of something, we would be able to do things better. It is time we rejected such defeatist, shortsighted views. It is time we faced up to the fact that the decision attitude toward problem solving that dominates management education, practice, and research favors default alternatives and locks us into a self-perpetuating cycle of mediocrity.

A design attitude to problem solving does not have to cost more — and is the best alternative we have for breaking out of the path-dependent replication of familiar patterns of management. A design attitude can bring us path-creating ideas about new ways to use technology, new materials, and new work processes that can change the definitions of cost and efficiency, making better solutions attainable at less cost. What attitude toward problem solving should guide us in our work? A decision attitude that chooses from among the alternatives that are already at hand or a design attitude that strives to construct a more satisfying solution than what has so far been proposed? A design attitude fosters an acceptance of and a comfort with a problem-solving process that remains liquid and open, celebrating new alternatives as it strives to develop a best design solution.

FRANK GEHRY'S DESIGN ATTITUDE

Frank Gehry's approach to design is distinctive in that he constantly works from multiple perspectives. He works with multiple models on multiple scales and works with both sketches and physical models simultaneously. Finally, he brings software into the process only at a late stage, working first with hands and materials to shape his design ideas.

Like most architects, he starts with rounds of interviews — in our case, with faculty, staff, and students. He also asked us to write a short statement about our image for the learning environment we desired. From those, a program for the building was developed, showing the various functional needs and the amount of space dedicated to each, such as faculty offices, PhD areas, student study and lounge areas, classrooms, seminar rooms, communal gathering areas, and staff areas. The relative sizes of these required spaces were then translated into sets of wooden blocks of various sizes colored by function. Combinations of blocks were used to play with the massing of the building and to give an overall sense of how the functional areas might be distributed in the building. As a project's design progresses, the number of models grows into the hundreds. Some models are at the grandest scale, filling up one or more eight-foot-by-four-foot pieces of plywood base, and some are of much smaller scale, perhaps modeling just one window or a corner element of the building. For our project, we had dozens of models for faculty offices and many separate models for each classroom.

The Gehry design approach works from both the inside out, as in the massing-models, and from the outside in based on freehand sketches of the building by Frank Gehry, such as shown in Figure 1.1. These are meant to be spontaneous and evocative of both form and emotion. A constant problem he recognizes is how to keep the feelings of the initial sketches as the architects proceed through the design. An important strategy in that process of trying to keep the feelings alive is to work with their hands, making models of the exterior and interior elements out of paper, metal, plastic, waxed cloth, or whatever material gives them both the form and feeling that they are seeking. There is an important lesson here for management. As Edwin Hutchins demonstrates in *Cognition in the Wild*, thinking is not something done exclusively inside the head, but is often accomplished in interaction with other people and with our tools. Spreadsheets are one example of how managers use tools for thinking, and tactile, material models are another, relatively unexplored possibility. The more ways of thinking we have available to us, the better our problem-solving outcomes can be.

Both the interior spaces of the building and the exterior form have a logical as well as an emotional ideal that is being sought. In looking for inspiration on these dual faces of the building, Gehry draws on paintings, sculpture, music, and nature for inspiration. For the exterior of our building, he was working with an image of water flowing over rocks, as well as an image of metal and brick melting into one another. At the same time as the work on our building is proceeding, he is working on other projects, and one can see in his studio

FIGURE 1.1   An early Frank Gehry sketch of the Peter B. Lewis Building

how there is a family resemblance among them. As he says, "You cannot escape your vocabulary." But he puts significant effort into trying to do just that, by looking outside of architecture for inspiration and guiding concepts. The sense of discovery is palpable in their studio.

The three-dimensional software they use to refine the design and work out the details of how the structure is to be built only comes into play after they have arrived at a model they are satisfied with as their "final" design. But realizing that it is final only in a tentative way, always subject to change as they continue to find better solutions to the many layers of problem solving reflected in the design. Once at this stage of the physical modeling, they digitize the model, both interior and exterior, and begin working with the software system to add the specifications and details that will make it build-able. Many technology advocates will see this practice as anachronistic, noting that you can sketch free form and also model in three dimensions with a computer interface that can essentially replicate whatever medium you prefer to work in. Gehry Partners thinks this is a mistake and that the use of the software as a design tool too early in the thinking process works against their commitment to openness in their search for best solutions. The software will inevitably favor some ways of approaching the design problem over others and some ways of working with the tools over others, both of which are to the detriment of the design process. They believe that keeping the connection between the initial sketches and the physical models as close as possible, with both being an intimate, tactile form of work in which mind, hand, heart, and materials are a closely integrated instrument of cognition and creativity, is the best way to maintain the desired feeling in their work from start to finish.

This illustrates another way in which managers can begin learning from the work practices of successful designers to reorient their own thinking. When exactly should an organizational process be embedded in computers and information systems? What parts of the process are better handled outside those systems, relying upon the kinetic and holistic interaction of participants with materials and with one another? These are questions we do not ask ourselves often enough.

THE USE OF MODELS IN DECISION AND DESIGN

When the Peter B. Lewis Building project began, we thought we understood what the process would be like. The Lewis Building project was broken into stages running from an initial feasibility study, to a detailed definition of the program requirements, to the conceptual design, to the detailed design, to the construction drawings, to bidding, and finally to construction. Each phase had a clear objective and led to a well-specified outcome and set of deliverable documents. And the project did follow that structure—but the architects' design attitude brought the process to life in a unique way.

After the school's requirements were identified and while the architects were in the initial design phase, Frank Gehry visited us with a model to show what he was thinking and get reactions. We were under the impression that his first model was a rough version of the finished project—that it would be refined and perfected over time and eventually become the final design. But that's not what happened.

We had anticipated that the essentially favorable reaction that the faculty had to the initial model that Frank Gehry presented, coupled with various suggestions the faculty had made, would lead the architects in a process of refining that initial model to perfect the original idea that was latent in it. So we could not understand the architects' reluctance to take the initial model as seriously as we did. Frank Gehry and his senior partner, Jim Glymph, would say things like, "this is just a place to start," or "it's the beginning and it will change." And of course we thought we knew what they meant by saying it would change, but in hindsight we realize that we didn't. The next model we saw was very different from that first one, and this process continued through several rounds before you could say the underlying form had stabilized and we were working with models that were indeed becoming refined with each iteration.

14   It struck us that he was using models in a very different way than what we were used to. He sees a model as a kind of three-dimensional sketch to stimulate thinking and explore ideas about possible ways that the project could go. We, in contrast, tend to use the concept of model as a theory of a situation and its solution. When we model, it is much more serious and stable — meant from the beginning to be a kind of truth that captures a situation in an abstract, compressed way.

For Gehry Partners, the model was a physical tool for thinking, not a representation of the building they were designing. Frank Gehry would often point to the model, saying, "This isn't what we are doing — it's not the building." And it took a very long time for us to begin to realize what he really meant. Faculty approached the model assuming it was the abstract essence of what the completed building would be like. We expected that the work to be done with the model was to improve it against all the many criteria that had been established, in light of the aesthetic statement that the architect intended for it. It was this expectation of our decision attitude that Frank Gehry was saying no to. His model was not the building because his search for a solution was still ongoing in a fundamental sense. The model did not contain an essence of the building, and we as faculty were not prepared to understand that.

The two examples of their design practice that we have seen, and the one that opened the article in particular, show us something that is central to Frank Gehry's design attitude, which is his relentless search for openness. His commitment to openness is evident in his attempts to bring in influences from many other domains during a design project and also in his determination to not allow a problem to be closed prematurely.

CALL FOR A DESIGN VOCABULARY

Simon argues that how we describe what a manager is and how a manager should think, what a problem is and how it should be approached, and what a good and true course of action is and how it is to be achieved, are all dependent upon our vocabulary. Good designers show an awareness of their own vocabulary and what it does to their work. Part of engaging in good design is choosing a vocabulary or language to use in defining the design task, generating alternatives, and making judgments of balance, fit, and scale. The awareness of one's own vocabulary and its impact on one's design work makes design an ideal vehicle for creating dialogue across specialized professions. It enables diverse professionals to engage in discussions about the qualities of their vocabularies, the creative experience of designing, and the criteria for making design judgments.

One thing that struck us in the project with Gehry Partners was the frequency with which they used the word *vocabulary*. They meant it in a broadly embracing way to include not just the words they were using, but also the strategies of problem solving they were drawing upon, the kinds of imagery they were being inspired by, and the materials, shapes, and textures of the design elements that formed a kind of language for the project. It was a language unique to that project, and the vocabulary of the project was a distinctive one with its own feelings, tensions, and inner logic. Any new element in the design entered into the context of that vocabulary and was judged not in its own terms, but in light of how it fit with, resonated with, contrasted with, or clashed with that vocabulary. This awareness of their language and their work practices as a vocabulary is a very important difference between the design and the decision attitudes toward problem solving. An awareness of one's own vocabulary is the first step to questioning it with a design attitude and exploring how different vocabularies yield more creative problem representations and enable the development of better designs.

We should make it clear in this discussion that we are not just talking about creativity. Creativity is certainly a good thing, and creativity is necessary for improvement in all our human endeavors. But creativity is not sufficient for a design attitude to problem solving, just as it is not sufficient for a decision attitude. The questions really should be: Creativity in what problem space? And creativity toward what end? Consider, for example, the inventory decision-making process discussed above. Much creativity has gone into the refinement and elaboration of the decision models for inventory control. Creativity itself is not going to bring us to the organizational, product, or process innovations we require. Creativity needs the guiding energy of a design attitude in order to focus our efforts on results that will be truly innovative and produce long-lasting organizational betterments. Design is in that sense larger than creativity. Design provides a context for creativity by channeling it toward humanly satisfying purposes, and that is why we cannot allow calls for increased creativity and techniques for enhancing creativity to take the place of increased attention to a design attitude in management practice and education.

At the Weatherhead School, we are rethinking the familiar vocabulary, images, and frameworks of management education and reviewing its evolution over the last fifty years. In doing so, we see that the late 1950s were a challenging time in management education, but of a different sort than the difficulties we face today. At that time, advances in the physical and behavioral sciences were showing the power of quantitative analysis and analytic thought processes in those domains, and management education was definitely behind the accomplishments of other academic disciplines. The Carnegie Commission and the Ford Foundation had undertaken major studies of management education and both had concluded that it was in dramatic need of

16 increasing the amount and rigor of quantitative analysis and analytic techniques in the curricula. The Ford Foundation established a number of PhD fellowships to encourage training of new faculty in the application of quantitative and analytic approaches from economics and behavioral sciences to research on management issues. Similarly, the Carnegie Commission outlined a program for strengthening the study of statistics and mathematical techniques in management schools. So the late 1950s and early 1960s proved a turning point in management education, marked by a recognition that the pendulum of teaching and research had swung too far away from the quantitative and analytic approaches of the sciences and too far toward the detailed practices of management.

Today the pendulum has once again swung too far and is in need of correction. An emphasis on quantitative methods and analytic techniques is fine, as long as you are already dealing with your best ideas about the situation you face and the alternatives open to you. But the more turbulent and chaotic the environment of business becomes, the less likely that is to be true. In those conditions, something else is needed — something that will help put better ideas and alternatives on the table for analytic consideration and quantitative assessment. We propose that a design attitude toward problem solving can do that.

Even seemingly nonquantitative frameworks that are central to our curricula today, such as Porter's strategy model or Kaplan's balanced scorecard model, share some of the characteristics of the most advanced analytic techniques. They enable managers to take extremely complex, ambiguous, and multifaceted situations and bring them under a conceptual apparatus that breaks them down into component pieces in order to apply logical operations for thinking through difficult decisions. This seems eminently sensible, but it springs from a mind-set and approach to management problems that is in part to blame for the sad record of management performance. They are the latest default alternatives for thinking through complex situations. The ideas and alternatives for action to be considered in a decision are to a large extent already embedded in those frameworks. They do enable the surfacing of the ideas inherent in them, but they are a constraint to generating new and different ideas. This is, of course, even truer for more highly quantitative and analytic techniques.

A WORKSHOP ON MANAGING AS DESIGNING

As a first step in encouraging management to take a more balanced approach between the decision attitude and the design attitude, a workshop on managing as designing was the inaugural event in the Peter B. Lewis Building, sponsored by the National Science Foundation and the S. Rose Corporation. We were pleased to see the widespread interest in bringing design thinking into management practice and education reflected in the outstanding quality of participants who agreed to write a contribution for the workshop and for this book.

The workshop began with a keynote presentation by Frank Gehry in which he discussed his design process and his approach to managing his own firm, Gehry Partners. That presentation, along with the question-and-answer sessions that followed, seeded the vocabulary and issues for discussion over the next two days. On the second day, Karl Weick gave a keynote that brilliantly applied Frank Gehry's process of architectural design to the problems of organization design facing managers today.

Participants had written and circulated short provocations before the workshop and developed them into the chapters that follow. These capture central themes of the workshop discussion and emphasize that architecture and other design professions have much to offer managers who are looking to increase both the logic and beauty of the organizations that they create through their day-to-day problem solving. Among the themes explored in this volume are:

- Managers, as designers, are thrown into situations that are not of their own making yet for which they are responsible to produce a desirable outcome. They operate in a problem space that has no firm basis for judging one problem-solving move as superior to another, yet they must proceed.

- Design thinking is evident in the history of management methods and organization structures and processes, especially as they relate to ensuring control of an organization. Design thinking is also at the core of effective strategy development, organizational change, and constraint-sensitive problem solving.

- Managing as designing is a collaborative process, not the work of a single, heroic maestro. Innovative methods of collaborating across disciplinary, functional, and organizational boundaries are essential to the design of successful new products and processes. Good dialogue and persuasive argumentation, along with the physical handling of artifacts, contribute to the quality of design ideas.

- Better organizational environments for successful, value-creating designs can be achieved both at the organizational and the societal level. And better approaches to the education of managers in design thinking can also be achieved. These remain as unmet challenges for the next decades on a global scale.

- We are always trapped by our vocabulary. The familiar vocabulary of management brings premature closure to problem solving by, for instance, shifting focus to discounted cash flows and calculations of cost and profit, almost before a design process has started. This can turn a design process that is best kept in a liquid state into a crystallized one and closes design inquiry.

18

– Using multiple models of a design problem and the working ideas for its solution can bring out different aspects of the design problem, different difficulties to be overcome, and a different sense of what a good solution might be — all of which contribute to a higher quality solution.

– Sketching, mapping, and storytelling are potential complements to models, both physical and analytic, in keeping an evolving understanding of a design problem in a more liquid state.

– Beware of falling in love with your ideas. In a difficult situation, the pressure is intense to find a solution, and the first good idea you encounter will hold great attraction. It is hard not to fall in love with an attractive idea, especially if it is your own, but a good design solution requires that you remain open to letting it go as alternatives arise.

– Seek functional solutions that meet the widest possible meaning of *functional*. A design solution is only truly functional if it meets the design criteria of all who are affected by it, including customers, employees, neighbors, publics, and future generations. This turns the criteria of functionality into an endless search because all the competing demands can never be met, and helps keep our approach to a problem in a liquid state.

– Above all, try! Try to break from the default solution. Try to solve each design problem in a better way than before. Try to expand the advantageous, innovative use of technologies, including those that are emerging, as well as those that are forgotten. Try improvising with available technologies and ideas as a form of innovation. Try to strengthen the range and power of your design vocabulary, including the metaphorical imagery and narratives you draw on to inspire your thinking. Try to set the highest standards for design excellence and refuse to settle for unnecessary compromises.

REFERENCES

Simon, H. A. 1996. *The sciences of the artificial*, 3rd ed. Cambridge, MA: MIT Press.

2

REFLECTIONS ON DESIGNING AND ARCHITECTURAL PRACTICE

Frank O. Gehry

WHEN AN artsy type like myself is confronted with going to a business school, I wonder how to talk about things that would be of interest to business school people. It's easy to think, "Well, business is a bunch of greedy guys who are just trying to make a lot of money, they'll do anything for a buck." Business has gotten a bad name in the course of the last few months, which is something I hope you all are going to correct in the near future. But I've read through the papers that you've written for this workshop and I'm staggered by the depth of thinking in them, by the literary references, and by the art references. The papers are brilliant and wide-ranging. The breadth of interest represented here is humbling to me. I'm very impressed with them. So I know very well that I am in the presence of a very serious group of people who are agonizing about things that are in a way very similar to the things that I agonize about, although our language, our vocabulary, is different. In your papers, you are asking, among other things, what is good design? Let me start by saying that I don't know if the Lewis Building is any good or not. At this point, after several years working with the faculty, having the presidents and deans change several times, and having just completed the building, it's hard to know if it's good or not.

The client is very important to me because you need a partner. It can't be the sound of one hand clapping. The best building, the best work, is done in concert with the client. The right client was an important part of making the Guggenheim Museum in Bilbao, Spain a success. The Basque government

Frank O. Gehry, *Gehry Partners, L.L.P.* This chapter is an edited transcription of Mr. Gehry's keynote speech at the Managing as Designing Workshop.

made a business decision to change the persona of the city in order to attract more people. They selected Jim Sterling, who was alive then, to do the railroad station. He was a really brilliant architect in London. They selected Norman Foster to do the subway, a thirty-kilometer underground rail. They selected Santiago Calatrava to do the airport, and he also did a bridge across the river, near my building. They had a competition to create a new museum and made an agreement to develop it with Tom Krens of the Guggenheim, who was looking for a way to globalize his collection. He was a painter and he has an MBA, so he's got a background in both disciplines that he's playing with, and he's quite brilliant at it.

On this project, Dick Boland has been the stalwart, has been the constant for me. In my mind, he's been the client, the person who is most interested in and most excited about the project. In the Lewis Building, I'm looking for a way to have the architecture complement the issues that the faculty are concerned about and also the issues that you discuss in your papers. The Lewis Building was intended to be a background that is not predictable — you can get lost in it. When it's filled with students, it should be pretty exciting. It's a simple plan. It's really a box with offices around the perimeter and classrooms in the middle. The circulation patterns, the ways that people will get around in it, are built in a way so that students and faculty will collide with each other — will come across each other in unexpected ways. They will find certain places where they want to go when they need to sit down and talk. Those places are going to be their niches, their favorite places to be with each other. And that's what a building needs to do. It has to facilitate that type of spontaneity and comfort of interaction and that was the intent here.

When I make a building, I tell clients at the start that we are going to be in a liquid state for a lot of the time. In the liquid state, there is information gathering and agonizing about program issues like adjacencies, land use, materials, and bureaucracies that we have to deal with. During that liquid period, we make a lot of study models, and some of the models are pretty scary looking. When we show them to a client, they get pretty nervous. We call them *schreck* models. It's a Yiddish expression for making people nervous. I do that so they can follow along with the trajectory of my thinking, which I believe is linear, actually. It's not predictable, but it is linear. I push something here, and then I see something, and then I take that and incorporate it. I think it's an opportunistic kind of process that evolves with the inputs that I'm getting from the client and the world around and all of the issues that have to be dealt with to bring a building from the beginning to the end. As it crystallizes, I tell the clients, it's more difficult to go back. Because by the time the building becomes crystallized, the ineffable has become more precise, and by then we've invested in engineering and we've invested a lot of time in model making, and to start retrofitting at that point is costly. So we try to keep the process liquid in the early stages — liquid, but with direction because we've got to produce a building. We know that. We have a goal to produce a building that has got to cost X, has to stand up, has to keep the rain out, and all of those things.

Staying liquid allows the freedom to make choices for quite a long time in the process so that there are a lot of opportunities for the design of the building. Some of my colleagues work quite differently. They will come in at the beginning with a kind of idea and then later show a finished model of it and say to the client, "This is it." And the clients, in many cases, prefer that because they don't want to think about it. It's over their heads. They can't really think that way. They're not trained for it and they're scared. They don't want to show their ignorance. If you do work for corporate America, you almost have to do it that way and that's why I don't do a lot of corporate work. On corporate projects, you are always working with the executive vice president, and when you are finished, you go to a meeting with the president. The president hasn't been involved in the process and comes in and looks at this thing and says, "Are you kidding? We're not going to build that." And it's just because they are not complicit in the process.

In our process, I require that the person who is going to make final decisions be involved in the process all the way through, so I don't have that terrible day of meeting with somebody who hasn't been there but has the final decision on the project. When the decision makers are complicit in the process, they are involved in the design with me. They have seen the *schreck* models. They understand the choices. They understand the priorities that were set and why they were set. And they understand that their money is being spent in a prudent way for the things they are interested in.

For example, when I started working with MIT on their building, I had a seven-hundred-person client. I had the president of the university, two hundred-some faculty, and four hundred students. They were suspicious by nature of architecture. They said, "Architects spend money on their ego trip and it's going to be at the expense of my office. I'm not going to have the office I want." They all care about their office. We took a big risk and created a Web site that all seven hundred people could access. At the end of each week, we put all of our thinking on the Web site — as raw as it was and maybe unreadable to a layperson. They had our email and they could respond to what was on the site or anything else. In the first year, I got a lot of hate mail, and they were relentless. Some of them even went so far as to interview old clients, back to twenty years before, and reopen old wounds and post that on the site. But by the end of the design process, the letters were constructive and bordering on sympathetic. They went the other way and were begging for more architecture. They were begging for more sculptural forms.

We showed MIT in the first three or four months what their budget would allow. It was a brick box, with a hole in it. Most clients start out with budgets that are unrealistic. They have a contractor or developer on their board who says, "Oh, I build buildings for $100 a square foot. Just double it and we can do whatever we want." So, you take people through and show them what their budget will allow, and that's not why they came to me. Then you develop what a normal budget would be for a building of their type. You can find that out on the computer, of course. You can say, "Cleveland, Ohio, business school building, X number of square feet." You push the button and they will give you the range for all the comparable buildings that have been built. Those costs are then indexed for the day you are going to start the construction and they will tell you that the range for the Lewis Building would be from $300 to $400 per square foot. I think we are somewhere in the middle of that range. We had a construction cost of about $340 per square foot. When we started, the budget was $240, so we had to make that budget become real. The biggest variable is the marketplace, and when we began the Lewis Building, the marketplace was hot. You couldn't get bidders for concrete and steel. Those are the two big industries that you can't corral. They're too big. So you are left to the winds, and those are the main things that fluctuate. If you get just one concrete bidder like we did for a building in Boston, they just put any price on it. So there is de facto collusion in this industry. And when the Lewis Building was bid, we talked to our architectural competitors and we were all getting 20–30 percent overpriced across the board in our projects. Now the economy is slowing down, and although prices are starting to become more reasonable, the donors are disappearing. So I think there is always a difficult balance in these projects.

In your papers, I think it was Paul Kaiser who made a reference to John Cage and the role of randomness in design collaboration, and I would like to comment on that. On a building, I don't know where I'm going when I start. If I knew where I was going, I wouldn't go there, that's for sure. It's not interesting to me to go do something that is preordained. And the randomness is part of an opportunistic process of working with the clients and with the constraints and the way they stimulate you in developing the buildings. The problem is that when Mies van der Rohe developed his vocabulary, he followed a line of work that began in the nineteenth century. In developing his corner detail, he drew from his teacher, Schinkel, who had borrowed from Behrens. If you go back to Schinkel at the Altes museum, you'll see that corner detail. And if you go back to Behrens House, you'll see the beginning of that same corner detail. And Mies developed it into a language that he used on almost all of his buildings. When you start messing with the kinds of shapes we have in the Lewis Building and the collision of forms we have here, it would be difficult to develop a vocabulary for each and every collision that has the refinement that went into what Mies did in his corner detail. When I come to the Lewis Building now, I see all of those collisions of forms as being very raw and unresolved — and I cringe because they are embarrassing in places. Over the next three years, I'll probably end up thinking they are very positive things in the end and wonder: "How could I have thought of that?" But right now I'm cringing at those things. So it's that kind of process.

Clients are complicated, too, like we are. When I went to interview for the MIT project, I told them a story about doing a psychiatric clinic at Yale for schizophrenic adolescents. As part of my research, I asked the doctors to let me be included in the patient groups, and I met with all of the different groups from young kids to teens and up into their early twenties. When I got to the oldest group, I sat in a sort of living room in their old facility, and I was the only person in the room who wasn't schizophrenic, I guess — at least not diagnosed as schizophrenic. I went around the room and they explained to me what they would like in their new building I was designing. They were very intelligent young people, and one quite beautiful young lady, who was very well dressed and obviously from a wealthy family, described what she thought were the important issues in the new building. And I was the only one who realized what she was doing. She was describing in detail the room we were in, with impeccable detail down to the moldings. It was scary — I was sitting there holding on to my seat. At MIT, I told them that when they would tell me what they wanted, they would do the same thing. I got the job anyway. Once we started the work, I met with eight or ten faculty representatives to discuss what they wanted. Before the meeting I had my office make a photographic dossier on each one of their offices. When they spoke, they actually did exactly what the young lady did. They described in a very detailed way their own offices. And I threw it on the table and I said, "See, I told you. You don't even know you're doing it."

At that point, they said, "Okay, but how do we bust out of this? What do we do now?" So we said, "Let's examine the cultures around here and how you deal with communal spaces where people have to work together and live together." We said, "What if you took the idea of a Japanese traditional house, with the shojis sliding panels?" We made a model putting their department in such a building, and we showed them how it did everything they said they wanted. They said they wanted to be alone, and they also wanted to be together. And so we showed them how they could have their own little rooms, and how they could just push the walls away and be together. They hated it.

24   So we tried a colonial house. In a colonial house, you come into a central space, the stairway goes up, and the rooms are around the top. So we laid them out, putting the senior people up in the rooms around a balcony with the students and their assistants in the space underneath. They looked at that and they hated it. They couldn't see themselves in that. Then we went to an orangutan model where the older orangutans are up in the trees, similar to the colonial house, and everybody else is down on the ground, and they can see each other and get down. We also did a hedgehog model with the offices below and trenches where people can come up. We tried a bunch of things that bordered on idiocy, and we made models of each of them and tried out separate departments in each of them. In the end, they built the orangutan village, although they didn't know it.

But I don't think we got very far from where we started with them to where we ended. Clients are often an immovable body. What we got is a building that has an image, like this one does — they are each different, but they both have a persona. People will come from all over and gaga over them. On the inside, though, they will have a building that will do what their president and faculty said they wanted. They will have a building for seven departments that need to talk to each other. The reclusive ones among them will find ways of interacting and the building will function to facilitate that interaction. It's simple. Just putting the cafeteria in the middle and putting their breakout space in view of the cafeteria means they can see when other professors are going to lunch and say, "Oh God, I'd like to talk to that guy. He's going to lunch, I'm going to go to lunch." It's that dumb, and I think it's going to work that simply.

We did a cafeteria for Condé Nast in New York and Sy Newhouse asked for the same exact thing. He had Anna Wintour and David Remnick and other high-profile editors. They were all people who don't want to meet with the other editors. They have their own little fiefdoms, they are all famous, and they are all well known. When they go to lunch, they meet whichever fancy designers they want to meet with at Four Seasons or some other restaurant, and interaction between the editors didn't exist. We created a cafeteria that made fifty or more power tables. You know how people go into a restaurant and look for the corner? Well, I put fifty of those places in the cafeteria. By making the walls glass, you can see each other. And because the cafeteria had an architectural persona, the people who have lunch with Anna Wintour ask her, "Can we have lunch in your cafeteria?" People cannot go into the cafeteria unless they go with somebody that works at Condé Nast. It was set up so that was the only way to get in, and since it was publicized everywhere and everybody wants to go there, it has worked. Newhouse could have built a cafeteria for $6 million, but he spent $12 million. He says it was worth every penny because it does work. They all come there and they all meet. And he said that, believe it or not, David Remnick and Anna Wintour occasionally have lunch together. Their people are interacting. But one important thing, and I think this may be more important than the architecture, is that Sy Newhouse has lunch there every day as well. That is critical to the issue. So architecture can facilitate and play a role in helping to create desired interactions.

Why then is there so much mediocrity in our landscape? Why then doesn't the world at large realize it? I'd say 98.5 percent of buildings are mediocre — I call them *buildings* because I wouldn't even list most of them as architecture. It's dangerous to say but I don't see much architecture on this campus. And maybe I'm being a snob, but it's just not among people's priorities, I guess. The amount of architecture in the world is getting better just because a lot of us are being publicized more. Popular press has gotten more interested in it. People are going to Bilbao, and the popular press is excited about Bilbao. It gets a pretty high mark. The architectural critics and my colleagues try to disparage it, try to knock it. You've heard the words *star architects, starchitects,* or some other despicable term. One of the philosophers started using the term *spectacle architecture*. That's a value judgment. I go to a client, and they say, "You make spectacle architecture. I don't really need a spectacle, or a Bilbao effect." Maybe the world thinks of those as positive things. I think of them as disparaging. Because Bilbao was done with a lot of heart and soul, working with the community, and trying to make a building that would fit in, and that worked for art. I've gotten hundreds of letters from artists who don't find the building threatening to art. Bob Rauschenberg, who hates architects, came over to me and even kissed me on the lips and thanked me. He said he was going to make better art at his old age. And a lot of them said that Bilbao is a building that challenges them. There is a serious intention in making these buildings. There is a very serious intention in the Lewis Building to create a building that does the things that Dick Boland and his colleagues are interested in.

I want to say something about how I run my world. Because it is very business-like, and you will probably be shocked to hear that. People think that we're flaky artists, and there is no bottom line, but I have a profitable office. I started in 1962 and for the first fifteen or so years, I did not have the backup that was needed and I couldn't attract the technology we have now. Because the ideas were strange to the worlds of architects, the people that I had working with me were not the very technical guys who knew how to put such buildings together. The technical guys wanted to work with an office where they had a predictable future. And they knew that I would work on a project until I had it right, regardless of anything else, and that the end product was more important to me than the money. That was the perception.

In fact, it was not exactly that way. I started my office with very little money. I didn't have a rich uncle or father or anybody. I established a discipline in 1962 that whatever fees I got, and they weren't very much at that time, would have to pay for the work. I could work day and night myself for free, as long as everybody working for me was being paid. When they are starting out, lots of architects use student labor because it's very easy to recruit kids who will work for nothing. A lot of my friends do that. That's like taking drugs. Once you're on it, you can't get off it. And you develop a culture of that. It fits the system of job-getting, though, because more and more projects are gotten by competition. Clients have found out that for very little money they can get five architects to jump through hoops and give them models and drawings, and they think they are getting something because they have a lot of choices. And then they pick somebody. The reality is that for me to do a competition, for a building like the Lewis Building, would cost me a half million dollars. The normal stipend for competition for a building like this is about forty or fifty thousand dollars per architect. So the pressure to use freebee students is great. From the beginning, I was somehow blessed with the problem that I couldn't do that.

I also insisted that people who worked for me got a Christmas bonus, a cost-of-living increase every year, vacations, and all of those things. That was built into the culture from the beginning and it exists to this day. As that business practice became apparent to the architectural world, and that took about fifteen years or more, I started to recruit technical expertise. We now have an office that has 120 people. The last two years, the younger people have noticed that I've gotten older, and they've asked, "What happens to us now? Where are we going?" I said there is no way that, if I leave, this office is going to be able to do what I do. It's a very personal kind of work. I design every building now, although I have fantastic people. Edwin Chan, who worked on the Lewis Building with me, has been with me for eighteen years. He is a very talented designer. He could do work on his own. For reasons that I don't understand, he has stayed with me all these years and I am grateful. If I left tomorrow, he could design a very nice building on his own. His buildings would be different. They would start out maybe nodding in my direction, but they would take off. Just because his mind is that inquiring. I know he pushes me all the time, to push somewhere else, so I would guess if I wasn't there, he would just go fly off into his own land. The office is now called Gehry Partners. It's got seven partners, plus me. Two of them, Edwin Chan and Craig Webb, are the designers, the rest are project management and technical people. Jim Glymph, who worked on the Lewis Building, is a senior partner.

I'm seventy-three. Most business people retire by seventy-three, or by sixty-five. In order to facilitate my getting out, although I'm not planning to get out, I've separated the office so that there are fees to the Gehry Partners for architecture and then a design fee that is allocated for Frank Gehry, for me. For now, all fees are in the same pie. I don't take the design fee for me. It's all shared. We've been doing this for five or six years and the clients have been very receptive to that idea that there is a separate fee for what I do. And that sets the stage for when I leave. Say that next year I decide to only work half time. At that point, I would take the design fee for the two projects that I do, which would be more than adequate to cover my lifestyle, which isn't very fancy. And it would allow the office to grow as Gehry Partners, but with its technical expertise and with the younger designers front and center. What I've done in the press over the last few years is identify the young designers so that they are known by the architectural press and the universities. I've encouraged them individually to go around to the schools and lecture and create their identity and write their papers and we support that.

The office has a major commitment to the computer and Jim Glymph has led that effort. It started because I couldn't figure out how to delineate some of the curves I was playing with in a way that they could be built. When you go to Rome and visit San Ivo or San Carlo by Borromini, you see curves that would be difficult to do, even today. I haven't a clue how he figured out how to build them. He must have been on the scaffold himself just visually making them because you couldn't represent some of those shapes and the twists that he played with. Jim went to the aircraft industry way back—fifteen years ago— and he hired aircraft engineers and I think that was fairly unprecedented in an architect's office. We developed the process using three-dimensional Catia software that Dassault Systemes had developed for the aerospace industry. At the time, we thought it was pretty much useless to the rest of the world and that it was only relevant for the kind of work I was doing. So we didn't think there was any future for it in architecture. In our projects around the world, we work with local construction companies and associate architects, who we train with our system. When our project is done, we track what they do and find that they continue using our system. So there seems to be a continuing use of this software and process. And it's not just the software. It's the way we use the software, it's the way we helped change the software, and it's the way we integrate it into our work process.

28   What we are doing now is we set up a small subsidiary that will train people to use our process. We are also developing new processes for incorporating the computer into project management for detailed design and construction of our buildings. Now you should know that I'm illiterate on the computer. I know how to turn it on. I barely know how to use my cell phone. I don't know how to retrieve messages, I can't turn on a VCR, I don't know how to do all that stuff. I knew years ago that at some point you become obsolete, but right now, the State Department of the United States government, who wouldn't in their wildest dreams ever hire Frank Gehry to do a building—never, never, never hire Frank Gehry—has come to us for training in our process. They are amazed by how we control the complexity in my buildings with our computers and our process, and they want to know how we do it.

You would imagine that offices like Skidmore, Owings and Merrill or KPF have this kind of business-oriented practice. I worked with a lot of those firms, and we are way ahead of them on these issues. We are way ahead of them technically, we're way ahead of them organizationally, and it's startling to me when I go to work with them. I just can't believe it. I'm starting to say, "Wait a minute, what am I missing?" I always thought of them as the business guys. I always thought of them as having their organizations together. I never thought of myself doing that. I think it just happened because I set these very simple rules for myself. That I wouldn't borrow money. That everybody was going to get paid. And that I had to get enough peace to do the work the way that I wanted. Dumb simple, but it has led to what we are doing. And it is a very comfortable kind of process. Architects are supposed to make 20 percent profit. We are lucky if in a year we make 7, 8, or 10 percent profit. But doing the work, having the kind of pleasure doing it that we do, that's very adequate. If you put the bonuses that we pay back in, the profits would crumble even more. Irrational, but that is my story. I think I've talked too long. Are there any questions?

LUCY SUCHMAN: *Thank you for the story. It was wonderful. My question comes out of an idea from studies of technology about agency. The ways that we talk about how things happen tend to emphasize single people, such as yourself, being the source of the creation. But another way of thinking about it says that your agency is distributed in all sorts of interesting ways across all these people that you told us about as well as the technologies, and I wondered if you could reflect on that a bit. If that makes sense to you. I think there is an interesting tension between the ways in which you are actually working and are at the same time seen as a single agent in your buildings. You did design the Lewis Building. And at the same time, you didn't.*

I'm not sure I can formulate it, but when we work together, it is play. When you are a kid, your play when you are a child is the beginning of work. Those patterns of interaction and accomplishment in play are the patterns that establish how you are going to work. Creativity, the way I characterize it, is that you're searching for something. You have a goal. You're not sure where it's going. A serious CEO, you would imagine, does not think of creative spirit as play. And yet it is. And that CEO, you could also imagine saying, "Let's take senior management up to whatever lodge and play around." They use the word. And business people are creative, I always thought, when they let themselves be. So when I meet with my people and start thinking and making models and stuff, it is like play. On Disney Hall, when I was getting excited, there was a Frankie Laine song from the television series, *Rawhide*, that I played. I got the record and I had a little tape machine and when we were rolling, I would put it on, "rollin', rollin', rollin'." The whole office heard. It was characterizing the excitement we were having to more people and it brought more people into it. The people who aren't architects wanted to know what the hell was going on. I heard Peter Lewis talk about similar issues in his business, worrying about how he can bring people willingly and with excitement into the game — into the play.

Now, Edwin, who I mentioned earlier, is incredible. The first five years working with me, he sat there and didn't say a word. He was in awe, I guess, that he was there. Then I would say to Edwin, "What do you think about what we're doing?" He would look at me and say, "I don't know, what do you think?" That went on for the next five years. Then I realized he became a monster. He started moving stuff around. We have a joke because in doing a project, a building becomes like a Rubik's cube. You start moving one thing and everything else starts to go. We were doing a project in Korea that never got built, but every time I went on a trip and came back, he had moved the auditorium. He was impeccable. He had incredible reasons for it. He's really brilliant. He doesn't sleep at night and he comes back the next morning and moves the auditorium. Now, we rely on him to do it. I said, "Edwin, I'm going out of town. You just move the auditorium and I'll be back." And he does.

The funniest thing is to see this group trying to design our new office. Without a client, it's hilarious. Luckily, I left, and Edwin moved the auditorium and he faxed me and he claimed it was just dumb simple. We have a culture that invites a lot of interaction and it pushes me and I love it because it keeps things going. It keeps my mind going, and I'm open to it. At some point, I freeze like everybody does, and I am caught in my own inability to move. I am not infinitely able to free-associate. I do fall in love with the thing and that's dangerous for me and I recognize it. I do lead in that kind of way. I do rely on Edwin or somebody to change the game, change the rules, because the dangerous thing for us is to crystallize before we have all the information, before we know what the issues are, and if we've addressed all of them.

MARIANN JELINEK: *I'm very curious. I'd like to bring you back to the earlier statement about the State Department. I would love to have the State Department work with you. But I'm curious about why they want to get involved?*

The government agencies that build buildings are inefficient. They have a process of building where there is a battery of stuff you go through and they are all written in documents. It's frozen in time, but in an earlier time. And it's based on a culture of how our buildings were built. And the culture of how buildings get built has evolved with the American Institute of Architects. The AIA has developed documents and processes to protect the architect, but it's become overprotective. It is like overprotecting your kids and then finding that they don't learn and grow, and that's what happened in the architecture profession. The government contracting system has built into it this infinite democracy. It's created a very complicated world that adds money to the process. It adds time to the process and time is money. When they see me riding away above that, they ask, "How do you get away with it? How do you build those things?" Real people are willing to pay for them, and *Engineering News Record* has pointed out that the construction industry has learned from our processes. And they are interested in where we are going because I think inevitably we are going to a paperless process. We did it in Seattle at the Experience Music Project, where about one-third to one-half of the building was done paperless. We went from computer to computer, and the steel was fabricated from our program. You could print the paper if you wanted, but they didn't have to. And so they are trying to figure out how we do it because I guess there aren't many other people doing it. We have tied into our group some of the best structural engineers in the world. We haven't got a formal partnership with them, but we have an intellectual partnership.

LES GASSER: *I'm really interested in something that you haven't spoken so directly on and that is the effect of time on a building because it exists without maintenance or without evolution. It doesn't stay as a solid, stable thing forever.*

Well, when I was starting out, I thought a lot about that issue. I thought about flexibility and felt that buildings should be nondenominational. If you look at Versailles as a model, the rooms are interconnected in a linear way. The king had his bedroom, and when it was winter, he moved his bedroom to the south side, and when it was summer, he moved his bedroom to the north side. They didn't have plumbing that tied them down, so they would bring the bedpans and all that stuff with them. There was this kind of flexibility and ability to move, and that was nice because the character of the room was different. You had variety, change, so there was flexibility. Once I designed a store for Joseph Magnin, and the store was designed with Cyril Magnin, who was alive then. He was a great entrepreneur and merchant. We spent hours talking about the industry and the changes and problems that he faced. The fashion industry has rapid flips. In six months, it goes from one thing that is hot to another thing that is hot, and the fixtures had to change. The minute it was built, it was obsolete. And that is why I started making cardboard furniture, because it represented a disposable fixture. By the second store, it was completely changed. They wanted to change the color, change the graphics, do a lot of stuff that Rem Koolhaas did at Prada. But it was done decades ago. I had a series of columns with carousel projectors and a wall 150 feet long above your head, where the projectors could project images of their models. It was like a moving picture. Two years after the store opened, I told Joseph Magnin how we had failed Cyril. I asked him, "What did we do wrong?" He said, "I don't know but I noticed they haven't changed the projected displays." They invited us to a staff meeting of a store we did. I listened to each person and toward the end, the young display guy requested $200 per month more for his $400 per month display budget. And I put up my hand, and I said, "Young man, is this the reason you haven't changed anything?" And he started crying. He said, "Yes, Mr. Gehry, I know this place is like a wonderful instrument. I could play it like a violin. I'm dying to do it. But they won't give me the money to do it. I can barely change a light bulb with the budget." So I said, "It's easy. Triple his budget and we're all set. It's not that much money." And the store manager said, "It's not in my profit-and-loss accounts. I can't do it. It's not in my budget. I can't do it." And I think the same thing could happen with the Prada store in New York. If they are going to keep changing, they have to train somebody to be an advocate during the continuous use of the building, someone who advocates and gets a priority from the management to have enough money spent doing that.

What will happen in the Lewis Building is that this room will become obsolete, but these rooms will last and become relics because people will have nostalgia and say, "I went to school here. You can't change it." That's when you get the environmental and the protectionist agencies that are going to protect every inch of the building, every screw. We are working on one of the Hughes

32 buildings at Playa Vista. It's an old, nondescript building, but there is a corridor in the building where Howard Hughes walked and the historic preservation guys won't let you move that corridor. That's ridiculous, you know?

As far as the maintenance issues that you bring up, technology does change and there are new materials. Titanium, which we used in Bilbao, is inert. It's an element. It's a pure element and doesn't rust or corrode. But the architectural world goes back to the history of Vetruvius who talked about commodity, firmness, and delight. That's our architects' mantra. When we go to school, we learn about Vetruvius: commodity, firmness, and delight. And that's what an architect's job is to do. And there are architectural groups that have fastened onto firmness. And firmness has become a fixation for using stone. But they somehow don't factor in that the great monuments of the world that were made in stone are deteriorating, and they are very difficult to keep clean because of pollution. I attended a conference in Switzerland a few years ago where they were trying to argue that guys like me are irrelevant. We shouldn't be doing this stuff. We should go back to stone, to what is solid because that represents the real thing. At that meeting, I got up and talked about how a third of a millimeter of titanium would be longer lasting than all the stone they ever had. Then Jean Nouvel got up and talked about his glass buildings, which look fragile, but aren't. He was much more poetic about it than I was and talked about how glass is more lasting than stone and doesn't change.

DICK BOLAND: *I have heard some of your colleagues say that there are many really brilliant, creative architects. But, only a few of those really creative architects become really great architects because they compromise and that you do not compromise.*

Well, what is compromise? I mean, we compromise all day long. I'd rather be on a beach somewhere or on my boat than here, so that's a compromise to come here. The point is you strive for certain excellence. You have a sort of model in your head of what it is you are going to do and you stick to it. I stick to it because I can't do the other. And when I have to do the other — whatever the other is — to get the job or to do anything, my body doesn't do it. It's not constructed in that way, it doesn't allow me to. I've developed ways of working where I can talk openly with my clients and they are all happy with the process we follow and how we work with them. And they would say I have listened to them.

So I have developed behavior that endears me to the people who pay money to get me to do work. That's a kind of pandering to the audience. I try to make buildings that feel good, so that's pandering. There are architects' frames of mind and there are artists' frames of mind that are very critical of things I do. For that reason—because I have a particular personality. I like people. For me, the building of a building, the process of working with people, is more exciting than the final building. I can prove that endlessly in my life. I have built a way of working that includes dealing with the world in the way I want to deal with it, and there is compromise in that.

I could have come to the Weatherhead School and said, and I have the power for the most part to do it, "You build it the way I want it or forget it." And I could have built an incredible sculpture that had nothing to do with the faculty and students. There are many buildings that don't function. Some architects sell buildings that are irrational and irreverent about how people use a building. That wouldn't happen to me. I do listen. I compromise, and I compromised here. I spent time listening to the people on campus. I worry about the neighborhood. You may not think I did, but I spent a lot of time worrying about the law school. I listened to their objections and made the building as a result more interesting. I compromised in a way. So I think the word compromise is not so pure. I'm very happy with the building. I don't think I compromised my level of where I wanted to be with it, so I can be proud of it. Steve Litt, the architectural critic, is here. He's going to tell me whether it was any good, as will others in the press. There are things they can argue about, things that are failures and that are not failures. I think the word compromise is a difficult one.

As an aside, I am so excited that this room works for a seminar discussion like this. Because we spent a lot of time on this room. This is an old model, but only Dick and Scott at the time were willing to try it. Everyone had trepidation about it. There are a lot of examples of it in the world, but to me it came from Thomas Jefferson's conference table at the University of Virginia, which is this shape—an oval. You have the ability to see each other and hear each other around such a table, and I hope to build one in our new office, too. A rectilinear room wouldn't be doing this. And a circular room spins somehow. There's kind of a quieter feeling of this shape, and I'm just sitting here so pleased with myself.

FRED COLLOPY: *Later we will all be putting words on the board that should be part of a manager's design vocabulary. What word would you put up?*

Well, I would put the word *functional* up, and I would urge you all to think about the word *functional*. Because traditionally, architects use the word *functional* and clients use the word *functional* when they look at a building and say, "This guy produced a very functional building." And it means to them that they can use it, that it works. But that doesn't say anything about how it brings emotionality to the table and doesn't consider if it is human. Is it humanistic? Functional is boom! There it is, it's functional. Functional for me has a broader meaning than that. It means achieving a building that does all of the things we want as humans from our buildings. Building the Lewis Building, and having it here, right now, and using it, is functional, but that embodies all the processes, all the people, all the budgets, all of the building departments, and the whole history of architecture. All of those issues come together over time and arrive at a conclusion that stands here. It doesn't look like anything else we've seen, it has something to do with people's pride, I hope. People identify it as a nice place, something you want to come to, something that will attract students to come here, something that will make people think "Why is it like that?" and ask those kinds of questions. That's functional. I think in the world you're all in, you should expand the word *functional* to encompass more than just the simplistic notion of doing something well, but to encompass all these other issues. When I make a building I want it to feel easy on the hand for people. This means we give a lot of attention to all the little details of how the building will feel to them, from door handles to passageways. I think about how to give people a kind of handrail, so that the unfamiliar can become familiar for them.

Reading your papers, I was pleased to see that many of you do talk about those broader issues, and I think, given the crummy thing that has happened to big business like Enron, you should continue to do so. The business world is suffering, and I think that a commitment to being functional in this broad sense is something that will pull us out of this terrible situation. I'm encouraged that people in this room are interested in it.

I was raised in a Jewish family where I was taught the psalmbook by my grandfather and the psalmbook starts with "why?" I was raised to question always. The other important thing in the psalmbook was the story of Rabbi Hillel meeting a man on a road who asked him to explain the Jewish religion while he stood on one foot as a skeptic. And he believed there wasn't anything to it, so he said, "If it's important enough, you can tell it while I stand on one foot." Rabbi Hillel said, "Do unto others as you would have others do unto you." I'm not quoting Judaism because I'm totally outside of it and don't believe in religion at all. But isn't that the driving thing? The Golden Rule? In the end, when I make a building, I think of my neighbor. I try to. When I talked about this building the other night, the one thing that I agonize about and that I've been worried about, even though friends are reassuring me that it's okay, is when Ag Pytte, the university president, asked me to squeeze the building into a smaller lot. I realized I had to build a building that was out of scale with my neighbors. A lot of the angst in the design was to sort of make a design that pulled back and became a better neighbor even though it was out of scale. I am still very sensitive about that. As I look at it, I am very worried about that issue, although friends have said not to worry about it anymore. I don't know what Steve Litt will have to say about it, though. But for me, the important thing is to be a good neighbor. To not talk down to people. You give them back what they expect or what they deserve in your best work, but within the context of the Golden Rule, and it always has to be responding to the question, "why?"

I want to say something about Peter Lewis whose name is on this building. He couldn't be here, but I wish he was here. He was asked the other night at a symposium, how he managed. Because he started with a company that had one hundred people and now it's at thirty thousand—how did he do that? What he said was about how to deal with the future and how to build a company. He said that there are some core values that he started with. One of them was certainly honesty, which he is very much concerned about. And those core values are like the Ten Commandments. They can be stated while you are standing on one foot, like in Rabbi Hillel's story. Those core values have guided the expansion of the company. That's what holds it together. When new managers, new directors, and new people are brought in, they buy into and accept those basic core values, and that is how his company has expanded without him. He is now retired and the new guys who have taken over have tripled the value of the company. He feels it was because of those basic values that he passed on. Now that's a management thing that does deal with the future. I think you can get very complex about, and you can start to agonize about, all kinds of things about the future, but maybe it's simpler. Maybe if you start with a simple core of values. That's what I did. My office, with a few core beliefs, has grown very well. It's sort of dumb simple, but everybody's thinking of those values. It's not compromise. It's not a bad thing. It reflects nice values. It's that simple.

3

RETHINKING ORGANIZATIONAL DESIGN

Karl E. Weick

I WANT to begin these remarks by describing the concerns of two people who are troubled by issues of organizational design, Frank Gehry (the architect who designed the Lewis Building) and Dee Hock (the ex-CEO who designed VISA). Both of these designers are worried that when people get organized, the costs of coordination are too high. Their worries cut to the heart of any efforts to rethink the topic of organizational design. Let me briefly mention Gehry's concern and return to it later and spend more time setting the stage for our discussion with Dee Hock's concern.

First, Frank Gehry. Here's what bothers him about coordination: "From the very beginning I've been worried about the translation of ideas through the many people involved in the process of making a building. They frequently drain the strength and power out of an idea" (1999, p. 46). Scholars of organizational design themselves worry a lot about the fate of ideas that move through layers of people. But they worry about uncertainty absorption and the loss of details and premises and bad news. They worry much less about the loss of intensity. Thus, the question arises, what can designers tell Gehry that will help him reverse the tendency for ideas to lose their power as they move from person to person?

Dee Hock is worried about essentially the same thing. When VISA International was being formed in 1970, Hock worried that the strength of the highly original idea of a reverse holding company held by semiautonomous equals would get drained of its power by bankers with their inordinate needs

---

Karl E. Weick, *Department of Psychology and School of Business, University of Michigan.*

to be in control and avoid change. I want to describe in more detail the very moment in VISA's founding when these issues came to a head, because I think this moment contains most of the design issues that Gehry and Hock and scholars alike have to deal with.

Here's what happened at VISA. In the early 1970s, National BankAmericard Incorporated (NBI) turned around the Bank of America's faltering credit card business in the United States (Hock, 1999, p. 155). Soon thereafter, NBI was pressured by BankAmericard licensees in the rest of the world to do the same thing for them. The problems were formidable. Not only did each licensee have different marketing, computer, and operations systems, but each licensee also dealt with different language, currency, culture, and legal systems, all of which had to be transcended somehow. A technological fix was out of the question because banks were still using computer punch cards and tape, and there was no Internet. After months of tense negotiations, a meeting of the organizing committee was scheduled late in the second year of organizing. The meeting was to be one last attempt to resolve three deal-breaker disagreements. Positions had hardened and the organizers could think of no compromise that had any chance of being accepted.

Shortly before the final meeting, the chairman of the organizing committee, Dee Hock, reflected on how the international group had been able to get as far as they did. It dawned on him that "at critical moments, all participants had felt compelled to succeed. And at those same moments, all had been willing to compromise. They had not thought of winning or losing but of a larger sense of purpose and concept of community that could transcend and enfold them" (1999, p. 245). Hock and his staff hatched a plan for the final meeting. They contacted a local jeweler and asked him to create a die from which he would cast sets of golden cuff links. One cuff link would contain a picture of half of the globe and the phrase, "the will to succeed." The other link would contain the other half of the globe and the phrase, "the grace to compromise."

When the final meeting actually convened, as expected it was polarized, contentious. The Canadian banks refused to participate and withdrew, and Hock adjourned the meeting midday and said they would reconvene the next morning in order to plan how to disband. Before adjourning, Hock invited everyone to a grand dinner that evening in Sausalito in recognition of their undeniable efforts to try to make the organization work.

After dinner, there was brief reminiscing about shared experiences and obstacles overcome. Then the waiters passed among the diners and placed a small wrapped gift in front of each of them. Hock asked people to open the elegant boxes and examine the contents.

He then said quietly, "We wanted to give you something that you could keep for the remainder of your life as a reminder of this day. On one link is half of the world surrounded with the phrase 'the will to succeed' and on the second link is the other half of the world and the phrase 'the grace to compromise.' We meet tomorrow for the final time to disband the effort after two arduous years. I have one last request. Will you please wear the cuff links to the meeting in the morning? When we part we will take with us a reminder for the rest of our lives that the world can never be united through us because we lack the will to succeed and the grace to compromise. But if by some miracle our differences dissolve before morning, this gift will remind us that the world was united because we did have the will to succeed and the grace to compromise" (paraphrased from Hock, 1999, pp. 247–48).

Then Hock sat down. There was a full minute of absolute silence as people examined their gift. And then the silence was shattered by one of Hock's exuberant Canadian friends who exploded, "You miserable bastard!" The room erupted in laughter. The next morning everyone was wearing the cuff links. By noon, agreement was reached on every issue and VISA International came into existence.

Now, why is this a microcosm of design?

1. The incident is about the progression in designing from *purpose* (a binding intent worthy of pursuit[1]), to *principles* (how people will conduct themselves in the pursuit of purpose[2]), to *people* (who needs to participate), to *concept* (the set of relationships among people that allow for the pursuit of purpose in accordance with the principles), to *structure* (the charter that creates a legal entity), finally to *practices* (deliberations, acts, and decisions within the community that animate and update the design) (adapted from Hock, 1999, pp. 7–14).

2. The incident is about the limits of design. Because relationships are so complex, it is hard to agree on much beyond "intent, sense of direction, and principles of conduct" (Hock, 1999, p. 89). But those three are enough if people have the confidence, latitude, and expertise to self-organize the rest of the details.

3. The incident is about agreement (Hock, 1999, pp. 88–89), which is the elemental act of organizing. Wherever there is a need for agreement, there is ambiguity, differing points of view, conflict, and a desire for reconciliation. Effective designing makes it possible for people to move toward reconciliation and coordination. But this movement can be treacherous.[3]

4. The incident is about identities and structures that are reified into solidity yet can be undone and redefined if enough social pressure or power or attractive alternatives can be mobilized. The Canadian bankers are not just a reified financial institution in North America with strong self-interests. They also can envision themselves quite differently as semiautonomous equitable members of an international community that provides unsecured consumer credit. The image of "community" as the rudimentary form of organization is crucial.

5. The incident is about making do, improvising, and cobbling together a bricolage[4] of previously intact, self-contained, regional systems. The VISA system

was unprecedented. Furthermore, who could imagine that firms deeply committed to self-control and their own self-interest would be willing to give up their autonomy (Hock, 1999, p. 155) to an unproven system of governance tied together worldwide *before* the Internet? At the microlevel, there is certainly improvisation involved when Hock declares an impasse and the imminent disbanding of VISA, which sets conversations in motion that will unfold in uncontrollable directions.

6. The incident is about flow, motion, dynamics, updating, negotiating, and malleability.[5] The forms that impose order on the gatherings are transient forms that momentarily give meaning to shifting relationships. We gain here a glimpse of a parallel between organizations that are characterized as a blend of chaos and order (Hock calls these "chaordic") and Frank Gehry's architectural structures that capture the same blend of chaos and order, a blend he calls the "stationary dynamism of a flame" (Sorkin, 1999, p. 39).

7. And the incident is about feeling, intensity, passion, cunning, exploding. It is about heart as much as head.

CURRENT THINKING ABOUT ORGANIZATIONAL DESIGN

Before we dig deeper into the design issues implicit in VISA's formation, we should review how scholars of organization are positioned currently to understand such episodes. It is clear that most scholars do talk about organizational design, whether they intend to or not. This is evident when they talk about contrasts such as mechanistic-organic; differentiation-integration; clockworks and cogs; pooled, sequential, or reciprocal interdependence; and routines, rules, and mutual adjustment as means of coordination.

It is also clear that scholars seem to be developing the topic of organizational design in an unwieldy direction. As political scientist Paul Schulman puts it, the history of organizational theory is one of "moving from a belief that organizational behavior could be fully determined by a set of complete and consistent design principles, to a hard-won recognition that more and more variables come into play" (Paul Schulman, email, November, 19, 2001). The problem here is that, as the variables multiply, scholars say less and less about more and more. The net result is that we now function basically as a discipline of critics who lower confidence rather than as a discipline of designers who raise confidence. Repeatedly we find ourselves in the position where we say, "I'll know tomorrow why the things I predicted yesterday did not happen today" (Flyvbjerg, 1998, p. 44n7). And when we learn why our predictions failed, we typically add more variables to our frameworks. The problem is, we don't drop any of the variables that have been accumulated. Nor do we take seriously the possibility that greater reliance on something other than the language of variables[6] could facilitate intervention and design.

If you look closely at definitions of organizational design, you begin to see the obstacles that researchers have put in their own path. Consider a definition crafted in 1965 that remains accurate: "The design of an organization refers, of course, to its structural characteristics, i.e. those elements in the total picture of the organization's functioning that (a) remain unchanged over a sufficiently long period of time to be describable and (b) influence or constrain important aspects of the organization's total behavior. The use of the word 'design' implies a focus on aspects of structure that are prescribed by or at least acceptable to the formal authority of the organization" (Haberstroh, 1965, p. 1,171). Richard Butler's current definition covers the same ground: "the choosing of structures and associated managerial processes to enable an organization to operate effectively" (Butler, p. 384).

Both these definitions insert obstacles and limits into understanding because they restrict attention to such features as unchanging elements, the presumption of a central designer, alignment with formal authority, the organization as a material entity, details and constraint, the prescribed rather than the emergent, and choices rather than construction. These are all issues we need to put back into play if we want to reanimate the topic of design. We need to be more attentive to what Bate, Kahn, and Pye call "the paradox of organization design": "On the one hand design creates nothing. By itself, design is an empty vessel waiting to be filled with people, meanings, and actions . . . it is a dead form that has no life or energy itself. . . . Yet on the other hand, it creates everything since the organizational design will have a fundamental framing effect on people's expectations and perceptions, setting the context for the organizing activity—the social construction of roles and relationships—through which structure is enacted" (2000, p. 200). If designing is both everything and nothing, then we need to dig deeper to grasp it. Dee Hock gives us a little more breathing room when he describes design as "a mental concept of human relationships in a world of exploding complexity and diversity" (KPMG speech, September 27, 1999, p. 9).

Here's how I want to structure the breathing room that Hock makes available. I want to say a little more about the six themes culled from the VISA example. First, I want to look more closely at the changes that occur when designing moves from purpose to practice, changes that I will describe as "compounded abstraction." Second, I will discuss the effects of agreement and coordination on the loss of perceptual detail, a loss that I will describe as the "shareability constraint." Third, I will discuss the role of underspecification in design, something I will describe as "the charm of the skeleton." Fourth, I will describe how designing, as practiced by Frank Gehry, embodies all of the revisions for design that are implicit in what I have described. Then I will conclude with comments on the inevitable question, "So what?"

The artist Robert Irwin used the phrase "compounded abstraction" to describe the progression that is involved when people try to make sense of the world. His thinking is important for students of design if we assume that designs have to make sense. Designs have to be sensible themselves, and they have to help people make sense of the situations they face. The essence of compounded abstraction is found in one of Irwin's favorite maxims: "seeing is forgetting the name of the thing seen" (Weschler, 1982, p. 180). In Irwin's view, sensemaking moves through six stages, beginning with *perception* (synesthesia of undifferentiated sensations). The undifferentiated perceptions begin to take on meaning in the second stage, *conception*, where people isolate unnamed zones of focus. In the third stage, *form*, these zones begin to be named. And in the fourth stage, which Irwin calls *formful*, the named things are deployed relationally and are arranged in terms of dimensions like hot/cool, loud/soft, up/down. So far there is some fluidity in the process and some possibility of reversing and redoing and relabeling. But at the fifth and sixth stages, people begin to act as if the labels were immanent and discovered rather than extrinsic and imposed. In the fifth stage, which Irwin labels *formal*, patterns of relations begin to be reified and treated as entities. For example, the formful relation of up/down now gets reified into the more formal relationship of superior/subordinate, master/slave. And in the sixth stage, *formalize*, the reifications dictate behavior and become taken-for-granted fixtures around which people organize their activities. By the time people formalize their experience they are essentially estranged from direct perceptual experience. At each step in this sequence of compounded abstraction, details get lost, the concrete is replaced with the abstract, and design options get foreclosed.

If we take this sequence seriously, it suggests that designs can preclude seeing and that labels need to be taken more lightly. By taking labels more lightly I mean that a crucial moment in designing is the questioning of labeled signs[7] that now stand in place of direct perceptions. Managing as designing means, in part, the monitoring, containing, and reversing of compounded abstraction.[8] The necessity to act this way becomes clearer when we connect the image of compounded abstraction more directly to the complexities of organizational life.

DESIGNING AS CONSTRAINED SHARING

The social psychologist Reuben Baron draws the same distinction between perceptual and conceptual processing that Robert Irwin draws. Baron argues that in the mode of direct perception, people develop knowledge by acquaintance through active exploration. Cognitive processing involves bottoms-up stimulus-driven processing in order to take action. Direct perception consists of on-line automatic processing. As a result of continued direct perception, people tend to know more and more about less and less, which makes it easier for them to "forget the name of the thing seen." By contrast, when people work in the conceptual epistemic mode, they develop knowledge by description rather than acquaintance, their cognitive processing is now schema-driven rather than stimulus-driven, and they go beyond the information given and elaborate their direct perceptions into types, categories, stereotypes, and schemas. Continued conceptual processing means that people know less and less about more and more.

The relevance of these shifts for organizational design becomes more apparent if we add a new phrase to the design vocabulary, "shareability constraint" (Baron and Misovich, 1999, p. 587). Informally, this constraint means that if people want to share their cognitive structures, those structures have to take on a particular form. More formally, as social complexity increases, people shift from perceptually-based knowing to categorically-based knowing in the interest of coordination. As demands for coordination increase, people begin to perceive one another in terms of roles and stereotypes, distributed cognition becomes more category-based in order to reduce differences and gain agreement, concepts become simpler and more general in the interest of transmission, and there is a greater aversion to inconsistency between interpersonal attraction and beliefs. While all of these changes facilitate coordination, they do so at the potential cost of greater intellectual and emotional distance from the details[9] picked up by direct perception. As we saw earlier, Frank Gehry worries about ideas being drained of their strength and power when they pass through too many people.[10]

In a reversal of Robert Irwin's maxim, people who coordinate tend to remember the name of the thing seen, rather than the thing seen and the thing felt. If crucial events occur that are beyond the reach of labels that smooth social life, then coordinated people will be the last to know about those events.[11] For this reason, reified designs can be dangerous because they encourage perceptual shortcuts such as normalization.[12] If people rely on such shortcuts, then they rarely feel any need to update their labels, categories, or inferences.[13] If a coordinated group updates infrequently, there is a higher probability that it will be overwhelmed by troubles that have been incubating unnoticed.[14] Highly coordinated groups are the last groups to discover that their labels entrap them in outdated practices.[15]

Entrapment is a major challenge for designers. If we assume that perception-based knowing is crucial for effective collective action, then designers need to moderate the demands for coordination in any organizational design. If the demands for coordination are reduced, this serves to increase the number of independent sensing elements that can be externally influenced by changes in the pattern of events (Campbell, 1988). This increased capability for sensing allows for perceptually-based knowledge to be stirred into an otherwise schema-driven coordinated world.[16] Small pockets of perceptually-based influence have the potential to update collective editing. Thus, it is crucial for designers to foster social mechanisms such as pooled interdependence (Thompson, 1967; Snook, 2000) with its limited demands for coordination, minority influence, partial inclusion, and loosely coupled systems, in order to weaken stereotyping, strengthen situational awareness, and restore adaptability. The goal would be, in Lanzara's words, to engage in designing based on transient constructs that produce "larger, loosely connected structures, that, taken as a whole possess a high degree of stability and resilience, but locally are always up for grabs" (1999, p. 343). What Lanzara has described is a recipe for modest coordination that maximizes perception-based knowing.

DESIGNING AS THE CHARM OF THE SKELETON

Regardless of the direction in which designing moves, whether it is toward the compounding of abstraction or toward the undoing of abstraction, there is a sense that unfinished designs have more vitality than do finished designs. Unfinished designs are present in Irwin's intermediate stages of concept, form, and formfulness. Unfinished designs are also present, literally, in Gehry structures that are under construction. Listen carefully to one person's reaction to an unfinished Gehry building. "The unfinished version has a special innocence, clarity, authenticity, and authority. . . . (T)he worry is that elaboration and growth inevitably equal loss" (Gehry, 1999, p. 29). Whether one is a designer of organizations or of physical structures, the trick is to add density to a skeleton while retaining the vigor, quirks, and visual charm of that skeleton.

This line of thought implies that a primary danger in designing is overdesign. Designers fail because they don't know when to stop. The trick in designing is to stop while the design still has life. Life persists when designs are underspecified, left incomplete, and retain tension. From this perspective, the presence of zones of focus that are tough to name and tough to relate may signal that a design is finished rather than just beginning. The organizational designers Paul Bate and Annie Pye are sensitive to this issue in their efforts to redesign hospitals. They observe that "design is a bare bones framework on which a more organic, emergent, social structure develops as people interact, argue, fall out, come together, and otherwise manage their day to day situation" (Bate et al., p. 199). Dee Hock was sensitive to this issue in designing VISA. He noted that purpose, principles, and people were about all he could set in motion. Once these three were in place he had to rely on self-organizing to flesh out the functioning. Notice that Hock in his role of designer stops just before he gets to the "good stuff" of specifying structures and procedures and practices, something that all managers, especially CEOs and founders, love to do. Although tempted to specify all of these details and reify his vision, Hock pulls back. He underspecifies the structure and allows others to add in density. By doing so, he increases the chance that the designing will retain vitality because people on the frontline customize the procedures and structures to meet the demands they actually face.

COMPOUNDED ABSTRACTION IN FRANK GEHRY'S WORK

These several strands can be pulled together and illustrated by Frank Gehry's style of working. Gehry starts with undifferentiated drawings that capture what he calls "a dream."[17] As Sorkin puts it, a Gehry building starts with a sketch that enacts an essence of ineffable character (p. 31). The dream and the drawings begin to take on form when zones of the drawing are isolated and then named (e.g., contours are labeled as folds similar to those in the sleeve of a dress, Friedman, 1999, p. 44). The zones continue to take on form when they are related (e.g., these folds shape the interior space but these other folds don't) and then formalized into 3-D computer renditions. At each step there is an increased potential for the original dream to be lost when it is named in the interest of coordination with engineers, contractors, and patrons. Thus, in a reversal of Robert Irwin's maxim, as the Gehry organization names the dream, it "forgets" the thing that Gehry sees.

Notice how Gehry tries to forestall this loss. He often builds multiple models of the same dream (see examples on pages 32–33 of Friedman, 1999). Different models of the same dream foster different zones of focus, different forms, and different relations. There is a tantalizing question of whether these models encourage different judgments of the object or different objects of judgment.[18] The beauty of Gehry's multiple models is that even though the original essence has been paraphrased by the Catia computer program into a more limited set of labeled relationships, the design is still not frozen. Instead, each model represents a different set of labeled zones of the original dream. Oftentimes, different features from different models are combined at this later stage. This blending is a fascinating mix of the renaming that is characteristic of earlier stages of abstracting and the relating and formalizing that are characteristic of later stages of abstracting. When separate designs are blended in the final version, this means that the final design actually embodies multiple designs, all of which started from the *same* place. The final design is a bricolage as well as a unity. In other words, the final formalized structure may be less fixed than it appears. Part of what has been reified is malleability itself.

The crucial point is that because of the way in which Gehry's designing unfolded, the final reification is not fixed. The final design embodies the tension between conception and perception that is a key primitive in designing. The pressure toward reification that is created in Gehry's studio by the need for coordination gets slowed by multiple models. This slowing adds richness and flexibility to the final design, and in doing so, increases the likelihood that the structure can update itself. A structure that contains a history of multiple models is not a single structure at all. Instead, it is many structures. In the jargon of the day, the structure is infused with the capability to be self-organizing.[19]

Let us be clear about how this self-organizing happened. The flexibility inherent in different zones of focus that are given different names was preserved until the last possible minute in the form of more than one model of the same dream. The final synthesis, which was actually a bricolage of fragments from different models, preserved alternative zones of focus, alternative names, and alternative relations in the final design, but did so in an orderly manner because all of those alternatives started from the *same* origin. In a way, designing is immanent in the design. Stages that unfolded between the dream and the outcome are compressed in the final design. But that compression can be reversed and drawn out in the service of updating the design. Said differently, a compounded abstraction can reinstate the compounding of the abstraction, thereby unfreezing what ordinarily looks fixed. But this outcome does not come easily. It requires tolerance of ambiguity, willingness to adopt multiple zones of focus and multiple models, reluctance to settle for simple labels arrayed in obvious dimensions, bricolage that breaks apart models that have their own integrity, and courage to advocate weaker coordination in the interests of stronger unique images.

So far we have looked at the compounding of abstraction and the distancing from original intuitions in the interest of coordination. There is the tacit prescription that multiple compounding, coupled with belated bricolage, produces a more resilient design. This is movement from the concrete to the abstract. It involves designing as wary abstracting.

DECISIVE GROUNDING IN FRANK GEHRY'S WORK

But the reverse direction of movement, from the abstract back toward the concrete, also is a crucial aspect of designing. We turn now to that direction,

46   which we will call, designing as decisive grounding. Here we focus on designing that runs from more formalized and formal back toward forms and concepts and perceptions. Again, we draw on Gehry and his style of working. This time we focus on Gehry's 1978 design of his own house. Mildred Friedman describes the house as a "dumb little pink Santa Monica bungalow (that) became a laboratory in which it was possible [for Gehry] to try anything, and he did" (1999, p. 8). What Gehry tried to do, in our terminology, was to move backward, away from reified notions of "house" toward forms and conceptions stripped of conventional relationships and names. That movement backward has been described in Michael Sorkin's essay, "Frozen Light": "Like a Chinese painting of a fish in which a stroke suffices to animate the shape, Gehry reanimates. He sees the orthodox formal vocabulary of most architecture as lifeless and gets to work, not with the production of an alternative system . . . but with the breath of new life injected into old forms. . . . With his own house . . . the box is not simply distorted geometrically, it's stripped bare. Gehry dances down the line of essence, inquiring how much can be removed and reconfigured before the house disappears" (p. 37).

Gehry's own description of the house shows vividly what happens when unnamed zones of focus come back into view as the orthodox house begins to disappear. He mentions having dinner in the house with Arthur Drexler who was the director of the Department of Architecture and Design at the Museum of Modern Art in New York. "When Arthur Drexler came here for dinner one night, he thought the house was a joke. Berta [Gehry's wife] told me afterward that he asked if the peeling paint was intentional. That's what was strong about it. You were never sure what was intentional and what wasn't. It looked in process. You weren't sure whether I meant it or not. There was something magical about the house. And I knew that the thing a lot of people hated or laughed at, was the magic" (1999, p. 57).

Here we get a glimpse of designing as a deliberate effort to question reification, a deliberate effort to restore unnamed zones of focus, and a deliberate effort to invite redifferentiation. I labeled this reverse progression as "decisive grounding" for a good reason. To ground anything is to cut through accumulated labels, and schemas, and stereotypes, and to move back toward original, natural, coherent wholes. In the case of the highly original organizational design that enacted the VISA corporation,[20] for example, these original coherent wholes were the purposes and principles that had become obscured in the banking industry when powerful people imposed their own names on the wholes and defined reality.[21] In doing so, they consolidated their control over less powerful players through reified structures that worked to their advantage. Dee Hock attacked these reified command-and-control structures in banking, unpeeled the onion of banking that had become reified by the powerful, and designed a community of semiautonomous equals who now collectively manage global transactions that involve $1.5 *trillion* a year.[22]

SO WHAT?

Where is managing as designing in all of this? If we continue to view organizational design as structuring for stability and predictability, then the potentially irreversible shift from perceptual wholes to conceptual particulars that has concerned us throughout this essay is no big deal. Quite the contrary. If managers keep imposing machine metaphors and mechanistic assumptions onto events in an effort to stabilize them, predict them, and control them, then categories, stereotypes, schemas, routines, and formalization seem like useful tools. This is a pervasive scenario in organizational design, clearly visible in contemporary command-and-control systems, not unlike those found in Gehry's own firm.[23] This scenario of machine models is pervasive in theory as well as in practice. Institutional theorists attribute machine-like processes of conformity and mimesis to fluid events, and network theorists attribute machine-like nodes and connections to dynamic relationships. The picture in both cases is the same, a picture of static clockworks that can be designed correctly. This is the world where, in Dee Hock's words, "Management expertise has become the creation and control of constants, uniformity, and efficiency" (1999).

The problem is, that version of managerial expertise is no longer what we need. Instead, "the need has become the understanding and coordination of variability, complexity, and effectiveness" (Hock, 1999, p. 57). This switch can be seen clearly in medical care, which has seen a dramatic shift from the "old days" when medicine was simple, ineffective, and relatively safe, to the current days when medicine has become complex, effective, and potentially dangerous.

If managers need to understand and coordinate variability, complexity, and effectiveness, then they need to create designs that mix together perceptual and conceptual modes of action or move back and forth between these modes or rely on multiple compoundings of abstraction. Designs that fit these requirements are best achieved if design is recast as designing that uses transient constructs, bricolage, and improvisation.

I began these remarks with the observation that Frank Gehry and Dee Hock both are troubled by the way their ideas lose intensity when they get translated in the interest of coordination. If we as designers try to solve their problem, the solution turns out to be pretty much what both of them are already doing. Our solution reads, if you want to recapture intensity, moderate the demands for coordination. As demands for coordination diminish, conceptual labels become easier to revise, zones of focus become more malleable, and patterned events are seen more clearly. The easiest way to reduce the demands for coordination is simply to stop before names overwhelm the thing seen. The charm of the skeleton, with its stable incompleteness that supports a variety of names, is lost on the zealous designer who never thinks to stop. In the name of pinning down all of the particulars of structure and process, the designer tries to do work that is best left to designers on the frontline. The overzealous designer forgets that the density of the skeleton can be worked out in real-time through self-organizing that preserves intensity.

Design is a battle of sorts between naming the thing and losing the dream, and keeping the dream but losing the name that stirs others to make the dream happen. Names (and variables) have the potential to freeze and edit and fracture the wholes that designs start with.[24] To reanimate designing, we need to move upward slowly, away from zones of focus toward the naming that begins to compound our abstractions. And we need to move downward steadily, away from reifications back toward zones of focus that can be renamed with labels that are imperfect in new ways. When we move in either direction, either away from the certainty of a dream or away from the certainty of a reification, we move toward greater uncertainty in the form of increased possibility. In a true upending of organizational design we find ourselves engaged, not in uncertainty absorption, but in uncertainty infusion. We give up clarity and take on confusion, we give up intention and take on thrownness, and we give up anticipation and take on resilience.[25] These may seem like strange choices when design is supposedly about some sort of stability. The wisdom of these actions lies in their alignment with flowing, changing, variable contexts of life, contexts that are not of our own making, and contexts that are not within our control. But this alignment does not mean that we give up stability. Instead, these choices focus the activity of designing on zones and forms and relations, which is to say, they focus the activity of design on sensemaking rather than decision making. When people make sense of flows, they impose labels that are good enough to move their projects along. But they hold those labels lightly and update them without apology and return again and again to perceptions and exploration and dreams. Thus, updating and repeated sensemaking become a testimony to the soundness of the design, not an indictment of its flaws.

This is a portrait of designing that scholars of organizational design should take more seriously. Why? Because Frank Gehry has already demonstrated that it works.

1. The rudimentary design that seems to provide the infrastructure for Dee Hock consists of semiautonomous equals affiliated for common purpose (p. 263).

2. Traditional treatments of design, such as that of Richard Butler, that discuss the use of "values" in design, cover similar issues to those that Hock seems to have in mind when he describes "purpose" and "principles."

3. Use of the word *treacherous* is not intended as hyperbole. Instead, we are concerned with the early detection of errors when they are easiest to correct. To spot an unfolding error, in its earliest stages, requires attention to small, nuanced details. Machiavelli frames the issue thusly: "As the doctors say of a wasting disease, to start with it is easy to cure but difficult to diagnose. After a time, unless it has been diagnosed and treated at the outset, it becomes easy to diagnose but difficult to cure. So it is in politics" (Machiavelli, *The Prince*, in Hock, 1999, p. 117). Error signals at VISA included signs that command-and-control designs were becoming ascendant, that authority was being consolidated at the top of hierarchies, that commitment was diminishing, that self-interest was being reasserted, and that efforts to control behavior with formal procedures were going too far. By the time of the cuff links episode, the diagnosis had become easy, but the cure took an extraordinary burst of originality.

4. Bricolage figures prominently in the following discussion (see "Designs as Bricolage" in Weick, 2001b, pp. 62–64). Bricolage is a design strategy that unfolds when people work with what they have at hand, suggesting both that people work *with* the ruins of a previous structure, not *on* the ruins, and that sunk costs are recoverable (Lanzara, 1999, p. 346). Jacques Derrida in "Structure, Sign, and Play in the Discourse of the Human Sciences" (in Derrida, 1978) paraphrases Levi-Strauss's idea in these words: "The bricoleur is someone who uses the 'means at hand' that is, the instruments he finds at his disposition around him, which are already there, which had not been especially conceived with an eye to the operation for which they are to be used and to which one tries by trial and error to adapt them, not hesitating to change them when ever it appears necessary, or to try several of them at once, even if their form and their origin are heterogeneous." Examples of bricolage would be people who cook with leftover food and those who cobble together computer code from assorted fragments.

5. Malleability is one of Dee Hock's favorite criteria for effective organizational design. He refers to a principle of design in VISA as the requirement that "it should be infinitely malleable yet extremely durable. It should be capable of constant, self-generated modification of form or function without sacrificing its essential nature or embodied principle" (Hock, 1999, p. 139).

6. It is not clear how one goes from "it all depends" to a specific design, unless there is a focus on designing, updating, transient constructs, plots, and sequence. An alternative language to the language of variables is the language of narratives. To encode perceptions in variables is to separate oneself from referent events (variables don't act), but to encode them in narrative is to engage the referent and the relations that comprise it. "When a good narrative is over, it should be unthinkable for a bystander to say so what" (Flyvbjerg, 1998, p. 86).

7. The use of the word *sign* here may seem confusing. Sign usually means details

and cues whereas *symbols* usually mean abstractions that summarize subsets of details. Thus, to move from perception to formal conception would normally mean to move from signs to symbols. However, a clue to potential problems in design lies in the fact that compounded abstraction collapses the distinction between sign and symbol. When perceptions become formal, formalized, and reified in conceptions, people treat their labeled conceptual summaries as if they were perceptual details. When people do this, they fail to see that labels screen and edit their attention and make it more selective. They forget that the map is not the territory and instead, treat the map as the territory. This confusion is a product of reification and is a weakness of stable designs in changing environments. If we focus attention away from design toward designing, then we begin to drive a wedge between maps and territories. As maps become better differentiated from territories, territories become newly available for reinterpretation and maps become newly available for updating and regrouping.

8. Weick and Sutcliffe (2001) note that a hallmark of high reliability organizations is their "reluctance to simplify interpretations" (pp. 59–62).

9. The word *details* should not be read as synonymous with the word *elements*. Instead, by details I mean the unnamed wholes that people have partitioned into zones of focus. A better word than details may be *configurations* or *gestalts*. Whatever the better word, my referent here is the primitives in both perception and design that can be grouped and named in several different ways. In everyday life, people get closer to details and farther from reifications when they maintain "situational awareness," focus attention on the here and now, reach a state of mindfulness as described within Buddhism, and/or gain access to William James's "stream of consciousness." Given the opposing pulls of socially affirmed reification and socially diverse experience, designing may best be seen as an ongoing effort to reconcile shareable cognitions with idiosyncratic experience.

10. This suggests that the concept of "uncertainty absorption" is drawn too narrowly. Gehry fears "intensity absorption," the loss of passion as ideas move from person to person, rather than the loss of detail. This suggests that the top management may make bad decisions not only because they are shielded from bad news and from premises, but also because they are shielded from passion, both as a signal of what matters and as a motivating force for their own action. In the well-known Bartlett serial construction task, where a message moves through several players and is sharply edited, investigators may have focused on an overly narrow set of issues. The question is not just, what happens cognitively to details that are assimilated and sharpened, but also what happens to affect? Do people care more at the conclusion of a serial reconstruction task, which is possible because the edited story is readily grasped, or do they care less, which is equally possible because the story has become conventionalized and is no different from most other stories they have heard. The loss of intensity is also a puzzle if that outcome is compared against the outcomes of studies of mobs, deindividuation, group polarization, the risky shift, and the emotionality of groups. This body of work suggests that intensity is often amplified rather than dampened in collective settings. A Gehry project is rarely a mob, but project meetings could encourage an escalation in willingness to take risks, which should make a big difference in outcomes depending on the stage at which participants shift in the direction of greater risk (perception, conception, form, formful, reified, taken for granted).

11. The basic model being assumed here is that designing for coordination (transmit, receive), affects cognitive processing (cognitive tuning), which affects grasp (high and low differentiation), which affects activity.

12. Diane Vaughan (1996) shows how reified launch routines in NASA were preserved when anomalous events produced by inadequate seals, events that should have been singled out and given a distinctive label, were normalized as acceptable deviations that fit within the preexisting labels and routines.

13. This failure has been described by Langer as "mindlessness." Weick and Sutcliffe (2001) argue that an obsession with updating tends to be found in effective high reliability organizations where mindfulness is a central thread throughout their processes and culture.

14. This is a central theme in Turner (1978) and Weick and Sutcliffe (2001).

15. Dee Hock makes a related point in his first law of management: "Everything has both intended and unintended consequences. The intended consequences may or may not happen; the unintended consequences always do." (KPMG speech, p. 4).

16. The "stirring" together of perceptions and schema is illustrated by Charlan Nemeth's (1986) finding that persistent minority influence stimulates those in the majority to reexamine their positions and to puzzle over why someone would so persistently espouse a contrarian point of view. The fact that the puzzled people are the majority means that their understanding is schema-driven. The fact that the majority also puzzles over perceptions that don't fit means that they are simultaneously attentive to stimulus-driven assertions. It is this hybrid of schema-driven belief and stimulus-driven doubt that exemplifies "ambivalence as the optimal compromise" (Weick, 2001a).

17. The image of a "dream" is also found in Dee Hock's suggestion that dreams, determination, and liberty are prerequisites for meaningful organizational design (pp. 182, 192).

18. This distinction comes from Asch, 1952.

19. The notion of "self"-organizing contains a nest of questions that are beyond the scope of this chapter. When self-organizing is triggered, it may be a beneficial source of design for reasons of motivation (it activates intrinsic motivation), it taps skills at which people have developed considerable expertise. Counterpoised to this straightforward implication is the more knotty issue that selves are multiple, transient, grounded in shifting reference groups, and fabricated from the images reflected by others.

20. The design has been described as a "reverse holding company."

21. It is important in the context of design to recall Nietzsche's powerful insight, supported by Flyvbjerg's research, that power makes people stupid. "According to Kant, 'The possession of power unavoidably spoils the free use of reason.' On the basis of the case of Aalborg bus terminal, we may expand on Kant by observing that the possession of more power appears to spoil reason even more. One of the privileges of power, and an integral part of its rationality, is the freedom to define reality. The greater the power, the greater the freedom in this respect and the less need for power to understand how reality is constructed. The absence of rational arguments and factual documentation in support of certain actions may be just as important indicators of power as the arguments and documentation produced" (1998, p. 37). Designs that increase options, encourage review of concepts and forms, and resist reification may undermine determination of reality solely along lines of power differentials.

22. What is so noteworthy about this example of organizational design is that it was set in motion *before* the Internet was in place, before complexity theory was available to map the designing, and while people were benchmarking on visible command-and-control forms such as General Motors (see Hock, 1999, p. 141).

23. Frank Gehry's efforts to pull engineering and contracting back inside his firm illustrate the pervasiveness of command and control designs and their attractiveness: "Control is back where it belongs, in the hands of the architect as master-builder" (p. 18n4).

24. A similar idea is found in Richard Rorty's observation that "the way to re-enchant the world is to stick to the concrete" (cited in Flyvbjerg, 1998, p. 129).

25. This circumstance resembles what has been described as a "cosmology episode" (Weick, 1993), suggesting that a moment of confusion can lead to a failure as at Mann Gulch or a success as at VISA.

REFERENCES

Asch, S. E. 1952. *Social psychology*. Englewood Cliffs, NJ: Prentice-Hall.

Baron, R., and S. J. Misovich. 1999. On the relationship between social and cognitive modes of organization. In *Dual-process theories in social psychology*, edited by S. Chaiken and Y. Trope, 586–605. New York: Guilford.

Bate, P., R. Khan, and A. Pye. 2000. Towards a culturally sensitive approach to organization structuring: Where organization design meets organization development. *Organization Science* 11 (2): 197–211.

Butler, R. 1995. Organizational design. In *Blackwell encyclopedic dictionary of organizational behavior*, edited by N. Nicholson, 384–90. Cambridge, MA: Blackwell.

Campbell, D. T. 1988. *Methodology and epistemology for social science*. Chicago: University of Chicago Press.

Derrida, J. 1978. *Writing and difference*, translated by Alan Bass, 278–93. Chicago: University of Chicago Press.

Flyvbjerg, B. 1998. *Rationality and power: Democracy in practice*. Chicago: University of Chicago Press.

Friedman, M., ed. 1999. *Architecture + process: Gehry talks*. New York: Rizzoli.

Gehry, F. 1999. Commentaries. In *Architecture + process: Gehry talks*, edited by M. Friedman, 43–287. New York: Rizzoli.

Haberstroh, C. J. 1965. Organization design and system analysis. In *Handbook of organizations*, edited by J. G. March, 1,171–1,212. Chicago: Rand McNally.

Hock, D. 1999. *Birth of the chaordic age*. San Francisco: Berrett-Koehler.

Irwin, R. 1977. Notes toward a model. *Exhibition Catalog of Whitney Museum*, 23–31. New York.

Lanzara, G. F. 1999. Between transient constructs and persistent structures: Designing systems in action. *Journal of Strategic Information Systems*, 8: 331–49.

Nemeth, C. 1986. Differential contributions of majority and minority influence. *Psychological Review* 93: 23–32.

Snook, S. 2000. *Friendly fire*. Princeton, NJ: Princeton University.

Sorkin, M. 1999. Frozen light. In *Architecture + process: Gehry talks*, edited by M. Friedman. New York: Rizzoli.

Thompson, J. D. 1967. *Organizations in action*. New York: McGraw-Hill.

Turner, B. 1978. *Man-made disasters*. London: Wykeham.

Vaughan, D. 1996. The Challenger launch decision: risky technology, culture and deviance at NASA. Chicago: University of Chicago Press.

Weick, K. E. 1990. Fatigue of the spirit in organizational theory and organizational development: Reconnaissance man as remedy. *Journal of Applied Behavioral Science* 26(3): 313–27.

———. 1993. The collapse of sensemaking in organizations: The Mann Gulch disaster. *Administrative Science Quarterly* 38 (4): 628–52.

———. 2001a. The attitude of wisdom: Ambivalence as the optimal compromise. In *Making sense of the organization*, edited by K. E. Weick, 361–79. Oxford, UK: Blackwell.

———. 2001b. Organizational redesign as improvisation. In *Making sense of the organization*, edited by K. E. Weick, 57–91. Oxford, UK: Blackwell.

Weick, K. E., and K. M. Sutcliffe. 2001. *Managing the unexpected*. San Francisco: Jossey-Bass.

Weschler, L. 1982. *Seeing is forgetting the name of the thing one sees: A life of contemporary artist Robert Irwin*. Berkeley: University of California Press.

4

Management and Design

Interaction Pathways in Organizational Life

Richard Buchanan

THE IDEA of managing an organization by design thinking is both provocative and puzzling. It is provocative because the popular understanding of design tends to reduce it to a self-expressive artistic activity associated with the appearance of graphic communications, industrial products, interior spaces, and buildings. The prospect of bringing this kind of design into the business of managing organizational life seems at best metaphoric and at worst frivolous. However, the popular understanding of design is not the understanding held by many leading designers. They regard design not merely as an artistic activity but as a deeply humanistic and intellectual activity that focuses on the creation of practical, effective products that serve human beings in all aspects of their lives. It is humanistic because it focuses on the human experience of products. It is intellectual because it requires direct or indirect knowledge of all of the factors that must be integrated in a successful product, whether the product is a communication, an artifact, a service or management activity, or an environment. Design provides discipline in finding and solving problems in practical life through the creation of products that have intellectual integrity as well as emotional and aesthetic satisfaction.

The early forms of design — found in the practices of graphic design and industrial design, interior design and architectural design — have an important place in organizational life. Each form of practice yields products that serve organizations in reaching their goals and objectives. In its best form, graphic design yields clear and effective communication, whether for advertising, for

Richard Buchanan, *School of Design, Carnegie Mellon University.*

presenting information about products and services, or for any other communication with customers, employees, and stakeholders. Similarly, industrial design yields the artifacts that are the core of manufacturing: consumer products, machines, tools, and equipment. Interior design yields pleasing retail spaces for customers and effective workspaces for employees, whether in the office or the factory. Finally, architecture yields the buildings and structures within which the work of business is carried out, often providing a symbolic expression of corporate or organizational identity.

If this were all that one understands in the concept of managing as designing, further exploration would lead to significant benefit for organizations. The reason is that businesses and other organizations make surprisingly little use of the traditional forms of design practice for advancing their goals.[1] Better understanding of the potential of traditional forms of design practice and the articulation of new methods for integrating design as a strategic tool in organizational life should be one of the goals of management education. Indeed, schools of design also should explore these matters, preparing designers who can participate more effectively in higher levels of management. There are numerous examples of successful organizations that have made strategic use of design, and there are also new educational programs that are exploring these issues. However, there is a clear need to consolidate what has been learned in practice and in academic exploration, and there is a need to set a new agenda for research that will build from what has already been accomplished.

One example of a significant problem that requires interdisciplinary collaboration between management and design is new product development. A growing number of corporations regard the management of design and new product development as a matter of great concern. The reason is not difficult to discover. When technological innovations spread quickly among competitors, design is one of the key factors of product differentiation in the marketplace, elevating one company over another in the minds of consumers.[2] Properly integrating design into a complex organization is one of the important challenges faced by management today. For this reason, *design management* is an emerging specialty within management itself. This is particularly important for corporations that are founded on an engineering culture because engineering often neglects the human dimensions of technology that are essential for success in the marketplace. But it is important for all organizations, whether in the private or the public sector (Blaich, 1993).

However, managing the traditional forms of design and product development is only one aspect of the emerging theme of *managing as designing*. In a deeper sense, managing as designing challenges us to think of the services

56   and activities of an organization, and indeed the organization itself, as consciously conceived and directed products in human culture. The question is how design thinking can help us along this path. Are there concepts and methods of design that can concretely affect the way we shape and develop our organizations?

Traditional design practice may offer some insight, but we are correct to be skeptical about how much may be learned and applied in managing an organization. The metaphor is exciting, but the specific new practices are vague. It is better to look toward new forms of design practice, particularly the new approach known as "interaction design," for ideas about managing as designing. This approach emerged quietly perhaps two decades ago around the problems that human beings face when working with computers and digital information systems. Early work focused on improving the "interface" of computers, but the work has gone far beyond interface design and has led to significant progress in making computer systems more accessible to ordinary people. This is what Geoffrey Moore meant by the phrase "crossing the chasm" in computer technology (Moore, 1991). What had been the private domain of computer programmers and early technology adopters, occupying a narrow market segment, expanded into the wide market segment of general consumers, most of whom have little direct knowledge of the software and hardware that operates behind the scenes. Interaction design provides the new concepts and methods that are transforming computer systems into the devices and tools of ordinary social practice for living, working, playing, and learning.

A similar transformation of organizational systems and management is what we seek in the idea of managing as designing. As organizations become more complex, there is a growing need to focus and clarify their operation for customers, employees, and managers. Interaction design offers this possibility as a strategic discipline of management.

The bridge to interaction design is not difficult to discover. The first span of the bridge is a recognition that human-computer interaction is only a small area of all of the other interactions that human beings have in their daily lives. Fundamentally, interaction design is about how people relate to other people and how products mediate those relationships. It matters little whether the product is a document, an artifact, a computer or a computer program, a service, a business activity, or an organizational environment. All of these *classes of products* and their specific *families of products* are open to design thinking that is based on facilitating the relationships among people to reach specific goals and objectives.

The second span of the bridge is recognition of the diverse kinds of knowledge and specialized expertise that are needed to design and execute organizational operations, whether such operations are external service activities—relationships with customers, suppliers, and government—or internal planning and management activities. Design that fails to understand the critical importance of accounting, finance, human relations, strategic planning, and vision building is doomed to irrelevance. Similarly, design that fails to understand the value of knowledge from the social and behavioral sciences—knowledge about the social and cultural context of an organization—will merely revert to traditional management practices. To be effective, interaction designers must immerse themselves in the reality of an activity and the supporting ideas that surround it.

The third span of the bridge is exploration of the discipline, methods, and techniques of interaction design as they may be applied to managing a complex organization. Interaction design is a strategic discipline in the sense that it seeks the integration of specialized knowledge around the performance of an action. It is task-based and, therefore, human-centered: it seeks to facilitate human beings in the accomplishment of their goals. This is more than a vague idea that the customer is always right in what he or she wants to do. Customers may or may not know what they want to do, but typically they do not know how to do it in a complex organization. One of the goals of interaction design is to make organizations accessible to all of the people who must interact with organizational systems.

An example in communication will illustrate the point. A social service agency in a midwestern state provides a twenty-page booklet to explain eligibility and procedures for accessing state funds to ameliorate a health problem. It is a classic example of bureaucratic communication, written in highly technical language that attempts to represent all of the rules and regulations as they are conceived by legislative policymakers. Employees of the agency find the information difficult to understand and apply, and clients—ordinary citizens—find it almost impossible to read. In one sense, this is a classic problem of information design and graphic design. A response may be that the booklet should be redesigned, perhaps with "plain language" as well as improved layout and typography. With this approach, there would probably be some improvement in comprehension, but it would be marginal.

In another sense, however, the current booklet is a sign of the new problem faced by many organizations. It reveals a systems problem, directly related to the core vision of the organization. The current booklet clearly demonstrates to any reader that the social service agency is designed primarily to administer and enforce rules and regulations. Failure to understand the booklet is blamed on the employee or the client—much as failure to operate a new computer

58   software program is often blamed on the user rather than on the software programmer or the company that produced the software. Traditional redesign merely reinforces the regulatory vision of the agency, not the service vision that presumably inspired creation of the agency.

Interaction design would approach the problem in a different way. The first step would focus on the vision and goals of the organization. Does the agency want to reinforce a rules-based culture or does it want to help people accomplish a task related to their health and welfare, while meeting all necessary rules and regulations? In short, should the communication be rules-based or task-based? If efficiency and satisfaction are goals of the agency, then the communication should facilitate action. What would follow is a new design of the booklet from the perspective of employees and clients, with features that reflect the realities of navigating through complex information to reach a successful and satisfying conclusion. These features may well include a new information architecture of questions and answers relevant to the client and the employee, greater use of images and diagrams integrated with text, as well as changes in language. One would find the best features through user research, scenarios of use, ongoing user testing and evaluation of effectiveness, and a variety of other methods now available to interaction designers. All of the agency rules and regulations would be maintained, but they would enter as needed along the pathway of applying for aid.

The role of an organizational champion in this process is essential. Leadership is needed to initiate the project and maintain its forward progress with the cooperation of employees, for whom cultural change may be painful. If the champion is a local manager, success will attract attention and curiosity from superiors. If the champion is at a high level in the organization, the interaction design process offers the opportunity for leaders to bring their personal vision of organizational change into concrete and specific reality. The daunting task of changing a system becomes focused through specific interventions in operational interactions.

Managers may use the opportunity and new insights afforded by the interaction design process to rethink other aspects of agency subsystems related to service operations—training of employees, supporting computer systems, physical facilities, and even the "brand experience" of the agency. A knowledgeable manager may even employ similar interaction design methods to rethink other agency operations, within the regulatory constraints of the organization.

This example is not far-fetched. It is one of several cases where large organizations are using the concepts and methods of interaction design— known by this name or by other names—to rethink the pathways of organizational life.³ Today, these cases typically begin in a problem of communication, similar to that faced by the social service agency. But as managers begin to see the potential of interaction design for revealing further problems and solutions in an organization, they see new opportunities for reshaping the work of the organization.

The discipline of interaction design involves several phases, each with relevant design methodologies and techniques developed by different practitioners and design researchers.⁴ The first step focuses on *vision*, seeking to clarify, understand, and sometimes help shape the governing ideas of an organization.⁵ The second step focuses on *strategic planning* and *strategic design planning*, where the task is to assess the environment and circumstances of organizational operations and then determine the most significant area for product design and development.⁶ The third step is preparing and exploring a *specific brief for interaction design work*. The fourth step is *generating ideas* for design solutions and selecting the most viable solutions. The fifth step is *planning and prototyping* one or more solutions and *evaluating* their effectiveness through ongoing user research and testing, ultimately leading to the selection of one design for *final realization*. The sixth step is *delivery* of the final prototype, along with documentation and production specifications, where relevant. The seventh step is *implementation*, which presents its own special design issues for managers who must organize human and other resources and plan how a new design will be produced or carried out, ranging from manufacture to marketing and distribution.

In addition to the phases of the discipline of interaction design, several features further distinguish interaction design from other management approaches. There is an emphasis on *visualization* throughout the process. Interaction designers employ a wide variety of visualization techniques to facilitate individual and collective understanding of ongoing work, ranging from concept mapping and sketching to visual collage and other forms of imaging. There is a *team approach* because the product is complex. There is an emphasis *on collaborative and participatory* design, involving both employees and customers. *Rapid and frequent prototyping* is common, allowing all participants in the process to critique the progress of work and contribute ideas for improvement. *User research and user testing* play an important role, allowing designers to go beyond the broad market segment analysis that is common in marketing and beyond the limitations of focus group techniques. Task-based *scenario building* is common to discover the real issues of user experience. Issues of *brand experience* often emerge through interaction planning, helping to inform the design work with the broader vision of the organization. In addition, the work process tends to allow *horizontal distribution of responsibility*, based on the local knowledge of those who are most directly involved with the issues under consideration; vertical management structures are typically low. In short, a variety of tools and techniques, some new and some old, inform the discipline of interaction design and encourage creativity and shared ownership of the results.

Explorations of interaction design in the context of organizational management face all of the challenges of pioneering efforts. The two greatest obstacles are lack of management education in the best practices of interaction design and cultural traditions rooted in old practices. Ironically, the roots of design thinking run deep in the literature of management and organizational behavior. In *Models of Management*, Mauro Guillén identifies three major paradigms of organizational management that emerged in the twentieth century (Guillén, 1994). In order of historical development, they are *scientific management, management of human relations*, and *management through structural analysis*. As Guillén explains, these are paradigms in the sense of "systems of interrelated ideas and techniques that offer a distinctive diagnosis and solution to a set of problems." Significantly, Guillén also identifies *religion* as a fourth major influence on organizational behavior, an influence that, he remarks, has been relegated to the background or totally neglected in studies of management and organizations. For Guillén, religion does not offer a paradigm of organizational behavior in the sense of the other three models, perhaps because religions vary so widely among nations and cultures.[7]

Without elaborating these models or explaining their specific application in organizations, one should recognize that they provide alternative frameworks for thinking about the design of organizations. The most explicit evidence for this is found in the work of Herbert A. Simon, whom Guillén regards as an early and influential proponent of the "management through structural analysis" paradigm. One of Simon's most important books, *The Sciences of the Artificial*, makes an explicit argument for regarding management —and all other kinds of professional behavior—as a form of design thinking. For Simon, design is the science of decision making, and it matters little whether the product of decision making is an organization or a consumer product. Better understanding of cognitive processes, he believes, will improve decision making in all areas of professional work.

Whereas Simon's work presents a formal connection between management and other forms of design, one can easily demonstrate that the other models of management bear a strong affinity with corresponding approaches to graphic and industrial design that have emerged over the past century. Scientific management has its analog in engineering design and in the application of knowledge gained in diverse subject matters of science, including ergonomics and psychology. Management of human relations has its analog in two seemingly distinct, but actually complementary, approaches to design. The first approach is grounded in the creation and projection of personal meaning in graphic and industrial products. It emphasizes the self-expressive voice and style of the individual designer. The second approach is grounded in the transactions of human communication that are made possible through all types of products. It emphasizes not the individual designer, projecting meanings into the world, but the interactions that take place when such projections are viewed in a social and cultural context. It relies on social psychology and anthropology to provide frameworks for the creative activities of the designer. Religion, too, has its place in design thinking, though this influence has been neglected in design theory as much as it has in organizational theory.[8]

While design thinking is implicit in management and organizational theory, the reason for going further in exploring managing as designing is clear. On the one hand, the large systems of management described by Guillén and others have lacked a thoroughgoing design discipline to effect their goals. Methods of implementation have tended to emphasize analytical tools without the corresponding synthetic skills for integrating specialized methods in new programs of human-centered action. Where synthesis has taken place, it has been more by chance and individual initiative than by discipline. The theory of organizational learning is a step forward in this direction, but the methods that support it remain significantly underdeveloped as a design discipline.[9] On the other hand, the traditional disciplines of design have tended to focus on a specific and concrete set of design products—graphics, artifacts, interiors, and buildings—without adapting the design process to actions and pathways of organizational life. Designers have been thoughtful about the place of their work in organizational life, but until recently they have not synthesized their experience in a form that is directly useful to management. In short, the potential of design thinking for organizational life has not been fully developed.

As organizations grow more complex, one may see an analogy between the organization and an urban landscape. The landscape is a complex system of systems, encompassing communications, tangible artifacts, human transactions, and competing values and visions that may shape the future. The city map is before us and systems analysts provide excellent descriptions of the interdependencies of the systems and subsystems. However, apart from these descriptions, the systems analysts and systems consultants offer only general ideas about how to redesign the system. The problem is how to intervene in this complexity through specific actions and design thinking in order to adapt to changing circumstances. Interaction design suggests that we shift our perspective from the massive totality of the system to the pathways of individual human experience — to our major pathways through the city and through the organization to accomplish our goals. These pathways we can know in a way that we can never know the totality of a complex system except through abstractions that distort reality. Whether our focus is internal pathways of leadership and management or the pathways of customers and clients, we can use the methods and concepts of interaction design to rethink how the organization does its business and gradually rebuild its systems in the dimensions of human experience. This is the promise of exploring managing as designing.

NOTES

1. In his keynote address to the Forty-fifth International Design Conference, Tom Peters offers this remark: "I think the world is awash in look-alike, taste-alike, and feel-alike products and services, and that the ability of design to transform an institution is not yet as widely accepted by top management as he [John Kao] suggests. To make that point, I want to speak tonight about institutions that do get it. Those that do, though there is no perfect model, exhibit a series of thirty-five traits that add up to what I call *design mindfulness*" (1996, p.16).

2. There is a small but growing literature in the area of new product development. For one of the recent and more successful efforts, see Cagan and Vogel (2002).

3. Among the projects now underway to apply the methods and concepts of interaction design to organizations, two deserve special note because of their scale and their location in government. One project is the redesign of the Australian Taxation System, regarded as the largest systems-design project in Australia since the Second World War. The other project is the transformation of the *Domestic Mail Manual* of the United States Postal Service. The task of the design team is to redesign the core legal document (currently approaching 1,000 pages) that presents mailing standards and the products of the USPS and governs operations of the corporation. In both cases, issues of vision as well as pathways of interactive experience are central matters of attention. The author is involved in both of these projects.

4. The discipline of interaction design is a new area of academic research and education, but it grows out of a variety of intellectual influences throughout the twentieth century. The interaction design programs of the School of Design at Carnegie Mellon University are among the first to consolidate and expand the theory of interaction design through teaching and research.

5. Tony Golsby-Smith, principal of Golsby-Smith Associates, is a pioneer in "strategic conversations" to clarify and shape corporate vision among the leaders of an organization. Darrel Rhea, principal of Cheskin Research, also works at the high level of management to clarify organizational vision and objectives.

6. Among designers who are exploring strategic planning and strategic design planning, the late Jay Doblin and, subsequently, Larry Keeley, now principal of the Doblin Group, are pioneers. Tony Golsby-Smith has also developed new methods for corpo-

rate planning and decision making, based on a simple, clear protocol for assessing issues and determining courses of action. Darrel Rhea, drawing on the historical excellence of Cheskin Research in marketing research, also employs new design methods for strategic design planning. There are also several design consultancies whose work bears directly on strategic planning and strategic design planning, including Ziba Design, Fitch, IDEO, and Design Continuum.

7. For example, Confucianism and Buddhism generally endorse the idea that there are intrinsic satisfactions in work, while Christianity tends to emphasize extrinsic rewards to work. Yet, religion has had far-reaching influence on business thinking around the world. It preceded the three commonly explored paradigms of organizational behavior, and it continues to exert considerable influence on some, if not all, of the models.

8. The Herman Miller Corporation provides one of the best examples of how religion has influenced both organizational behavior and the use of traditional design thinking about products. See Abercrombie (1994, pp. 83ff.).

9. In *The Fifth Discipline: The Art and Practice of the Learning Organization* (1990), Peter Senge characterizes the CEO as a designer. But the actual discipline of design thinking possessed by the CEO remains descriptive in key areas of practice.

REFERENCES

Abercrombie, S. 1994. *George Nelson: The design of modern design*. Cambridge: MIT Press.

Blaich, R. 1993. *Product design and corporate strategy: Managing the connection for competitive advantage*. New York: McGraw-Hill.

Cagan, J., and C. M. Vogel. 2002. *Creating breakthrough products: Innovation from product planning and program approval*. New York: Financial Times-Prentice Hall.

Guillén, M. 1994. *Models of management: Work, authority, and organization in a comparative perspective*. Chicago: University of Chicago Press.

Moore, G. 1991. *Crossing the chasm: Marketing and selling high-tech products to mainstream customers*. New York: HarperBusiness.

Peters, T. 1996. Design mindfulness, in International Design Conference in Aspen, *The New Business of Design*. New York: Allworth Press.

Senge, P. M. 1990. The fifth discipline: The art and practice of the learning organization. New York: Doubleday.

II   FOUNDATIONS OF
MANAGING AS DESIGNING

THIS SECTION EXPLORES *a wide range of theoretical underpin-
nings to inform our consideration of managing as designing. Alexander
Tzonis begins with a discussion of ways that managers can learn from
the poetics of architects and thereby add to their repertoire of professional methods. Karl Weick follows with an essay that draws inspiration
from Martin Heidegger and considers ways in which the condition of
thrownness characterizes the manager's design situation. It shapes the
possibilities for being a designer and helps us to understand how designs emerge in a social context. John King then provides a very challenging discussion of form and function, debunking the notion that
form does or should follow function in our design acts. Nicholas Cook
follows with a consideration of the incompleteness of language in design, using musical notation as the prime example. He demonstrates
most engagingly how different languages (or methods) of notation inevitably leave empty spaces in our ability to specify and play a musical
composition. Wanda Orlikowski then challenges us to consider who is
benefiting from a design and encourages us to be more reflexive on the
constitutive role of design in organizations. Yrjö Engeström provides
some answers for Orlikowski's questions by proposing a theory of argument that will be useful in helping managers reflect on and improve the
dialogues that characterize managing and designing.*

*Barbara Czarniawska then proposes that Gehry's design of build-
ings is best understood as the construction of action nets. She argues
that our familiar conceptions of organizations, action, and networks are
not adequate to capture the unique process of organizing found in his
projects and its implications for understanding organizations and innovation. Richard Boland then considers Herbert Simon's notions of intelligence, design, and choice as core components of management action
and explores the different sequences in which they can be used to punc-*

tuate a stream of experience and construct narratives of managing. Mariann Jelinek follows with a call for multilevel theories of organization that recognize the way environments, theories, and actions of managers all have design antecedents and consequences in a kind of interactive dance. Hilary Bradbury joins with a number of female executives in asking how the future of these socially constructed environments, products, and organizational forms could be reshaped to benefit our children and future generations. Joseph Goguen then provides a philosophical approach to these questions that does not resort to a reductionist vocabulary. It accepts that the organizations, products, and environments that we take as given and stable are constantly being reconstructed through the interaction of their members — creating a groundless world of process in which compassion and ethics become primary sources of judgment.

Miriam Levin and Keith Hoskin conclude this section with two chapters that root the preceding arguments in a historical context. Levin argues that it was in the Enlightenment that the grounding of management and the dream of a rationally controlled social order came to fruition. The grounding came from considering material objects as carriers of information that could be orchestrated to control society through communication in a kind of cybernetic dream. Hoskin analyzes management designs for organizations and control systems that are often assumed to have come from the railroads. He argues that they were instead informed by disciplinary educational practices of West Point during the nineteenth century. The two chapters are a striking historical vision of management as control and discipline and suggest the scope and depth of entrenched practices that we will have to confront in pursuing an agenda of managing as designing.

5

EVOLVING SPATIAL INTELLIGENCE TOOLS, FROM ARCHITECTURAL POETICS TO MANAGEMENT METHODS

Alexander Tzonis

THERE ARE many fascinating things about architecture seen from the point of view of management. Starting with Herbert Simon, many people in the management community have been captivated by architects' noticeable ability to "imagine," to "synthesize," and to "create" in conceiving buildings. Behind these general abilities that architects appear to have, there are specific intellectual tools and unique design methods for conceiving buildings — or the *poetics* of architecture. It is the ingenuity of these methods and our potential to reuse them in other domains that makes architecture so interesting for other disciplines today. In the context of the present discussion, there are two important questions to investigate: Which of these architectural methods are the most promising to be transferred into other fields such as management? How can they be conveyed?

We will touch upon three ideas here: the building metaphor, diagrammatic sketching, and recruiting precedent schemes.

BACKGROUND

Interest in transferring methods from architecture to management is new. The situation was the very opposite half a century ago. To be more exact, since the middle of the 1960s, an important number of architects involved in teaching and journalism reacted against what they saw as the opaqueness and lack of

Alexander Tzonis, *Department of Architecture, University of Technology of Delft.* Some of these ideas have been presented in a series of courses given in the College de France, May 2001, and also appear in *Designing, a Cognitive Theory,* Cambridge: MIT Press (forthcoming).

rigor in architectural thinking and began introducing into their profession ideas from management. It was management thinking that was revolutionizing architectural methodology, bringing to it concepts and techniques intended initially to improve organizations and industries. And this, despite opposition from many architects who believed that the privileged place management gave to the objectives of efficiency and effectiveness was "contaminating" the creative, disinterested, and critical character of their profession. More significantly, management contributed in shifting the focus of architects from design products to design process, a problem-solving, decision-making process that had to be tamed and rationalized with the support of analysis.[1]

However, as we came closer to the end of the twentieth century, management also had its anxieties. The highly abstract, factual, quantitative models developed through history that management had employed routinely were perceived now as reductive, "value-free," "value-absent," and deprived of *vision*. Effective in the short term, they were powerless to confront value-laden problems of innovation and radical modernization — situations characteristic of the last two decades of the "new world order," environmental crisis, and "globalization." In addition, as Simon remarked in his writings, although highly advanced in techniques and methods dealing with *analysis*, quantitative models of management could not deal with *synthesis*. They had techniques to solve industrial problems of rational resource allocation, but they were helpless to solve problems dealing with culture-bound, informal human organizations. On the other hand, as the oeuvre of Le Corbusier, Calatrava, or Gehry suggests, architecture possesses mental tools that can produce visions and achieve synthesis.

THE BUILDING METAPHOR

From a very early age, people appear attracted by the manner buildings are put together, used, or demolished. There is something extremely familiar and fundamental about them that invites people to use them as metaphors in a wide variety of situations to figure out how to plan novel, complex actions that are difficult to grasp. Perhaps their spatial structure can be applied to represent formally problems such as the conception of abstract organizations and institutions, problems management is busy with.[2] Perhaps conceiving sustainable organizations, plans, and policies can become more familiar if they are seen "as if" they are buildings, that is to say, made out of components like supporting structure, enclosing skin, and contained locations, going through phases like the construction of foundations, bearing skeleton, and roof as well as maintenance and demolition. Perhaps the intimate and vital relations buildings have

with humans (containing, protecting, imprisoning, possessing humans or being possessed by them) prompts buildings to be gainfully applied by analogy
to develop working hypotheses about the relation between institutions, their
employees, and their public. Perhaps, the way humans use buildings (entering, moving through, embedding objects in them) or the architectural, functional interrelationship between room and corridor — or rather "serving" and
"served," to remember Louis Kahn — makes building metaphors good vehicles for communicating, elucidating, and even justifying new complex ideas
about the distribution of power, arrangement of control, structure of information, and other tasks management struggles with. In other words, management
thinking can be aided by architectural spatial-functional thinking by offering
at the early heuristic stages of an inquiry a fast "insight" into complex, un-
identified, and untried problems before analytical methods take over. One can
see systematic procedures developed, employing architectural metaphors as
heuristic devices at the early stages of a management inquiry. In addition, one
can see them applied as communication vehicles in an inquiry that requires
multi-agent collaborative problem solving.

THE ARCHITECTURAL SKETCH

Architectural sketches are a kind of diagram. Like architectural metaphors,
sketches are used by architects as a means for communication in aiding design collaboration. They are a powerful tool that helps architects to abstract
attributes of hypothetical provisional design solutions and summarize their
complex patterns, thus enhancing the design process. Sketches have, to cite
Herbert Simon who pointed out the importance of diagrammatic reasoning,
a "low search, and recognition cost" (Qin and Simon, 1995). For this reason,
to paraphrase a much-quoted saying, one architectural sketch is "worth
10,000 words." The sketches that architects use are extremely powerful in com-
pressing vast amounts of information. Walls, windows, corridors, and level
changes are meshed with circulation channels, modulations of light, and variations in hydrothermal conditions. In "one glance," sketches articulate hierarchies of importance of issues immersed in a given project. They account for
objects in movement and states in flux and express the simultaneous presence
of multiple factors of form and function relevant to a project, manifesting constraints, and interdependencies between them. Architectural sketches are able
to do all that by *mixing* different modes of representation (pictorial, iconic,
topological, and algebraic), as well as by *superimposing* concurrently multiple
frames of formal-functional interrelationships with these frames of spatial reference. The effectiveness of architectural sketches becomes evident, as Asaf

Friedman (2003) studied recently, if they are compared to current computer-based navigation programs in expressing a sense of movement. The sketch offers a rich experience while the navigation programs, being reductive in terms of spatial frames of reference offer a "flat" one. And this happens even if the program provides highly realistic pictures in terms of perspective deformations, shadows, and color.

We can conjecture that systematic procedures could be developed to transfer mechanisms of representation from architectural sketches as heuristic devices at the early stages of a management inquiry. Mechanisms used originally by architects to construct diagrams and to map situations and problems relevant to the design of physical structures can be adapted and developed to represent settings and predicaments related to the conception of nonspatial organizational schemes. Such visual, spatial reasoning can be very supportive in the creation of working hypotheses for interpreting problems that are neither visual nor spatial and for that reason difficult to formalize or comprehend through other existing methods. In combination with the above metaphor of an organization or a plan *as a building*, they can be also applied to communicate—illustrate and exemplify—complex abstract ideas in the case of collaborative, dialogical problem solving where more than one expertise is needed.

UNDERSTANDING ORGANIZATION THROUGH SPATIAL-FIGURAL REPRESENTATIONS

Like the *building metaphor*, the *architectural sketch* can make solving organizational and management problems easier. They ease the burden of working memory in carrying out mental operations involved in solving such problems. They both offer a space-based type of representation, which is simpler to recognize and keep in memory. Both help to describe dynamic interrelationships between multiple nonvisual elements—such as changing aggregations of actors, events, resource budgets, and multiple objectives all operating simultaneously—that are notoriously challenging to understand or remember. It is possible to carry out this change of representation because, as recent research has shown, spatial schemata are similar to time schemata and spatial-functional structures and time-process structures are cognitively homologous (Boroditsky, 2000). Space-based representations, either through building metaphors or through diagrams, appear to be particularly good in dealing with data concerning intriguing structures of sequencing, as one has in complex schedules, or with overlap and inclusion, as in the case of multiple administrative responsibilities and controls. In such circumstances, expressive sketches can be much more efficient and effective than verbal or mathematical descriptions.

One of the most interesting supports that sketches offer in architecture is in fore-grounding subtle morphological or operational similarities between two different building projects. They are used routinely and informally for recalling from memory precedent design solutions and reusing them to solve new problems. Yet, architects, more than any other professionals, have gained an almost mythical reputation for being "creative"[3] and innovative even though they have been systematically generating their ideas by recombining precedents recruited by analogy. The myth was renewed during the romantic period and has been perpetuated up to our time. This contributed very little to the understanding of the cognitive mechanisms enabling architectural creativity and obscured the understanding of the role precedents play when architects design seemingly unprecedented architectural schemes. Architecture is not the only discipline or profession that uses precedents to provide answers by analogy to new problems. Certainly, law schools, military academies, and, relatively more recently, business schools have been using prior cases for educating students in solving problems. On a more theoretical level, psychology has carried out considerable research to identify the thinking mechanisms and to establish the heuristic value of using knowledge by analogy in creative research and invention in general.

However, one has to recognize that architects are usually more daring in their analogies than most other disciplines. They recruit sources from very distant domains (Tzonis and Lefaivre, 2001; Tzonis, 2001). Furthermore, architects recall precedent cases to extract from them only parts of an entire scheme, which they proceed to recombine in new wholes in highly surprising ways. For example, to develop a new prototype for high-rise housing, the famous Unité d'Habitation, Le Corbusier did not hesitate to recruit from precedents as diverse as a liner, a bottle rack, and a primitive hut (Moraes Zarzar, 2003; Tzonis, 1992). In many respects, this artificial intellectual process resembles the process of evolution of life.

Again one can imagine the development of algorithms employing the processes of recalling, partitioning, extracting, and recombining design precedents as heuristic devices at the early stages of a management inquiry, drawn by analogy to similar methods of architecture. Reasoning through precedents can accelerate the formation of working hypotheses for dealing with unfamiliar, complex, and hard to formalize situations.

POETICS, POTENTIALS, AND POSSIBLE ERRORS

However, one must keep in mind that there are neither explicit protocols nor authorized lists of rules for the conventions used in representing forms or functions in architectural sketches. Since the beginning of the Renaissance, conventions of representation of architectural diagrams have evolved and adapted slowly through usage. Architects, through history and today, learn how to interpret them or how to signify and communicate through them by means of practice and not by being taught explicit rules. The same is true for the use of precedents. Thus, translating or transferring the methodology of architectural diagrammatic sketches or reuse of precedents to other domains of knowledge or practice such as management will not be an easy task without taking into account concrete practices and even institutional settings linked with architectural practice.

A second major problem associated with the use of architectural diagrammatic sketches is that they are notoriously ambiguous and fuzzy. If one is interested in transferring to another domain such tools, one must keep in mind that architects themselves complain about their misuse in architecture. Professional standards of spatial and functional exactitude are at risk because of extensive — one might say addictive — use of diagrams by young architects. Excessive dependence on precedents can also frustrate innovative experimentation.

An even more important problem emerges when architects rely uncritically on sketches to take important, "pre-parametric" decisions at the outset of the design process. As J. H. Bay (2001) has shown in one of our research projects, heuristic design tools — and sketches are such a tool — can lead easily to illusions, deceptions, and biases, similar to the type Tversky and Kahneman (1974) have studied. Thus, uncritical trust in sketches can have a negative impact on design thinking. Similar problems of bias and error may appear if the heuristics of design by analogy to precedents is not controlled through rigorous testing. On the other hand, as the same research has shown, in the case of sketches, if they are appropriately constructed, they can be used preventively and even "therapeutically" to neutralize the very illusions the wrong kind of sketches generate. They can be mobilized as instruments for design de-biasing.

THE INTRIGUING QUESTION AND CHALLENGE

The intriguing question is how through history architecture employed general purpose spatial-functional intelligence with which all humans are endowed to develop unique habits of the mind, specific methods that are still used professionally in the conception of buildings. The challenging question is if and how the potential of such methods of architectural poetics can be transposed successfully in other domains, such as management.

1. Interestingly, one of the very first academic "challenging teaching assignments" of Herbert Simon as a young man (Simon, 1991) at Illinois Institute of Technology in 1942 was to introduce management and economics ideas to architects. But it has been only since the middle of the 1960s that a visible movement has appeared that tries to transfer explicit ideas from management to architecture. By the end of the 1960s, one finds new courses in several schools of architecture in the United States proposing such techniques that management initially applied to the organization of industrial production or administrative work. Characteristically, Maurice Kilbridge, a professor from the Harvard Business School was appointed dean of the prestigious Graduate School of Design in the early 1970s.

2. The possibility of mapping processes and social organizations into spatial structures has been argued extensively by Ray S. Jackendoff (1983 and 1994).

3. Architects as well as clients perpetuated the myth of architects as "demigods," emulating *par analogia* God — a term used in the Middle Ages and the Renaissance.

REFERENCES

Bay, J. H. 2001. *Tropicalism, design theory and biased belief systems.* Delft: Design Knowledge Systems.

Boroditsky, L. 2000. Metaphoric structuring: Understanding time through spatial metaphors. *Cognition.* 75: 1–28.

Friedman, A. 2003. *Poetic time, the representation of movement-based scenarios in architectural models.* Delft: Design Knowledge Systems.

Jackendoff, R. S. 1983. *Semantics and cognition.* Cambridge, MA: MIT Press.

———. 1994. *Patterns in the mind: language and human nature.* New York: Harvester Wheatsheaf.

Moraes Zarzar, K. 2003. *An evolutionary model for architectural practice.* Delft: Design Knowledge Systems.

Qin, Y., and H. Simon. 1995. Imagery and mental models in problem solving. In *Diagrammatic reasoning: Cognitive and computational perspective,* edited by J. Glasgow, N. N. Narayanan, and B. Chandrasekaran. Menlo Park, CA: AAAI Press.

Simon, H. A. 1991. *Models of my life.* New York: Basic Books.

Tversky, A., and D. Kahneman. 1974. Judgment under uncertainty: Heuristics and biases. *Science* 185: 1,124–1,131.

Tzonis, A. 1992. Huts, ships and bottleracks: Design by analogy for architects and/ or machines. In *Research in design thinking,* edited by N. Cross, K. Dorst and N. Roozenburg. Delft: Delft University Press.

———. 2001. *Le Corbusier, the poetics of machine and metaphor.* New York: Universe.

Tzonis, A., and L. Lefaivre. 2001. *Santiago Calatrava, the creative process.* Basel and New York: Birkhauser.

6

DESIGNING FOR THROWNNESS

Karl E. Weick

DESIGN IS usually portrayed as forethought that leads to an intention. But on closer inspection, design may be less originary than it looks. One reason is because beginnings and endings are rare, middles are common. People, whether designers or clients, are always in the middle of something, which means designing is as much about re-design, interruption, resumption, continuity, and re-contextualizing, as it is about design, creation, invention, initiation, and contextualizing. What separates good design from bad design may be determined more by how people deal with the experience of thrownness and interruption than by the substance of the design itself. All of these complexities are likely to be given more attention if we stop talking about organizational design and start talking about organizational re-design. The reframing involved in such a shift is illustrated by Adrienne Rich's description of life as music and Martin Heidegger's description of life as thrownness.

Here is Rich's commentary on being in the middle: "No one ever told us we had to study our lives, make of our lives a study, as if learning natural history or music, that we should begin with the simple exercises first and slowly go on trying the hard ones, practicing till the strength and accuracy became one with the daring to leap into transcendence, take the chance of breaking down in the wild arpeggio or faulting the full sentence of the fugue. . . . And in fact we can't live like that: we take on everything at once before we've even begun to read or mark time, we're forced to begin in the midst of the hardest movement, the one already sounding as we are born" (Rich, 1979).

Karl E. Weick, *Department of Psychology and School of Management, University of Michigan.*

Heidegger captures his own version of Rich's insight by unpacking the word *geworfenheit* (*werf* = to throw, *geworfenheit* = being thrown), which has been translated as "thrownness." Heidegger treats being-in-the-world — Rich's taking "everything on at once" — as "the prereflective experience of being thrown into a situation of acting without the opportunity or need to disengage and function as detached observers" (Winograd and Flores, 1986, p. 97).

Two examples of thrownness are the plight of a chairperson at a contentious meeting and the plight of the incident commander at the scene of a disaster. At a contentious meeting, such as trying to decide whether to adopt a new computer system, the chairperson is thrown into the midst of a garbage can organizing process of ongoing agendas seeking support and animosities looking for an airing, without much control or sense of history and with little opportunity for detached contemplation or any assurance that detachment would help anyway. Here's what it feels like to be a thrown chairperson:

1. You cannot avoid acting. Your actions, including the action of doing nothing, affect the situation and yourself, often in ways that run counter to what you intended.

2. You cannot step back and reflect on your actions. You are thrown on your intuitions and have to deal with whatever comes up as it comes up.

3. The effects of action cannot be predicted. The dynamic nature of social conduct precludes accurate prediction, and rational planning is not much help.

4. You do not have a stable representation of the situation. Patterns may be evident after the fact, but at the time the flow unfolds there is nothing but arbitrary fragments capable of being organized into a host of different patterns or possibly no pattern whatsoever.

5. Every representation is an interpretation. There is no way to settle once and for all that any interpretation is right or wrong, which means an "objective" analysis of that into which one was thrown is out of reach.

6. Language is action. Whenever people say something, they create rather than describe a situation. This means it is impossible to stay detached from whatever emerges unless you say nothing, which is such a strange way to react that the situation is deflected anyway (adapted from Winograd and Flores, 1986, pp. 34–36).

An analogous situation is that of an incident commander at the scene of a disaster. Imagine being the first commander to arrive on the scene at the burning World Trade Center on 9/11/2001. Just such an arrival was captured on film by French documentary filmmakers Jules and Gideon Naudet. What is evident on the film and in other occasions of incident command is the challenge of thrownness. Rhona Flin (1996), a leading researcher of incident command, argues that the challenge for the incident commander is to continually make sense of an unexpected and dynamic situation that is characterized by unfamiliarity, scale, and speed of escalation (p. 105). She says that a person thrown into a fire scene faces (1) extremely difficult decisions, (2) ambiguous and conflicting information, (3) shifting goals, (4) time pressure, (5) dynamic conditions, (6) complex operational team structures, (7) poor communication, and that (8) every course of action carries significant risk (p. 37). The situation of the commander is not all that different from the situation of the chairperson, and neither situation is all that different from that of designers and clients in general.

In situations such as these, designing unfolds in a world that is already interpreted where people are already acting, where options are constrained, where control is minimal, and where things and options already matter for reasons that are taken-for-granted. These taken-for-granted reasons are lost in history and hard to retrieve, if retrieval were even an issue. The question "why are we doing this" seldom comes up in the mood of thrownness because acting with what is at hand is primary and detached reflection secondary. Regardless of whether designing occurs in the context of living a life without a rehearsal or creating a building that is a work of art or crafting a meeting that doesn't explode or coordinating people to control damage, the common thread is that people in each setting share a mood of "disclosive submission" to the world (Dreyfuss, 1995, p. 173). In such a world, understanding occurs through acting, not through isolating and categorizing phenomena, and people act their way into understanding. This is existentialism with a twist. If existence precedes essence, then thrownness is existence whose essence is gradually disclosed as a small subset of all possible options for expression and interpretation. The tiny subset that defines "essence" is the residue of a larger set of possibilities edited down by culture, institutions, socialization, habitats, and labeled experience. Designers thrown into the middle of a contentious meeting, or a nation's nightmare, or a business school's aspirations, or a Spanish city seeking renewal will cope more or less adequately in a preinterpreted world depending on how skillful they are at bricolage, making-do, updating transient explanations, staying in motion in order to uncover new options, improvisation, and tolerating ambiguity. The same varying success in coping holds true for other participants who are thrown into the preexisting designs of a meeting, the crumbling Trade Center, the Peter B. Lewis building, or the Guggenheim museum in Bilbao. Thrownness puts a premium on recovery, resilience, and normalizing, without calling attention to the fact that these moods are at a premium.

The concept of thrownness seems useful within a vocabulary of design because it articulates the context within which designs will be more or less effective. The concept does this in at least five different ways. First, if we take thrownness seriously, it means that designing starts with a different set of background assumptions. The mind-set is not one of designing as if one faces a blank slate and a greenfield site, but instead it is designing as if one faces a population thrown into a determinate situation characterized by limited options, unreflective submission, continuous acting, occasional interruption, unquestioned answers, ready-made categories for expression and interpretation, and disjunction between understanding and explanation. Second, thrownness suggests that design is incremental even when it aspires to be much more. It is incremental because designers are thrown into an already interpreted world of the client, a world that they typically extend rather than upend. Design is also incremental because clients assimilate and normalize new design and bend it to whatever is already underway so that their action can continue. Third, good design gains meaning from its resonance with the condition of thrownness, which means that good design counteracts some of the features of a "determinate situation" mentioned earlier. The counteraction created by good design may enlarge a limited set of options, reduce blind spots, facilitate brief reflection, reduce the disruptiveness of interruptions, encourage trial and error with safety, refine primitive categories into a more nuanced set of distinctions, and tighten the coupling between existence and interpretation. Fourth, good design supports the mood of thrownness. Support means that the experience of thrownness is enriched when improvised actions are rendered stronger and more appropriate. In the case of a contentious meeting, for example, good design takes the edge off thrownness by providing affordances that make it easier to generate wise action, reflection-in-action (Schon, 1987), action that can be fine tuned and reversed so that prediction is unnecessary, increased situational awareness with decreased dependence on stable representation, richer interpretations, and more differentiated and nuanced language. Another way to describe support is in terms of what Frank Gehry calls "handrails." Handrails are familiar details in an otherwise strange setting that give people a feeling of safety and heighten their willingness to wade into someone else's preinterpreted world and try to become more attuned to what is already underway in it. Fifth, the assumption of thrownness in a preinterpreted world spotlights the potential value of design that stirs up those preexisting interpretations, throws some of them up for grabs, and encourages people to redecide what matters.

Frank Gehry's architecture is interesting when viewed through the lens of thrownness because it is compatible with so many of its tenets. A Gehry building does not start with a clean slate, it incrementally extends preexisting tendencies, it counteracts thrownness by enlarging the determinate space, it enriches thrownness by inviting improvisation, it softens thrownness by including handrails, and it unsettles the preinterpreted by inviting people to ask, "What does this mean, how do we mean?" Exposure to a Gehry building is a

78   microcosm of thrownness. That exposure engages "the prereflective experience of being thrown into a situation of acting without the opportunity or need to disengage and function as detached observers," (Winograd and Flores, 1986, p. 97) but that exposure does not wholly forestall disengaged reflection. Neither does life.

REFERENCES

Dreyfuss, H. L. 1995. *Being-in-the-world.* Cambridge, MA: MIT Press.

Flin, R. H. 1996. *Sitting in the hot seat: Leaders and teams for critical incident management.* New York: John Wiley.

Rich, A. 1979. Excerpt from "The dream of a common language." *The Sun* 46: 37.

Schon, D. A. 1987. *Educating the reflective practitioner.* San Francisco, CA: Jossey-Bass.

Winograd, T., and F. Flores. 1986. *Understanding computers and cognition.* Norwood, NJ: Ablex.

7

People Mutht Be Amuthed

John Leslie King

People mutht be amuthed. They can't be alwayth a learning, nor yet they can't be alwayth a working, they an't made for it.
Mr. Sleary, in Charles Dickens's Hard Times,
Book 3, Chapter 8, 1834

LOUIS HENRI SULLIVAN said in 1886 that form follows function in the realm of architectural design. Although Sullivan's aphorism was more conjecture than observation, it has evolved into an is/ought confusion. Form might very well follow function some of the time, but that's no reason to conclude that it should do so. Frank Lloyd Wright said that the notion of form following function was a misunderstanding: that form and function "should be one, joined in a spiritual union." Then again, Wright himself reportedly said, in response to complaints that his Unity Temple in Oak Park didn't work well as a church, that he didn't give a damn how it worked—he wanted to build a building that looked like that.[1]

The question of whether form does or should follow function is at the heart of modern management thought. Unfortunately, the same confusion found in architectural design is found in management as well. The signature of that confusion is seen in the fixation on linking managerial function and organizational form, as in discussions of "cross-functional" management and "new" organizational forms. Untangling this fixation is a necessary step in understanding the relationship between managing and designing.

It sometimes seems that the things we know did not preexist our knowledge

John Leslie King, *School of Information, University of Michigan.* The help of Fred Collopy and Doug Kelbaugh is acknowledged and appreciated.

of them and that things older than our lives were always around. When rounding the bend of Wisconsin Highway 23 near Spring Green, and catching a first glimpse of Frank Lloyd Wright's Taliesin, the buildings seem completely normal and expected. It is easy to forget that they were a radical and jarring departure when they took form in 1911. The rightness of Wright's prairie style was an invention, but the rightness of it makes it seem as though it was always there. In a similar way, students of management are tempted to think that the phenomenon of management arose when the concept of management was formulated, and that organization design emerged when the idea of organization first dawned. Few people will admit to believing this, of course, but anyone who thinks that form follows function almost has to believe this. If form follows function, it cannot have preceded it. Our ancestors were obviously creating form long before function was named, and we can see from those forms that they were related to function. How do we account for this ability in our ancestors without presuming that they had sorted out their opinions on Sullivan's aphorism millennia before he did? We might assign them a kind of primitive but marvelous capacity, much like that of the cunning tiger: he hunts with fearful symmetry, but he does not *know* he is hunting. Only *we* know that. In this conceit, we are like Monsieur Jourdain in Moliere's *Le Bourgeois Gentilhomme*, delighted to discover that he had been speaking prose all his life and didn't even know it!

The challenge before us is to align our definitions of what we are with the reality of what we do. *Homo Faber*, we are told, is distinguished among the animals by our use of tools. That would be a useful distinction if not for all the other tool-using animals like ants and sea otters and lots of birds and primates. The important feature of humans is not *that* we use tools, but rather, what we are up to when we use them. Tools were found along with the ancient cave paintings at Lascaux and Chauvet-Pont-d'Arc, but the presence of the tools pales in comparison to the self-reflective evidence of the art. If the form of the cave art was to follow some function, then what, exactly, was that function? Put simply, to amuse.

The word *amuse* has a tortured history. Its contemporary meaning evokes diversion, distraction, entertainment, even deception. Its original meaning was quite different and might best be captured by the phrase, *to stare in amazement*. To be amused meant to catch a glimpse of something astonishing, something that reset one's expectations.[2] Amusement is a matter of separating figure from ground, of seeing something in stark relief against its context, in a manner that causes previously unseen connections to appear. The fact that the experience often evokes a delighted laugh is merely coincidental. Humans have evolved brains that reward us for learning new things, and the reward is pleasure.[3] Pleasure is a consequence of learning, so we seek to learn.

Hence to the question of whether form follows function, and more importantly, whether we ought to think it should. The first architectural forms certainly preceded their functional applications. Humans sought out caves to live
in, they did not dig them. When they began to improve on their cave dwell-
ings, they had some notion of form that, when empirically tested, revealed
whatever functional utility it might offer. From the perspective of the modern,
it is difficult to understand the amusement that must have followed the recognition of the connection between adding a "fourth wall" to a cave and the resulting improvement in security, warmth, and psychological well-being. It
seems plausible that early humans acted on a rational prediction when they
surmised that adding the fourth wall would produce these benefits. But it
seems at least equally likely that they first noticed that a cave is simply a hole
on its side, and that by modifying where the "opening" was, the cave could be
transformed. Although this abstraction might sound like a stretch for a primitive human, it is not nearly as big a stretch as the cave paintings primitive humans made of the animals they hunted (or admired or worshiped) with themselves looking on. The deep idea is not that one could remake the world to be
more functionally useful. It was that one could remake the world *at all*. As experimentation with form evolved, all kinds of functional utility *followed*.

So, what was Sullivan up to when he declared that form follows function,
and what should students of management take from that aphorism about
design? At best, Sullivan was issuing an admonition to the architectural designer to remember that design has consequences when put into action, and
that consequences can affect welfare. This notion is important and valuable.
Taken to logical conclusions, it shows up in engineering, which, at its most
creative, tinkers with form to determine how function follows. "Engineering
science" makes use of earlier discovery to guide its tinkering toward particularly desirable functional consequences, but engineering practice remains
largely a matter of learning by doing. In such work, form usually does not follow function, and the only reason for declaring that it does is to privilege the
notion of function. This is a salutary endeavor in many ways. For one thing,
it helps keep the wayward tinkerer's attention focused on the question of
whether anyone will want to buy what he or she has produced. But it can have
pernicious consequences for those trying to understand the processes of design and management.

The most compelling danger in presuming that form follows function is
the implicit assumption that "function" is received rather than constructed.
The very idea of functionality is imposed by humans upon the world, not derived from it. There are, of course, underlying laws and consistencies and
probabilities on which we base our expectations, and we use them all the time.
But a function arises only in the context of explanations about those things; it

82   is not inherent in them. In the context of architectural design, confusion arises when one thinks of a building's "foundation" as a device to distribute the weight of the structure appropriately to the earth. Designers of foundations become preoccupied with weight distribution. When a different kind of form comes along, such as Buckminster Fuller's tension structures (e.g., the Dymaxion House and the geodesic dome), the primary purpose of the foundation must be different: to prevent the wind from blowing the structure away.[4] In fact, Fuller's key contribution was in rethinking form in order to alleviate one of the traditional problems with earlier functional notions, namely that a building had to be heavy. The issue was not weight, it was strength, which could be accomplished by a sophisticated balance of tension and compression. Function followed form. After the fact, when the functional utility of the form became clear, it seemed obvious that the form had followed the function all along. The inventive character of changing form was subordinated to the rational expectation of achieving a functional objective.

This kind of problem shows up with glaring clarity in management. It goes without saying that humans have been doing management much longer than we have been teaching it. Yet, to read modern management texts, one would think management sprang full grown from the brow of Henri Fayol in 1916. Fayol's contribution was to begin the process of codifying the "functions" of the executive. Initially, this was little more than a "to do" list of things managers need to think about, but it had enormous impact on the emerging field of managerial education in the late 1930s when Luther Gulick and Lyndall Urwick synthesized POSDCORB (planning, organizing, staffing, directing, coordinating, reporting, budgeting), and Chester Bernard published his landmark book on the subject.[5] This "functionalization" of management was accompanied by an equally influential functionalization of the idea of the organization itself. This was an extension of the old concept of division of labor and task specialization, which first found its academic voice in the work of Adam Smith and gained prominence through Max Weber's work on bureaucracy. Most important, organizational functionalism emerged from the practices of industrial organization as they evolved in the early part of the twentieth century, especially in Henry Ford's invention of production engineering and Alfred Sloan's creation of the multidivisional organization at General Motors.

The significance of the resulting change can be seen in the shift in key signifiers used by management research and education. The faculties of management schools in the late nineteenth century were classified by their substantive focus (e.g., banking, transportation, manufacturing). During this era, the concepts of "the organization" and "the firm" were handy signifiers to denote going concerns that were the *objects* of study by management scholars.[6] By the 1930s management school faculties were beginning to be classified according to the organizational function in which they were most expert: finance, accounting and control, operations, and so on. The terms "organization" and "firm" had also been recast as abstract yet strangely real entities embodying clearly prescribed functions. Organization and firm had become the *subjects* of management study, and that study could be carried out in the absence of any actual organizations or firms. Ronald Coase nailed the thesis that organizational form follows organizational function to the cathedral door, and Oliver Williamson provided the reduced-form argument to "prove" it.[7] Once the functions of the firm were understood, the forms could be modeled without the need of messy empiricism involving actual organizations and firms. Function was inherent; form was enslaved to follow. This trope imposes direct costs on students of management. For one thing, it causes old forms to masquerade as new, simply because they inevitably arise from the same old notions of function. But the more serious problem is the opportunity cost we pay in the loss of undiscovered functionality that would arise from truly new forms, if only we were willing to think them up and try them.

Curiously, many would argue that the field of architecture has gone the other way, headlong into the pursuit of form without attention to function. In this, Sullivan might have been prescient and prophetic in calling for attention to function when he did. In any case, Frank Lloyd Wright's ideal of the "spiritual union" has proved to be elusive. Perhaps the most striking contemporary example of this is the transformation of Ludwig Mies van der Rohe's masterpiece of form, the steel frame and glass curtain walls of New York's Seagram Building, into the cheap but functional imitations that populate the dreary landscape of suburban office parks. Mies's beautiful form led to a sea of ugly function, while the quest for the inspiring form continues.

Deriving managerial insight from the field of architectural design is not merely a matter of bridging the nomenclature of professional fields, or of finding ways for managers to mimic the work practices of designers. It lies in overcoming the fact that both architectural design and management have fallen into the same hole, although from opposite sides. Until they can crawl out of it together, it is doubtful that either can lead the other. The glimmer of hope is that, like our ancient ancestors, both camps will recognize that the hole they are in is really just a cave on its side. If they remove one wall, a suitably amusing vista might appear.

84 NOTES

1. The origin of the idea that form follows function is generally attributed to Louis Henri Sullivan's line, "Form ever follows function," in his article "The Tall Office Building Artistically Considered," published in *Lippincott's Magazine* in March 1896. In fact, the same idea was articulated by artist and architect Horatio Greenough in 1852, and can be found in the chapter "Structure and Organization" in an anthology of his works edited by Harold Small and titled *Form and Function: Remarks on Art, Design, and Architecture*, published by the University of California Press in 1947. The quote on form by Wright is widely cited but the original report of his saying it is difficult to locate. His reported observation about the Unity Temple is even more difficult to locate.

2. The role of astonishment, or "wonder" as it might be expressed, played a crucial role in the evolution of western thought from the constrictions of medieval scholasticism to the breakthrough of the Enlightenment. Museums, which were the first scientific laboratories, arose from the sixteenth century *Wunderkammern*, or wonder cabinets, assembled by the earliest systematic naturalists (see Oliver Impey and Arthur MacGregor, *The Origins of Museums: The Cabinet of Curiosities in Sixteenth and Seventeenth Century Europe*, Oxford: Clarendon Press, 1985). Not all early architects of the Enlightenment were enthusiastic about this. Descartes in Article 73 of his *Passions of the Soul* (1649), said, "Astonishment is an excess of admiration which can never be but evil." However, Descartes' rationalistic sentiment was counterbalanced by his contemporary Francis Bacon's admonition to use libraries, zoos, wonder cabinets, and experimental apparatus to gain knowledge and "be left the only miracle and wonder of the world." (from *Gesta Grayorum*, 1594).

3. For a review of research evidence for this, see Ingrid Wickelgren, "Getting the Brain's Attention," *Science*, October 3, 1997: 35–37.

4. Fuller's exposition of this concept began in his article "Tensegrity," in *Portfolio and Art News Annual*, No. 4, 1961, and was elaborated in his books *Synergetics* (1975) and *Synergetics 2* (1979), both published in New York by Macmillan Publishing Co., Inc.

5. See Henri Fayol, *General and Industrial Management* (London: Pitman, 1916); Luther Gulick and Lyndall Urwick, eds., *Papers on the Science of Administration* (New York: Institute of Public Administration, 1937); Chester I. Barnard, *The Functions of the Executive* (Cambridge, MA: Harvard University Press, 1938).

6. A useful source for this discussion is Edward F. L. Brech, *Education, Training and Development for and In Management, 1852–1979*, volume 5 of *The Evolution of Modern Management: A History of the Development of Managerial Practice, Education, Training and Other Aspects in Britain from 1852–1979* (distributed for the Thoemmes Press by Chicago University Press, 2002).

7. Coase argued that organizations were created to provide consistent operating frames not available in the marketplace (see *The Firm, the Market, and the Law*, Chicago: University of Chicago Press, 1988). Williamson took this further and characterized organizations (hierarchies) as the result of market failures due to the inability to manage high transaction costs in routine operations (see *Markets and Hierarchies*, New York: Free Press, 1975).

8

IN PRAISE OF SYMBOLIC POVERTY

Nicholas Cook

AMONG AFFLUENT residents of Hong Kong there is a cynical belief that two maids get half as much done as one, three maids a third as much, and so forth. Slanderous or otherwise, this belief reflects the common experience that it is hard to get things done and proportionally harder the more people are involved; hence managers. And because we usually use words to specify what we want done, the problem becomes one of translating words into actions. That is where the trouble starts. When the words don't work, we try to fix them by means of more words. We use words to explain what we mean by words. We try and find words for every situation or combination of situations. We try to anticipate every contingency. We fail.

The very idea of translating words into actions should, perhaps, have been a warning of where things were going wrong. We generally assume that one language can be translated into another. Yet we know that thoughts formulated in one language may resist formulation in another or turn into different thoughts in the course of reformulation. If that is the case of translation between different languages, how should it be less the case of such different spheres as words and actions? Instead of thinking of one thing—a mission, action plan, or set of procedures—that can exist in the form of either words or actions, we might do better to think of two quite different things—words and actions—that we attempt, in an often improvisatory manner, to match up against one another. And, of course, they frequently don't fit.

I have already slipped in a musical metaphor, and it seems to me that music reveals the problem with singular clarity, as well as suggests what the solu-

Nicholas Cook, *Department of Music, Royal Holloway, University of London.*

86   tion might look (or sound) like. A piece of music consists of an extended sequence of actions involving a number of agents.[1] Within those musical cultures that employ written symbols — as most do, in one way or another — notation specifies these actions, whether directly or indirectly. Writers on the
Western classical tradition often celebrate the sophistication of its staff notation, meaning by this its ability to specify musical relationships to a high degree of determinacy, thereby enabling the design of highly elaborate and often
extended compositions. Our confidence in the determinacy of the notation
is such that we sometimes speak of the performer "reproducing" the score,
meaning this not pejoratively but just as a simple statement of how things are.
It is only when you compare Western staff notation to other notational systems
that you realize quite how much it leaves undetermined.

I can make the point by briefly outlining the notational system for the Chinese long zither or *qin*. It is a tablature, meaning that it specifies what the performer should do (by contrast, staff notation is more like a picture of how the
music sounds, so it specifies the actions less directly). The earliest form of this
notation (up to the tenth century) actually used words: the oldest surviving *qin*
score includes such directions as "put the middle finger about half an inch on
the tenth *hui* [stud] . . . . Hide the middle finger, and afterwards press it on the
thirteenth *hui*, about an inch [down], in the form of a hook . . . . Lift the second finger slowly" (Kaufmann, 1967, p. 270). Conventionalized ideograms
were subsequently substituted for words, but the principle remained the same:
each movement of the fingers is itemized, resulting (according to the diplo-
mat, crime novelist, and *qin* expert Robert van Gulik) in twenty-six different
types of vibrato (van Gulik, 1969, p. 2). In other respects, however, *qin* notation falls far short of the determinacy of staff notation: in particular, it represents the music as simply a sequence of notes, without saying anything about
the rhythm or tempo.

To a westerner, this appears an astonishing deficiency, such that one might
question whether the notation really encapsulates the composition at all. But
who is to say that the omission of rhythmic specification is a greater deficiency than staff notation's inability to distinguish between different kinds of
vibrato? (Classical composers occasionally specified "vibrato," or more commonly, "non vibrato," but the idea of *composing* vibrato has no place in the
Western tradition.) The truth is that both staff notation and *qin* tablature
are radically incomplete, making constant demands on the performer's tacit
knowledge of what is normal or appropriate within a given musical context or
style. (The point is not that Western composers do not care about the shaping
of vibrato, but that they rely on the performer's tacit knowledge of what vibrato
to use in what context.). The difference is simply in what is specified and what
is left unspecified.

It is a general principle, then, that musical notations specify some things but not others. Considerations of cognitive economy mean that it could hardly be otherwise; if you try and specify everything, you will overwhelm the performer with information overload, and besides, you cannot anticipate every contingency, every situation or combination of situations — especially when several performers are playing together. But that is to put it negatively. The positive way to make the point is that, far from being deficiencies, the gaps in the notation represent opportunities for creative interpretation and interaction between performers. And the reason we go on listening to "the same" music is that, in performance, it isn't the same at all: every performance combines the security of the familiar (the "reproduction" aspect) with the shock of the new, or if not that, then at least the sense that you never know exactly what is going to happen until it has happened. In short, it is the gaps in the notation — its symbolic poverty — that give it its value as a way of specifying the series of social actions and interactions of which any performance consists.

In the case of jazz, this is quite obvious because a lead sheet is so schematic; nobody would be tempted to see it as more than a blueprint for a process of real-time interaction between the performers. You can't play jazz by just playing your piece, so to speak, because the essence of jazz improvisation is that you respond to the other, and so, as Ingrid Monson puts it, "To say that a player 'doesn't listen'. . . is a grave insult." (Monson, 1996, p. 84). But the same applies, for example, to a string quartet playing Mozart. The quartet may well play exactly the notes that Mozart wrote. And yet they don't play them exactly as he wrote them because every note in the score is subject to the contextual negotiation of intonation, precise dynamic value, articulation, timbral quality, and so forth (and it is, quite literally, this process of interpersonal negotiation and accommodation that you are hearing when you listen to music). For example, the performers stay in tune not because each independently conforms to a common standard (such as equal temperament), but because each constantly accommodates her playing to that of the others, so that "in tune" is an emergent concept. Mozart writes a C♭, say, but it is the performer who makes it into exactly *this* C♭ played just so, and in this way you might say that the performer erases what is specified in the score as much as she reproduces it. (Like words and actions, what is written and what is played are two different things.) And because all this depends on the interaction between performers, it is just as much of an insult to accuse a classical musician of not listening as it is in jazz.

Music, then, reveals with singular clarity just how people can work together, and how it is possible to design a framework within which they will do so — one that can give rise to a highly elaborate and distinctive output (Mozart's String Quartet in G Major, K. 387, say), even though local decisions

88   are constantly being delegated to the individual and made on the spur of the moment. It is easier to understand this design process if we think of musical scores not as texts to be reproduced in performance, but rather as scripts that choreograph a series of ongoing social engagements — or to put it another way, as prompts to action that is in certain respects clearly envisioned, but in others, unpredictable and creative. And my claim, of course, is that the same applies to any form of complex, planned activity. Let me give a specific example from my experience as Dean of Arts at the University of Southampton, when I was trying to introduce faculty-wide standards in relation to things like teaching quality evaluation and academic load management. The obvious approach is to introduce standardized documentation that forces people into specific, predetermined procedures. People may accept this, but they do so grudgingly: you may win conformity this way, but you don't win people's hearts and minds, and so there is a limit to what can be achieved. The other approach is to specify the goals and leave each academic department (or, in some cases, each individual) to find ways of realizing them: this promotes ownership, it may win hearts and minds, but it results in a level of procedural diversity such that, as a manager, you can have little confidence that your objectives are being achieved in any consistent manner, if at all.

Procedural consistency or hearts and minds? That is like choosing between a musical notation that specifies virtually everything and one that specifies virtually nothing, or between a score by Brian Ferneyhough and so-called free improvisation ("so called" because no improvisation can be completely free, just as even Ferneyhough can't and doesn't specify everything the performers do). The vast majority of musical culture speaks (or sounds) against the necessity of such black-and-white, either/or choices: it shows how you can communicate not just broad goals but highly determinate frameworks for realizing them, without prejudicing the initiative and creativity that gives people an investment in their work — not least because creativity and initiative are as real when they operate on the small scale as on the large, as can be seen from the comparison between the strictly delimited freedom of a Mozart quartet and that of jazz. His K. 387 shows how you can at the same time script action and interaction, give people a part to play, and ensure the common ownership of the outcome that is so positive a feature of chamber music. Mozart's music may not tell you exactly *how* to manage people in such a way as to reconcile corporate goals and individual freedom — the solution to my academic management problem was, like most solutions, a combination of modest, local, and contingent measures — but it is lasting testimony that such reconciliation is possible.

Music, in short, shows how you get things done, not through the hopeless attempt to anticipate and comprehensively specify people's actions, but by finding ways to prompt their performance in real time. In this way, you invoke people's tacit knowledge, their ability to interact with one another and to improvise, within a shared sense of direction and purpose. And in doing this, you are making the most of symbolic poverty.

NOTE

1. In what follows, I talk mainly about ensemble music. But, as any concert pianist will confirm, even solo performance involves interaction with the audience and in that sense, multiple agency.

REFERENCES

Kaufmann, W. 1967. *Musical notations of the orient: Notational systems of continental, east, south and central Asia*. Bloomington: Indiana University Press.
Monson, I. 1996. *Saying something: Jazz improvisation and interaction*. Chicago: Chicago University Press.
van Gulik, R. 1969. *The lore of the Chinese lute*, 2nd ed. Tokyo: Sophia University.

9

Managing and Designing

Attending to Reflexiveness and Enactment

Wanda J. Orlikowski

> We shape our buildings, and afterwards our buildings shape us.
> *Winston Churchill, 1924, quoted in*
> *Stewart Brand,* How Buildings Learn:
> What Happens after They're Built

THE CHALLENGE proposed by the Weatherhead workshop is to develop a vocabulary of design for management education. Thinking deeply about the creative role of human action in producing social and material realities is a valuable effort. However, we should do so cautiously so that in the process of learning from design we don't succumb to the temptation to idealize it. Design can and sometimes does generate creative, exciting, inventive, and inspiring artifacts, but not always. As our experiences with poorly designed products, processes, plans, policies, services, tools, interfaces, infrastructures, and buildings attests, we are just as capable of ineffective designing as we are of ineffective managing. Like every human undertaking, the field of design brings with it both possibilities and pitfalls, inventions and conventions, enablements and constraints, and we should be attentive to these as we explore connections between designing and managing.

With this caution in mind, I want to question a key premise underlying the interest in remaking management in the image of design — the notion that managing and designing are different endeavors. I will argue instead that they are more similar than they are different. I will then consider how both man-

---

Wanda J. Orlikowski, *School of Management, Massachusetts Institute of Technology.*

agers and designers would benefit by being more attentive to the constitutive role of representations and the enactment of social and material realities.

CONSTITUTING REALITY

The workshop invites us to explore how we might make management more like design. In many respects, however, managing is already much like designing, at least, design as typically practiced in software development, policy formulation, urban planning, R&D labs, engineering firms, and architectural offices. The meaning of the word *designing* is given by its etymology—the Latin *de-* + *signer*—"to denote, signify, or show by a distinctive mark." To design, thus, is to make representations of the world. By this view, managing *is* designing, as is evident in the discourse of management, which reflects a preoccupation with operating on the world through symbolic means. Consider, for example, typical terms from a managerial lexicon: data, dimensions, exemplars, forms, functions, goals, measures, methods, models, patterns, perspectives, plans, problems, procedures, requirements, solutions, specifications, standards, strategies, structures, techniques, tools, and visions. That most of these terms are also common in design should not surprise us, as both design and management are engaged in the production of representations.

Boland (1985, p. 195) reminds us that a system of representations is "constitutive of the social world, not just a convenient operator on it." Activities of designing and managing, by reflecting and reinforcing specialized (technical, institutional, artistic) logics within particular representations of reality, thus serve to shape the very reality that they represent (Geertz, 1973). And they do so in remarkably comparable ways. Consider, for example, the parallels between the contexts and practices of design and management:

- Both occupy privileged, authoritative positions in our contemporary cultures and economies, positions that rely on expert knowledge, training, and socialization.
- Both have become institutionalized and professionalized domains of specialized activities and identities, with established rites of passage, distinctive repertoires, specific norms and forms of status, and considerable influence and power.
- Both tend to embody and employ a separation of conception and execution, which sustains a divide between the time, place, worldviews, norms, interests, values, discourses, and practices of those designing/managing and those using the design or being managed.
- Both tend to engage in social engineering, designing/managing the artifacts, spaces, or organizations that others engage with, thereby shaping/configuring the lives of these others.

92
- Both tend to be normative, presuming to know what others need/want/ should have and presuming to know ahead of time what will be required/ valued/useful over time.
- Both tend to produce representations that are, by definition, set apart from the embedded and embodied doing, being, and becoming of every-day life, tending to emphasize a priori canonical precepts at the expense of in situ noncanonical, lived experiences.
- Both tend to impose a formal, selective, and abstracted order on ambigu-ous, contested, multiple, local, and dynamic terrains.
- Both tend to downplay the influence of everyday actions in realizing the products of designing and managing.
- Both tend to neglect unanticipated consequences, assuming that designs/ plans will be implemented and used as intended and that they will (nec-essarily) generate the desired outcomes.

In producing representations, the fields of designing and managing pro-duce social and material realities. They both do so by describing, inscribing, prescribing, and proscribing how, why, when, and where others live their lives. Yet, neither field has a well-established practice of reflecting on its constitutive role, tending to deny or take for granted embedded ideologies of instrumental or aesthetic rationality. As Bowker and Star (1999, pp. 5–6) note, this is a dan-gerous thing:

> Each standard and each category valorizes some point of view and silences another. This is not inherently a bad thing—indeed it is inescapable. But it *is* an ethical choice, and as such it is dangerous—not bad, but dangerous.

Developing a practice of critical reflexiveness that acknowledges the constitu-tive nature of their activities could help both designers and managers be more attentive to the implications of their choices.

ENACTING REALITY

The Weatherhead workshop offered the following definition of design: "By de-sign, we mean the giving of form to an idea—shaping artifacts and events that create more desirable futures."[1] This begs the question "desirable for whom?" With a few notable exceptions, neither managers nor designers are known for their commitment to and enthusiasm for a constructive engagement with the actors who will use the artifacts and realize the events shaped by their designs over time. Some might argue that a close engagement may be counterpro-ductive—that the inventiveness of designers may be unduly restricted by the narrow demands of actors overly concerned with their immediate require-ments and that designers' creativity is best served by enabling them to push beyond local needs to produce breakthrough ideas and breathtaking aesthetics. As with all such dualistic arguments — that the designer must follow his or her own design sense or be totally responsive to actors' requirements — the value lies somewhere between these extremes. Good designers are inspired to create artifacts that *both* exhibit an enduring aesthetic quality *and* generate outcomes in use that people care about. Although designers may be held accountable for the aesthetic quality of their designs, they cannot be given the same responsibility for the outcomes that others care about. For that, we must engage the people who will be left with the design when the designer walks away, the people who will need to interact with it day in and day out to get their work done. And it is these people and the outcomes they care about that are too often overlooked in the discourses and practices of designing/managing. Changing that will require both fields of design and management to develop a deeper awareness of, appreciation for, and ability to engage with the generative power of human enactment.

Attending to enactment means that designers and managers come to understand the critical role that actors other than themselves play in realizing their designs. Designs are conceived and developed on paper, whiteboards, and computers, with models, graphics, and text, in software, hardware, foam-core, and mortar. They are representations of possible realities. However inventive, intuitive, brilliant, or beautiful these designs may be, their ultimate value is dependent on the engagement of others. They are incomplete until realized in action, until integrated into the everyday practices of human actors for whom the designs are a means to an end. And it is through understanding and engaging the everyday practices through which representations are enacted that both managing and designing may develop new, critical capabilities.

Recognizing the constitutive role of enactment in design means seeing that "good design" cannot be ascertained a priori — if by design we follow the workshop organizers in meaning the creation of desirable futures. Good design in this view is not an intrinsic feature, stable property, or static quality of the representation (the designed artifact, building, program, organization), but a recurrently enacted accomplishment provisionally and ongoingly achieved by human actors trying to use the design to get something useful done. Thus, as users of a computer program, occupants of an office building, and members of an organization live in and work with their designed tools, spaces, and procedures, they constitute, everyday and over time, the situated quality and effectiveness of those tools, spaces, and procedures to do their work. "Good design" is enacted. And recognition of such ongoing constitution opens the door for engaging the generative power of human actors to continue to achieve good

94   design in practice over time — as requirements change, opportunities emerge, components break down, new materials are invented, and both people and artifacts learn (Brand, 1995). No representational design can guarantee that (Suchman, 1987).

Taking enactment seriously suggests that designers and managers develop capabilities for relating to and reflecting on the everyday action of people that brings into existence (or not) particular outcomes. These outcomes may be suggested and promoted by the design, but they are not given by the design. They emerge from how people engage with the design in situated practice and over time. Outcomes depend on what people do, on how they enact the design, and such doing is never determined by the design, for in the liminal space of enactment there lies the opportunity for slippage, for resistance, for learning, for change — for people "to choose to do otherwise" (Giddens, 1984, p. 4) with the designs handed to them.

Dealing with emergence requires designers and managers to understand their designs in relation to those who will enact them in practice. It requires a commitment to co-create with these others whose lives will be shaped and changed by their engagement with the designed world. It requires an inquiry into what and whose desired futures are to be enabled and a willingness to be open to and be changed by that understanding. It suggests engaging the respectful interaction among people that can lead to transformed meanings, identities, and intersubjectivity (Weick, 1993, p. 642).

Learning from enactment requires designers and managers to understand and critically examine their assumptions, values, and practices, and how these may — even if inadvertently — silence some voices and strengthen some inequities. It suggests designers and managers be open to learning from a multiplicity of perspectives, as well as being willing to be less certain, less assertive, less directive, more provisional, more collaborative, and more experimental. It requires recognition of the limits and possibilities of one's knowledge and designs (Weick, 1993, p. 641). Wise designers and managers know this, reflecting in and on action to understand the cognitive, social, material, and structural consequences of their designs and then changing themselves and their actions as a result (Schön, 1983).

IN CLOSING

Making representations is what we as humans do all the time, and it is central to the creative role of human action in producing social and material realities. Examining and reflecting on that creative role would enhance the activities of both designing and managing. I have tried to argue here that a vocabulary of design that is insufficiently reflexive — that does not recognize the constitutive role of representations — will unintendedly reinforce privileged interests and values. Similarly, a vocabulary of design that is oblivious to enactment leads to a practice cut off from the everyday contingencies, opportunities, breakdowns, errors, improvisations, and learnings through which human actors accomplish good design-in-action. Designers and managers would thus both benefit from explicit attention to the critical influence of *reflexiveness* and to the generative power of *enactment* in the ongoing (re)production of social and material realities.

NOTE

1. "Managing as designing: Bringing the art of design to the practice of management," a workshop held at Case Western Reserve University, Cleveland, Ohio, June 2002, http://design.case.edu.

REFERENCES

Boland, R. J. Jr. 1985. Phenomenology: A preferred approach to research on information systems. In *Research methods in information systems*, edited by E. Mumford et al. New York: North-Holland, pp. 193–201.

Bowker, G. C., and S. L. Star. 1999. *Sorting things out: Classification and its consequences*. Cambridge, MA: MIT Press.

Brand, S. 1995. *How buildings learn: What happens after they're built*. New York: Penguin Books.

Geertz, C. 1973. *The interpretation of cultures*. New York: Basic Books.

Giddens, A. 1984. *The constitution of society: Outline of the theory of structure*. Berkeley, CA: University of California Press.

Schön, D. A. 1983. *The reflective practitioner: How professionals think in action*. New York: Basic Books.

Suchman, L. 1987. *Plans and situated actions: The problem of human machine communication*. Cambridge, UK: University of Cambridge Press.

Weick, K. E. 1993. The collapse of sensemaking in organizations: The Mann Gulch disaster. *Administrative Science Quarterly*, 38, pp. 628–52.

10

MANAGING AS ARGUMENTATIVE HISTORY-MAKING

Yrjö Engeström

HISTORY-MAKING IN EVERYDAY ACTIONS

History is made in future-oriented situated actions. The challenge is to make the situated history-making visible and analyzable. For studies of managerial discourse, this implies that we should look for ways of capturing how managers discursively create new forms of activity and organization.

There are different types of "distance" between practical activity and discourse (Engeström, 1999a). Small talk between accidental passersby represents one end of the spectrum where talk and practical activity seem entirely divorced. At the other end, there are instances where practical activity and discourse seem to merge almost completely: preachers, auctioneers, and talk show hosts would be examples of that. Most professional activities fall in the middle where practical activity is accompanied and complemented but not replaced or accomplished solely by talk. Physicians conduct physical examinations and perform physical procedures on patients by means of physical artifacts, necessarily accompanied by talk and text. Here the relationship between discourse and practical activity, or between linguistic mediation and tool mediation, becomes an interesting and tension-laden problem, for both practitioners and researchers.

Writing mission statements, brainstorming, and scenario work (see van der Heijden, 1996) are seemingly clear-cut examples of discursive history-making. The problem with these types of discourse is that they tend to be separated

Yrjö Engeström, *Department of Communications, University of California, San Diego, and Center for Activity Theory, University of Helsinki.*

from practical actions. The effect is well known: plans and scenarios do not easily translate into practice. In a sense, these types of discourse have an inherent tendency to become glorified small talk: big words with small consequences. Correspondingly, daily management decisions are often poorly argued but have big unintended consequences. History is made as if behind the backs of the makers.

To overcome the divide, Schön (1983) suggested that professionals engage in reflection-in-action. Momentary pauses or withdrawals from the ongoing action may signify that a professional enters into a "reflective conversation with a unique and uncertain situation," a "framing experiment," a reformulation of the problem at hand. Schön demonstrated how such framing experiments may be articulated in discourse between an experienced master and a novice. Schön's examples of the possibility and discursive dynamics of collective, future-oriented reflection-in-action beyond master-novice dyads were much weaker.

Various professionals conduct work meetings focused on problematic issues or cases. Such meetings typically not only reflect on the particular issue or case, they also include consequential decision making. In other words, they are both reflective and practical. What is commonly missing in case meetings is awareness of the fact that the discourse not only generates solutions for the particular issue but also more general new patterns of activity. One would expect that in management team meetings such an awareness is more present than in most other professional meetings. Such settings offer opportunities to capture how history is made in situated discursive actions.

A thoughtful attempt to conceptualize history-making as embedded in our everyday activities is the book by Spinosa, Flores, and Dreyfus (1997; see also the review by Jasinski, 1998). The authors argue that history-making is based on "the skill of uncovering the tension between standard, commonsense practices and what one actually does" (Spinosa, Flores, and Dreyfus, 1997, p. 23). They suggest that there are three basic ways to resolve such tensions, namely articulation, cross-appropriation, and reconfiguration.

In *articulation*, the basic pattern of the activity is not changed, but important practices or values that have become vague, confused, or lost are recovered and a new coherence is thus achieved. Articulation often takes the form of principled or persuasive speaking. In *cross-appropriation*, practices, ideas, or tools are taken over from other activities or social worlds. This may or may not change the whole pattern of the activity. Cross-appropriation typically manifests itself in interpretive speaking and personal narratives. In *reconfiguration*, a marginal aspect of the activity becomes dominant and the entire pattern is radically transformed. Reconfiguration requires constant awareness of anom-

98   alies. The notion of reconfiguration comes close to the concept of expansion elaborated in activity theory (Engeström, 1987).

> In cases of reconfiguration, a greater sense of integrity (as experienced in articulation) is generally not experienced. Rather, one has the sense of gaining wider horizons. (Spinosa, Flores, and Dreyfus, 1997, p. 26)

In a recent paper (Engeström, Engeström, and Kerosuo, 2003), we analyze how the three modes of history-making suggested by Spinosa, Flores, and Dreyfus are related to the types of discursive actions found in intense case-oriented discussions among medical professionals. It turned out that the relationship between two types of discursive actions, *making joint decisions* and *modeling*, was of crucial importance. The former refers to actual here-and-now care decisions, but modeling refers to future-oriented attempts to elucidate and stabilize the patient and her care in a new, expanded way. To put it crudely, making joint decisions represents articulative action; modeling represents reconfigurative imagination. At decisive points of breakthrough in the discussion, modeling began to approach and resemble making joint decisions. Our study indicates that *to overcome the gap between action and imagination in history-making, it may be necessary to bring closer to one another, and occasionally merge, articulative decision making and reconfigurative modeling.*

ANCHORING UP AND DOWN

Managing as designing can be understood as reconfigurative production of visions and articulative production of decisions. The challenge is to bring these two into fruitful interplay with one another. When that happens, when envisioning and decision making are dialectically intertwined, we see the potentials of management as design unfold.

What does it take to create management team meetings that combine off-line argumentative envisioning with on-line consequential decision-making? I argue that it requires two kinds of anchoring: *anchoring up* and *anchoring down* (see Engeström, 1999b). These two kinds of anchoring typically entail different kinds of language, epistemic actions, and representational tools. Bringing these different types of resources together in hybrid arrangements generates processes and outcomes that were not known ahead of time — a hallmark of good design.

Anchoring up relies on *paradigmatic language*: explicit concepts, systemic models, and historical analysis. Thus, anchoring up visions means asking for their historical value and potential. Anchoring up decisions means asking for their systemic consequences.

Anchoring down relies on *experiential and descriptive language*: cases, feel-

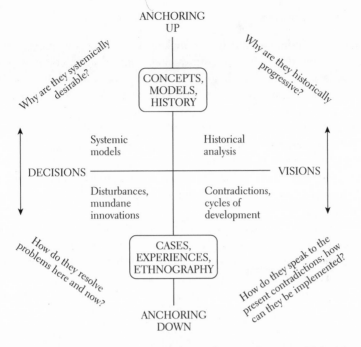

FIGURE 10.1   Anchoring up and down in the production of visions and decisions

ings, and ethnography. Anchoring down visions means asking how they will be implemented, how they will take the organizational life cycle a step forward, and how they speak to the contradictions presently experienced in the organization. Anchoring down decisions means asking how they will affect and resolve problems and generate innovative solutions in the organization here and now.

We may now represent managing as designing in terms of a cognitive field, schematically depicted in Figure 10.1. Argumentative history-making involves clashes, contrasts, negotiations and combinations between the subfields and corresponding modes of inquiry.

The cognitive field depicted in Figure 10.1 may be read as a metamap for assessing and developing managing as designing. If the work of management meetings tends to concentrate on one or two of the subfields in the map, neglecting or avoiding others, we may suspect that there is a built-in bias or block that needs to be addressed. Furthermore, even if the subfields are visited in a seemingly balanced manner, there may be a problem in handling transitions and dynamic relations between them.

Managing as designing and history-making takes, however, more than anchoring up and down. It also requires *anchoring sideways*, comparing, contrasting, debating, and blending one's own situation and point of view with those of partners and competitors. This corresponds to what Spinosa, Flores, and Dreyfus (1997) call cross-appropriation. As pointed out, cross-appropriation typically manifests itself in interpretive speaking and personal *narratives*.

Anchoring sideways visions means asking about the visions held by competitors and partners. What would be their conceptualizations and models of the historical potentials of the situation? What would be their descriptions and experiences of the impact and implementability of the vision under consideration?

Anchoring sideways decisions means asking what competitors and partners might do in the situation. What would be their conceptualizations of the systemic consequences of the possible decision? What would be their descriptions and experiences of the immediate impact of the decision?

Anchoring sideways is not restricted to thought experiments and exercises

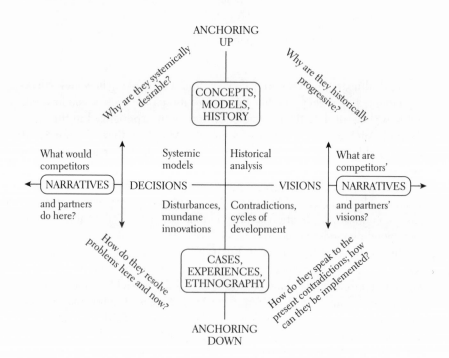

FIGURE 10.2   Managing as designing: anchoring up, down, and sideways

of benchmarking. Managers talk to their competitors and partners all the
time. The challenge is to bring this aspect of managing into interplay with the
other fields described. This challenge is depicted in Figure 10.2.

As can be seen in Figure 10.2, we may schematically characterize anchoring up as asking *why* questions. Anchoring down may be characterized as asking *how* questions. And anchoring sideways may be characterized as asking *what* questions. Again, the key is in the complementarity, interplay, and transitions among the different types of questions.

REFERENCES

Engeström, Y. 1987. *Learning by expanding: An activity-theoretical approach to developmental research*. Helsinki: Orienta-Konsultit.
——. 1999a. Communication, discourse and activity. *Communication Review*, 3: 165–85.
——. 1999b. Expansive visibilization of work: An activity-theoretical perspective. *Computer Supported Cooperative Work*, 8: 63–93.
Engeström, Y., R. Engeström, and H. Kerosuo. 2003. The discursive construction of collaborative care. *Journal of Applied Linguistics*. 24:3, 286–315.
Jasinski, J. 1998. Book review: History-making and the skills of world-disclosing. *Human Studies*, 21: 455–62.
Schön, D. A. 1983. *The reflective practitioner: How professionals think in action*. London: Temple Smith.
Spinosa, C., F. Flores, and H. L. Dreyfus. 1997. *Disclosing new worlds: Entrepreneurship, democratic action, and the cultivation of solidarity*. Cambridge: MIT Press.
van der Heijden, K. 1996. *Scenarios: The art of strategic conversation*. Chichester: Wiley.

11

MANAGEMENT AS THE DESIGNING
OF AN ACTION NET

Barbara Czarniawska

BEFORE I met Frank Gehry, I thought about design in what I daresay were conventional terms. To design was to conceive of an image in one's head and to reproduce it on paper or in a computer file. A creative activity — intellectual and individualistic.

After having listened to Gehry describing his work, and to others concurring with him, I think of design in a completely different way. True, the intellectual and individual activity remained as central, decisive, and unique, but I could see that it took a proportionally small amount of Gehry's time and energy. The work began later. It was necessary for him to explain his imagery to his collaborators and to present it to his clients on several occasions. Finally he, his collaborators, and his clients were required to explain to various types of contractors what had to be built, how it had to be built, when it had to be built, and so on and so forth. In order to translate the mental image completely and successfully into a beautiful building, it was necessary to design not only the building but also an *action net*.

An action net is a general concept referring not so much to entities existing in the practice of management as to a useful way of studying that practice. It suggests that organizing, and its special case, management, consists of connecting different social actions. This happens according to a pattern institutionalized in a given time at a given place. In contemporary culture, the action of producing is connected to the action of selling, which in turn is connected to the action of buying. Such actions are always social or collective,

Barbara Czarniawska, *Gothenburg Research Institute, Göteborg University.*

even when performed by individuals. But it also happens that new connections are created against the institutional grain (alternative banks omit the connection between savings and interest payments, for example); innovative or entrepreneurial connections are forged; old nets are reshaped or destroyed.

Is an action net an organization then? No, and the case of the construction of the Peter B. Lewis Building is a good example. There were a great many organizations involved, performing the various actions required. True, some connections among actions may become formalized by contracts, binding organizations rather than single actions, or part of an existing action net may form a boundary around itself, creating a formal organization. Such, I imagine, was the case when Frank Gehry became Frank O. Gehry & Associates, Inc.: a boundary was drawn around successfully connected actions and a net became a company.

Is an action net a network then? No, because a network, as it is popularly understood, is a set of connections among actors, whether people or organizations. Actors first connect; then they do something together. Actors come first; action comes second. From an action net perspective, however, actions come first and actors come second. There is a double meaning here: in the first place, actors acquire an "actorial" identity from actions, not the other way around. Frank Gehry's contractor became Frank Gehry's contractor not merely by being known as a contractor, but by promising to deliver what was needed to build the Lewis building. True, past actions build the reputations of actors, but it is only their stability that gives "character" to "actants" (that which acts or is acted upon, as defined in semiotics). Actors also take second place in the sense that, from the point of view of an action net, actors are exchangeable; whereas from a point of view of a network, actions are exchangeable. The Mafia is a network: when one type of activity does not pay, the network shifts to another, as long as the same people can be involved. When the same thing happens in the construction business, we speak of "cliques" and "corruption." Although friendship may be beautiful, it does not necessarily build buildings.

An action net is not the same as an organization field, or industry. Rather, it denotes actual connections among actions, and although these connections will likely occur within the same industry, they will certainly never involve the whole of it. It is more likely that they will include actions reaching outside one given industry, as in the case of business professors contributing to the designing of their school.

The architectural design is an excellent demonstration of the thesis that management equals the designing of an action net. Studying formal organi-

zations already in existence, we, as organization scholars, are usually intimi-
dated by those greater-than-life reifications of our own concepts. Who would
ever dare to imagine General Electric or World Bank as a mere action net!
And yet formal organizations arose from action nets, are part of action nets,
and host many action nets. To take an action net perspective reveals those
temples of modern capitalism as potential sketches on a sheet of paper that
might never have been built if appropriate connections among collective actions were not created and stabilized. Thus, the construction industry, the
main metaphorical culprit of our myopia, may repay its metaphorical debt by
shifting our attention from buildings to construction to design. Because no
matter how much is said about organizations as machines or organisms, the
ruling metaphor is still that of a building: people and things enter, and people
and things exit.

"Connecting collective actions" is, however, yet another abstract concept.
At any rate, it is easier said than done. How to "connect" such actions as the
financing of a building, the creation of a design, and the collective dream of
an ideal business education? They must be *translated* one into another, and
here I use the concept of translation in the sense given it by Latour (1986): not
only translations of words into other words—the language of architects into
the language of the users and the language of financiers—but also of things
into other things, of images into other images. Not everything can or must be
translated, in the sense of becoming something else when put into another
place. Some objects can remain where they are and can remain as they are;
seen from different points of view, they will, at any rate, be different objects.
Star and Griesemer (1989) call them "boundary objects," in the sense that they
remain between different realms, belonging to all of them simultaneously, but
seen from different points of view. Gehry's drawings are an excellent example
of such objects: works of art to us, plans of action to the builders, financial demands to the sponsors, and working objects for the architects. Boundary objects form both excellent connections among different actions and excellent
stabilizers of connections already in existence: "Have you forgotten what you
agreed to do for us? Look at the picture enclosed with the contract!"

Thus, a meeting between management and design can result in a common
image of both activities: management as the designing of an action net. It requires the replacement of an image of an intellectual, individual, and control-
fixated activity into an activity in which intellect and emotions never separate,
visions are adjusted as new circumstances arise, improvisation and bricolage
achieve high status, and connectedness—for better and for more difficult—is
the crucial point in management and in design.

REFERENCES

Latour, B. 1986. The powers of association. In *Power, action and belief*, edited by J. Law. London: Routledge and Kegan Paul, pp. 264–80.

Star, S. L., and J. R. Griesemer. 1989. Institutional ecology, "translations" and boundary objects: Amateurs and professionals in Berkeley's Museum of Vertebrae Zoology, 1907–39. *Social Studies of Science* 19: 387–420.

12

Design in the Punctuation
of Management Action

Richard J. Boland Jr.

HERBERT SIMON's *The Sciences of the Artificial* (1996) is one of the finest examples we have of a well-developed theory of managing as designing. Some key ideas from that classic book are summarized in Chapter 1 of this volume, and here I will elaborate on them slightly. In *The Sciences of the Artificial*, Simon conceptualizes the designed artifact, be it an organization, a policy, or a work practice as located at the interface between an inner and an outer environment. The design artifact mediates the demands of the outer environment through a set of operative principles in its inner environment. Successful designs are those that effectively and efficiently mold themselves to their environment. Simon views human cognition, as well as computers, as engaging in design thinking with a sequential, list-processing approach to generating and testing moves in its environment. The problem space a manager deals with is a product of the problem representation that is being employed. A problem representation structures the problem space with elements of the problem and its potential solution and is the most potent explanation for if, and how, a design problem will be solved.

Problem representations are indeed important and our vocabulary of representations is critical in determining how well or poorly we do as managers. How we as managers define our projects and problems, and the set of methods we employ for engaging them, as well as our notions of what constitutes a good and true course of action, are all rooted in and constrained by our vo-

Richard J. Boland Jr., *Weatherhead School of Management, Case Western Reserve University.*

cabulary. Good designers are aware of their own vocabulary and what it does
to their work. Part of engaging in good design is choosing a vocabulary or language to use in defining the design task, generating alternatives, and making
judgments of balance, fit, and scale. Developing an awareness of one's own vocabulary and its impact on one's design work can make design an ideal vehicle
for creating dialogue across specialized professions. As Simon argues, it can
provide a common ground for diverse professionals to engage in discussions
across the divide of their disciplines about the qualities of their design vocabularies, the creative experience of designing, and the criteria for making design judgments, all of which are sorely needed in our highly specialized world.

   Much of Simon's concern in *The Sciences of the Artificial* centers on the local and immediate experience of an individual who faces an environment that
is essentially unchangeable. It is a given to which the manager must mold the
organization. Accordingly, his discussion of language follows the "picture theory" of early Wittgenstein, in which words are assumed to point directly at
things in the world. If there is ambiguity in our language use, Simon argues
that it can be reconciled by clarifying the context of its use. This leaves managers looking very placid with concrete knowledge of the world they face and
a limited capacity for agency to transform the world. In a few of the later chapters, however, Simon considers longer-term, higher-level kinds of design projects by corporate and social policy makers. In these chapters, he seems to recognize the symbolic nature of language, and the inherently metaphorical and
ambiguous nature of words, thereby highlighting the role of individual actors
in constructing the very environment they face. The malleability of the environment is evident in his discussion of social planners as painters who, having
made a mark on the canvas, have in effect changed it and created a new design
problem to face. He uses the example of the Marshall Plan and the various
ways it could be named (a central bank, a clearinghouse, a market) to show that
those names bring different possible environments into consideration and suggest different design problems to solve. This heightened sense of agency for the
designer suggests a greater moral obligation on the part of the designer for the
kind of worlds she will be creating, as well as a heightened concern for questioning who is the client being served by a design effort. It also suggests that the
different narratives of action we bring to a representation (being a banker, negotiating in a market, serving as a trusted agent) are another, though for him
unexplored, quality of cognition affecting the outcomes of our design projects.
The way we narrate the story of our experience to ourselves and others as we
engage in a sequence of events gives meaning to the problem space we construct and the calculations we make within it.

108   With that brief background on Simon's conceptualization of design, I
would now like to put design into his larger vision of management action. In
his *New Science of Management Decision* (1977), Simon identified the three
major activities performed by a manager: intelligence, design, and choice. Intelligence is that activity that alerts us to the need for an intervention in order
to change the current state of affairs. It is the process of sensing and predicting
conditions that require action or signal that a change is required if we are to
achieve our desired goals. Design is the formulation of possible courses of action that can respond to the current situation in a way that makes the possible
course better able to serve desired human ends and achieve our goals. Choice,
in turn, is the process of selecting that design alternative that is most efficient
and effective in achieving our goals. These three are thoroughly interdependent and always take place in a way that finds them intertwined: intelligence
includes a critical view of a current design or a previous choice that proved un-
satisfactory; design includes an intelligence about materials, techniques, and
processes available, as well as numerous choices among design trade-offs; and
choice includes a design sense for fitting alternatives with previous choices, as
well as an intelligence about the current conditions affecting each alternative.

Nonetheless, we experience each of the three activities as a separate mode
of action. Each is always engaged in a way that puts one in the foreground and
the other two in the background. In Polanyi's (1966) sense, we attend to any
one aspect from (or in light of) the others. While one aspect is in focal attention, the others are held in a subsidiary, or tacit, way. So that, although the
three are thoroughly interdependent, they are not simultaneously in focal attention, and we can therefore think of the three aspects as being punctuated
sequentially in management action.

Now my question becomes: what are the implications of the way that managers punctuate the sequences of their intelligence, design, and choice actions? In asking this, I am drawing on Karl Weick's formulation from his
Social Psychology of Organizing (1969) that an individual engages in sensemaking of the "blooming, buzzing confusion" of their ongoing stream of action by punctuating it into a sequential pattern in order to generate a plausible
and coherent understanding. There are six sequences in which the three aspects of intelligence (I), design (D), and choice (C) can be untangled from
the circular pattern of mutual influence depicted above and punctuated as a
three-step process:

1. Intelligence-Design-Choice/Intelligence-Design-Choice/....
2. Design-Choice-Intelligence/Design-Choice-Intelligence/....
3. Choice-Intelligence-Design/Choice-Intelligence-Design/....
4. Intelligence-Choice-Design/Intelligence-Choice-Design/....

5. Design-Intelligence-Choice/Design-Intelligence-Choice/ . . . .
6. Choice-Design-Intelligence/Choice-Design-Intelligence/ . . . .

Each of these punctuations of intelligence, design, and choice actions represents a way in which they are assembled to provide a story-based, dynamic sense of wholeness, combining a notion of moving forward, with the possibility of a feedback, learning relationship. As in any narrative, something happens first, even though there is a continuous stream of intelligence, design, and choice activities. The one that is seen as happening first serves as the beginning of each narrative episode of acting in the world — moving forward, learning, and making sense of the "blooming, buzzing confusion." As a narrative, our experience has the following shape: an intelligence, design, or choice event happens, then one of the remaining two, and then the final one that brings an end to the story and serves as a source of feedback to the initial event, allowing the cycle to begin again. It has the form: First, . . . Then, . . . Finally, ... One incident or element of the story leads to another. I will briefly explore each of these six possible punctuations as to the narrative sense that I make of them and their implications for understanding managing as designing.

NARRATIVE 1. INTELLIGENCE-DESIGN-CHOICE:
RATIONAL MAN ECONOMIC THEORY

The sequence of intelligence-design-choice is Simon's own punctuation in which intelligence recognizes a need for intervention, design makes alternatives available for consideration, and choice selects the best (satisficing) one. This is the classic view of rational man who is intentionally goal seeking and uses intelligence and forethought to guide organizational action. Our literature is full of examples showing that this model does not represent how humans actually behave. Simon "saves" this model for economists by posing that individuals are boundedly rational and do not seek best or optimal solutions as a strong economic model might suggest, but rather search for solutions until one that is "good enough" is found — the boundedly rational person therefore satisfices. This image of a satisficing human, as attractive as it may be, has an undesirable consequence that follows from its temporal dynamic. In light of Simon's own recognition of the importance of problem representation, we see that this punctuation of managing is easily trapped by the common wisdom of those in a problematic situation — its sequence begins with a pre-understanding of the situation that can promote a myopic circularity in which the way we happen to be thinking about things becomes institutionalized in the representation and definition of the world we face. My intuition is that this way of punctuating management action leads to a finer and finer attention to problem representations that grow increasingly irrelevant to the human condition. Welfare policy, education policy, transportation policy, and most public policy issues seem to fall prey to the traps of this form of punctuation.

NARRATIVE 2. DESIGN-CHOICE-INTELLIGENCE: THE "WHAT HAVE I DONE?" MANAGER

This mode of punctuation begins with ideas for shaping a situation that are ready at hand. Design alternatives are accepted as given and obvious, with a choice made among them, and intelligence applied to explain what has just occurred. Coming at the end of this punctuated cycle of action, intelligence is left with little to work with and generates self-escalating processes — refining the obvious and pre-given into organizational structures. Designs produced (perhaps unthinkingly) are accepted as the best we can do and subjected to an intelligence that tries to perfect them. Initial, premature choices become the building blocks for a process of self-rationalizing closure. This manager is forever involved in situations that were chosen in only the most generous use of the term, yet are being perfected and concretized. He goes through his day wondering how he got into this mess, but his punctuation of action, with intelligence reinforcing happenstance, results in less and less desirable outcomes — unless fate has brought him remarkably good luck. Many large organizations follow this pattern of punctuation in which the latest management fads are adopted, one after another.

NARRATIVE 3. CHOICE-INTELLIGENCE-DESIGN: THE EXISTENTIAL INTROVERT

This punctuation of experience as acts of choice, intelligence, and design provides us with another unhappy story, in which the manager begins down a path of existential choice in a vacuum. A way of being is asserted without prior design or intelligence. Later, this manager becomes engaged with an analysis of how to achieve the identity that was chosen and only later to deriving alternatives for doing so. The existential choice that begins this punctuation roots it in the moment of action, but it also leaves the manager floating free from reality. The manager who "fixes" things that aren't broken is one example of this narrative. An isolation and loneliness characterizes this punctuation of action, born of a disconnected sense of the environment or context in which action takes place.

NARRATIVE 4. INTELLIGENCE-CHOICE-DESIGN:
THE CHRONICALLY DISAPPOINTED MANAGER—
"IF I HAD ONLY . . . ."

This form of punctuation begins as the manager senses an environment and makes choices for action but only afterward has insights as to other courses of action that could have been followed. It is a failed version of the rational-man economic theory in which the actor, because of a severely limited (gagged and bound?) rationality is always second-guessing himself and later repenting for having acted too quickly. It is also probably the story of many familiar management failures, including most recently Arthur Andersen and Enron. From the outside, this form of punctuation seems sadly unable to think creatively about its situation. Are those convoluted, insider-owned self-trading structures really the best way that Enron executives could think of for doing business? Was the wholesale destruction of audit documents the best way that Andersen partners could think of for maintaining their professional status? It appears as moral bankruptcy, but is more likely due to a fatally delayed use of design in punctuating their engagement with customers and the world at large.

NARRATIVE 5. DESIGN-INTELLIGENCE-CHOICE:
KARL WEICK'S SENSEMAKING MANAGER

Here, we have design as the shaping of things while engaged with others in the flow of action, and the producing of outcomes that are surprising to even the individual herself. Interaction with others generates equivocal enactment that is then subject to a sensemaking process. During sensemaking, intelligence is applied to order those elements of the raw action in ways that make the situation meaningful, aesthetically pleasing, and morally acceptable. This intelligence is followed by a choice of which meanings and sensemaking structures to carry forward into future enactments. This is a cybernetic system modeled after an evolutionary process, much like Weick's sensemaking model with its pattern of variation, selection, and retention. Here, goals (if they are ever explicitly considered at all) are only understood retrospectively, and the raw, surprising enactments of design are the primary driving force of organizing. Weick's many years of research on the sensemaking model of organizing shows how powerful this view of punctuating action is for understanding organizing behaviors both successful and unsuccessful. It is, in a sense, the antidote to the rational man model of the first narrative, grounded in a phenomenological appreciation of human action.

NARRATIVE 6. CHOICE-DESIGN-INTELLIGENCE:
THE EXISTENTIAL HERO

This form of punctuation is the story of those who elevate existential choice as the primary drive of action. First they choose who or what they are, and then they design alternatives and perfect them based on self-defined criteria. The environment is not used as a source for feedback on goals, but is essentially ignored in favor of the egocentric choice of the individual. This leads to the self-certain, self-sustained hero who can endure hardship in the name of a chosen principle. Unfortunately, this "hero," being detached from the world, is as likely to be a Unabomber as a Trappist monk. As an organizational leader, this individual is at a disadvantage unless she is truly a visionary.

CONCLUDING THOUGHTS

Herbert Simon provides us with an overarching view of managing as designing that is rich in implications for educating future leaders and guiding our organizational research. His emphasis on design, when placed in the context of his larger model of managerial action, has allowed us to play with alternative ways that the core managerial actions of intelligence, design, and choice can be punctuated and made into a narrative in an individual's ongoing experience. The narratives arising from these different punctuations are argued to lead to different consequences in the world, and some examples have been presented for each. One conclusion to draw from this exploration seems clear: punctuations that put choice off to the last possible moment and that place design as the driving activity of managing (Narrative 5 — Karl Weick's sensemaking manager), or that place intelligence and goal-driven problem solving as the driving activities (Narrative 1 — Simon's satisficing manager), seem to be the most promising for a humane and survivable organization. Others lack an evolutionary capacity to learn through feedback or lead to unhappy outcomes of chronic inaction, second-guessing, excessive risk-taking, or premature closure of inquiry.

REFERENCES

Polanyi, M. 1966. *The tacit dimension*. London: Routledge & Kegan Paul Ltd.
Simon, H. 1977. *New science of management decision*. Englewood Cliffs, NJ: Prentice-Hall.
Simon, H. 1996. *The sciences of the artificial*, 3rd ed. Cambridge: MIT Press.
Weick, K. 1969. *Social psychology of organizing*. Reading, MA: Addison Wesley.

13

Managing Design, Designing Management

Mariann Jelinek

MANAGEMENT AS a deliberate and planned, intentional exercise is variously described as the contribution of the railroad managers of the mid-nineteenth century (Chandler 1965; Chandler and Salsbury 1974; Chandler 1977) or of George Whistler about 170 years ago, or from about one hundred years earlier, the time of the Philosophes and classical economist Adam Smith, among founding candidates. But the medieval cathedrals were built earlier, by hundreds of years, as massive social projects extending for decades and requiring the work of hundreds or thousands of craftsmen (King 2000). Earlier still by centuries, designers had achieved huge artifacts requiring the efforts of thousands of workers over decades — in Egypt's pyramids, the irrigation systems of ancient Iraq and Syria, and the temple cities of the Mayan empire, among others. Even earlier, evidence suggests that the prehistoric artworks deep in Lascaux Caverns required substantial support — food, materials, and light carried as much as a mile deep into the dark to create the enduring, magical images over many years (Chauvet et al. 1996). Every such effort was, perforce, "managed." In every one, a pile of rocks was envisioned as something else that might be, and the systematic efforts to achieve a goal, along with the parallel efforts of many others to support those whose toil moved, placed, and arranged the rocks or decorated them, was orchestrated.

Only when organizations became large and complex, and particularly when they began to operate over long distances, was management theory formalized in the mid-nineteenth century, later by far than management practice. In the past 150 years of management/organization theory, our managerial

Mariann Jelinek, *School of Management, College of William and Mary.*

114   practice has shifted from paternalistic, centralized, and hierarchical toward a
more pluralistic and inclusive, decentralized and egalitarian mode — in some
places, at some times, with many remaining organizations continuing to embody much older ways. In the same time frame, our metaphors have shifted
from mechanistic to organic to chaotic. Yet the metaphors matter: we think
through metaphors that reflect our experience as embodied beings who experience existence first through our bodies (Lakoff and Johnson 1980; Varela
et al. 1993). The metaphors embody our sense of where we think the action is,
and they shift as our focus shifts, and our intent. Our shifting metaphors say
we are seeking to solve different problems: from following orders to replicat-
ing a successful pattern, motivating others, dealing with change. Different
problems require different solutions, and in social organizations, different designs. What, then, does the metaphor of design signal?

Organizations — for profit and not for profit, government and nongov-
ernmental organizations, voluntary and coercive — are not machines. Their
"parts" (if by which we mean human participants) are reactive, often recal-
citrant, sometimes brilliantly creative in their support (or subversion) of the
stated or imposed vision: they enact *revision*, even as formal decisions are
made and remade, responding with informal decisions of their own (Homans
1950). Nor are organizations organisms: their parts change, as individuals flow
in, through and out, and as groups coalesce, merge, and dissolve. But there is
no natural life cycle, and organizations can revivify with new enthusiasm to
accomplish different goals with different members, technologies, and focus
points. (But the metaphor lives on in at least one scholar's call for "An Organic
Perspective on Strategy," Farjoun 2002). Beyond metaphor per se, the underlying assumptions and connections in the theory we create will condition
what we attend to or ignore, and how we comprehend organizations.[1]

Participants' shared understandings also evolve, emerge, and sometimes
dramatically shift with new information, new events, and new catalytic leaders (designers?). Our theoretical metaphors evolve as we seek to signify what
we see as happening. "Machines" are made entities, as are organizations. "Organisms" change, grow, and eventually die in a predictable time frame, as do
most organizations (typically coterminous with their founders).

But not all organizations die off so easily. Some long survive their founders,
continuing to exist for decades, even centuries. Organizations partake of
something more than and different from either machines or organisms in their
purposive quality, their potential for deliberate morphogenesis, and their
changing purposes over time. IBM today is not the organization it was five
years ago or ninety years ago. GE under Jeffrey Immelt has reemphasized research, science, and technology, signaling a move away from the financial ser-

vices that had been Jack Welch's focus. (And organizations can also be designed for fun, as emergent entities intended for no purpose other than the delight provided for participants by the interactions that constitute them, which may change at participants' pleasure: think of a group of classmates who become alumni, continue to meet and vacation, raise their families and build lifelong friendships—but shift their activities as members age.) That organizations and firms can so refocus is important because it invites us to consider both design and redesign, fit and refitting over time to new circumstances and ends. It also cautions us to note that what works in one era may well have to be reinvented to survive in another.

One central image in our time has been the computer, with organizations as "information processing engines" in an Information Age. Perhaps, however, we need a way to transcend these images again. Here, the design metaphor offers interesting insight. A genuine revolution of possibility flowed from the move between prior flat file systems into relational databases and, in computer systems, the hyperlinked nodes of the Internet. Similarly, the "virtual organization"—often pro tem, frequently voluntary, and broadly dispersed—is the iconic organization of our times. But how does one design it? Or should one perhaps instead invite it to emerge? Is the issue deliberate design, or is it design of a process of interaction that allows a collaborative process to emerge? What helps a virtual organization to emerge and to develop effective, useful, satisfying interactions? How shall we theorize about such organizations? What will such theorizing tell us about design in more enduring organizations? Or should we embrace the ephemeral organization as a new norm?

When such an organization does emerge, it may be both transient and protean. Theory to describe its dynamism will of necessity evolve metaphors of multilevel interaction, of autonomy coordinated by shared purpose, which itself evolves in interactions structured by the participants themselves (Jelinek 2003). The issues are forms, functions, and flexibilities in an interactive dance, all under the constraint (in most organizations) of getting something specific done, on time and within budget. In a virtual organization, the dance itself relies upon an underlying infrastructure that facilitates interaction, invisible (because taken for granted) energy, and a technological grammar that permits us to behave as if we were in one another's presence, that we might generate common purpose. In computer terms, the Internet relies upon Javascripts, html, or xml—and on electric power, file structures, conventions, and more. The virtual organization also relies on underlying structures, which, like the computer systems to which I've compared them, also evolve. To what extent are organizations well compared to computers, to knowledge engines that create, store, and facilitate access to expertise? To what extent are organizations and management illuminated by the design metaphor? If we speak of "an interactive dance" among elements, the design metaphor invites us also to consider both choreography and the larger Art of Dance as well.

Strategy hinges on dynamically stable commitments to purpose, communicated through levels so as to call forth emergent commitment (and enactment). These commitments are "stable" insofar as they endure long enough to achieve something like their intended goals. They are "dynamic" insofar as they do indeed shift in response to events, information, and people, and furthermore that their goals can and do change. They are "emergent" in that no strategy is real until it is enacted, made manifest in the actions of those throughout the organization whose actions constitute the organization itself, as well as enact its strategy. This was so despite the likely lack of such vocabulary around the pyramids: demands of weather, of feeding the workers, and of keeping intent visible were met; the pyramids went up, and by all accounts were glorious (even more so originally, with brilliantly white limestone sheathing, than in our own time, when they still inspire awe). So what is different? How are our designs different? How is our management different from the time of the pyramids? How *should* they differ?

The design metaphor invites us to consider a host of questions. Using architectural design as a framework for inquiry, issues of how ideas come to be, how they are shaped, whether opening them up to others attenuates or concentrates them, and who is entitled to participate all arise. Applying these notions to management and the design of organizations (or strategies), we are instantly alerted to the issues of power, collaboration, participation, and (joint) emergent decisions so frequently ignored by traditional organization theory. These issues seem especially urgent today.

I think what has changed in the past century and a half is our attention. Perhaps because we are awash in data and information (much of it noise), management theory is now more attentive to change, to the dynamism and evolutionary character of our intentions, and to the roles of information and cognition in shaping intentions. We are also heirs to a scientific inquiry method that has biased the tangible, material, and quantitative, sometimes creating a distinct disinclination to notice the intangibles. Scientific analysis has also alerted us to the importance of abstract patterns of interaction over time. Here organization and management theory has described how organization designs may differ. Both management theory and practice are familiar with such abstraction, where some fraction of effort is conventionally assigned to a department, a division, a laboratory, or a team, but eventually must come together with other fractions to accomplish a larger goal.

Consequently, we seek theories to explain to ourselves how it is that the magic happens. Despite changeable contexts of new demands, rivals, economic volatility, and life events intruding on our intended activities, we accomplish much. Yet sometimes it is success despite our theories' limits, because those responsible for action (even if not officially "in charge") find a way. How is it that organizations "learn," or enact strategies, or change their strategies over time? Beyond mere reification, or the mundane observation that "only people act," we need multilevel theories to address such collaborative design, such evolving real time social construction and understanding, and such information-driven processes among and between only intendedly rational, reactive beings. Here, design suggests deliberate attention to embedding the values of learning and the interactions, discourses, and reflections that lead to it, much more formally into the organization. To my ear, this sounds very much like the process that architect Frank Gehry describes in causing interactions among colleagues by virtue of his buildings' designs — embedded in deliberately created traffic flows, sight lines, and chance encounters. And process models are also relevant (Langley 1999).

Note the interplay here of epistemology with theory with practice, and of all of these with our formal consideration of them. If we believe that organizational decisions "should" be made by the Great Leader in splendid isolation, we structure organizations to localize power and information at the top and to fractionate the rest of the organization: "the mushroom theory of management" rules (i.e., "keep 'em in the dark and fertilize well"). Private offices, protected corner suites, long corridors, and formal clothing and interactions are to be observed as symbolic physical artifacts. By contrast, if we believe that organization members broadly must understand strategy in order to enact it and perceive relevant environmental information, we structure flatter organizations with open information flows, and more open physical surroundings, informal clothing, and interactions may be seen.[2]

At the most basic levels, as theorists and as practitioners of management, we are interested in behaviors and interactions to further desired outcomes. A design perspective directs our attention to the context that enables, stimulates, or encourages some behaviors while inhibiting or discouraging others. Elements of that design might include selection and training processes, physical surroundings, information flows, performance assessment, and incentives, among others. But beyond these factors, the actors themselves profoundly shape their environment and one another, in their interactions and their responses to them. Managers shape and reshape the contextual factors of their realm of work, seeking to improve outcomes (including performance and comfort, although not limited to these). As scholars, we seek to craft theory that embraces the phenomena of interest and guides further observation and interaction: we want to understand and to help others understand, too. To do so effectively, our theory must develop both a dynamic, interactive character and an awareness of how these levels interact, for we are *creatures* of our theories as well as *creators* of them. In short, we also design theories, beginning with the design templates, tools, and concepts of our training. Acknowledging this reality puts living flesh on Einstein's comment, "Our theories determine what we may see."

It seems to me that we might also productively acknowledge both design and redesign of our management theories. Then we would experiment to see how well the theories work for their intended purposes (and how their unintended consequences suit us) and redesign them subsequently. The historic account of management surely suggests that that's precisely what has already been happening for lo these many years as each new generation of management scholars and practitioners wrestles with "the" issues (and metaphors) of their time, from the "machine bureaucracy" (Henry Mintzberg's evocative phrase; Mintzberg 1979) through the organic organization, the matrix, and the networked organization to today's increasingly virtual firms. Transaction cost economics and Michael Porter's widely cited version of industrial organization analysis (1980) have directed a generation of managers and theorists to understand that organizational boundaries are firm and transactions between a firm and its suppliers and customers are all about the contest for a (fixed) margin. Fast forward to add information to the mix, and Dell Computers' virtual integration with both suppliers and customers comes into view, calling into question some of the fundamental elements of our traditional theories of organizations, transactions, and strategies (Magretta 1998; Madhok 2002).

Yet refocusing our attention on deliberate design (even the deliberate creation of circumstances to support emergent design, chaotic design, and fortuitous juxtapositions) might well refresh our understanding and potentials in the new context of our times. We need, I think, to manage our design process, too, building in the "innovation buffer" of time, resources, and attention to create the organizational contexts for now, rather than for yesterday and yesterday's challenges. We need both vision and revision as our needs, contexts, understandings, and goals evolve.

If our theory moves in these directions, the implications for management education are profound. Managers too would need to be much more attentive to the consequences for action and interaction, to the way that rules, incentives, practices, and goals affect people. Where is stability required — to respond to legal constraints, for instance? How can stability be achieved "on the fly," by responding to clearly out-of-control efforts, when something isn't working? Teaching managers and would-be managers about dynamic consequences of action will be challenging. But it's not the only challenging implication. Larger-scale management encounters the realities and conflicting interests and influences of politics. How can policy makers both envision and revision to avoid disasters like the partial deregulation of energy markets in California that apparently encouraged fraud according to widespread accounts? How can society comprehend the need for dynamic response, and yet reasonably hold policy makers accountable?

Nor is such dynamic response merely reactive. Managers will need reflexive attention to their organizations and to their actions. Where is innovation essential — to respond to changing competitive environments, new technologies, or emerging opportunities (or disasters)? How might managers intervene to encourage closure in a stream of decisions? And how might they intervene again to dissolve closure and return to "design" mode? Who gets to intervene or to decide when closure is "premature"? How can proposals, possibilities, and opportunities be "played with" — as obviously unfinished "*schreck* models" to invite collaboration — without undermining the legitimate need for assessment? How can we create theories that ready our students to manage in a constant iteration of closure and fluidity, openness and commitment, the ephemeral consensus of stability to accomplish one project without losing the mutability to address the next? In short, considering managing as design invites us to redesign our understanding of management, our theory of managing, and our management of theory.

NOTES

1. See Buckley 1967 and Boulding 1968 for some provocative early thinking on theory constraints, and Weick 1990 and Hargadon and Fanelli 2002 for more recent exemplars.

2. See "Smashing the Cube: Corporate Transformation at Ciba-Geigy" (Johnson and Collis 1995), HBS case # 9-795-041, for a striking illustration.

REFERENCES

Boulding, K. E. 1968. General systems theory — the skeleton of science. In *Modern systems research for the behavioral scientist*, edited by W. Buckley. Chicago: Aldine, pp. 3–10.

Buckley, W. 1967. *Sociology and modern systems theory*. Englewood Cliffs, NJ: Prentice-Hall.

Chandler, A. D. 1965. The railroads: pioneers in modern corporate management. *Business History Review* XXXIX (Spring): 16–40.

120 ———. 1977. *The visible hand: the managerial revolution in American business*. Cambridge, MA: Harvard University Press.

Chandler, A. D., and S. Salsbury. 1974. *Pierre S. DuPont and the making of the modern corporation*. New York: Harper & Row.

Chauvet, J. M., E. B. Deschamps, and C. Hillaire. 1996. *Dawn of art: The Chauvet Cave: The oldest known paintings in the world*. New York: Harry N. Abrams, Inc.

Farjoun, M. 2002. Towards an organic perspective on strategy. *Strategic Management Journal* 23(7): 561–94.

Hargadon, A., and A. Fanelli. 2002. Action and possibility: Reconciling dual perspectives of knowledge in organizations." *Organization Science* 13(3): 290–302.

Homans, G. C. 1950. *The human group*. New York: Harcourt, Brace & World.

Jelinek, M. 2003. Enacting the future: A time- and levels-based view of strategic change. In *Research in multi-level issues: an annual series*, vol. 2, edited by F. Dansereau and F. J. Yammarino. New York: JAI Press.

Johnson, E. W., and D. J. Collis. 1995. Smashing the cube: Corporate transformation at Ciba-Geigy, Ltd. Harvard Business School case # 9-795-041, Harvard University, Cambridge, MA.

King, R. 2000. *Brunelleschi's dome: How a renaissance genius reinvented architecture*. New York: Walker and Company.

Lakoff, G., and M. Johnson. 1980. *Metaphors we live by*. Chicago: University of Chicago Press.

Langley, A. 1999. Strategies for theorizing from process data. *Academy of Management Review* 24(4): 691–710.

Madhok, A. 2002. Reassessing the fundamentals and beyond: Ronald Coase, the transaction cost and resource-based theories of the firm and the institutional structure of production. *Strategic Management Journal* 23(6): 535–50.

Magretta, J. 1998. The power of virtual integration: An interview with Michael Dell. *Harvard Business Review* 76(2): 73–84.

Mintzberg, H. 1979. *The structuring of organizations*. Englewood Cliffs, NJ: Prentice-Hall.

Porter, M. E. 1980. *Competitive strategy: Techniques for analyzing industries and competitors*. New York: The Free Press.

Varela, F. J., E. Thompson, and E. Rosch. 1993. *The embodied mind*. Cambridge, MA: MIT Press.

Weick, K. 1990. Technology as equivoque. In *Technology and Organizations*, edited by P. S. Goodman, L. S. Sproull and Associates. San Francisco: Jossey-Bass.

14

WEBS RATHER THAN KEVLAR

Designing Organizational Systems

Hilary Bradbury

IN OUR effort to reconsider management as a design science (Fuller, 1971), let us not forget that *Titanic* was the product of a consciously managed design process. Fifteen thousand men, organized in a rigid bowler-hat-wearing hierarchy (with nary a woman in sight!), worked on the design of this ship. As the sold-out movies and exhibitions worldwide attest, *Titanic* continues to intrigue us for the very failure of its design. The design for *Titanic* exemplified the logic of modern industrialization, a logic that asserts that nature can, indeed must, be conquered.

VISA International, on the other hand (see also the discussion by Karl E. Weick in Chapter 3), intrigues us for different reasons. VISA was designed to operate as a global, flat, networked organization. It was designed to be resilient in the face of chaotic global markets, striving for order as a *chaord*, that is, as a combination of both chaos and order. Nature, a chaotic system, deeply informed the design of VISA (Hock, 2000).

VISA and *Titanic* offer us archetypes of two rather different products of design. The latter suggests the usefulness of looking to natural systems as we invigorate management scholarship and practice with a discourse of design. The implicit suggestion is that we have designed for too long as though seeking to

Hilary Bradbury, *Weatherhead School of Management, Case Western Reserve University,* with Sue Simington, Sara Metcalf, Anita Burke, Catherine Grey, Darcy Winslow, Sarah Severn, Chris Page, Denise Kalule, Catherine Bragdon, Sara Schley, Catherine Greener, Sheena Boughan, and Joyce LaValle, executives who meet regularly to discuss sustainability issues. The author's project participation and writing have been supported, in part, by funding from a National Science Foundation grant.

122 create organizational *Titanics*, that is, human artifacts increasingly out of place in the natural landscape and therefore unsustainable. We want to invite explicit reconsideration of nature as inspiration while we begin to design our organizations for a postindustrial era.

Janine Benyus (1997) explores innovations inspired by natural systems and points to numerous examples of product designers learning from nature. The title of this paper is drawn from one such endeavor, namely the efforts under-way to design a material with the properties of spider silk. Compared with Kevlar (found in bulletproof vests), spider silk is able to absorb five times the impact force without breaking. According to *Science* news reporter Richard Lipkin (1995, cited in Benyus, 1997), spider silk is so strong that on a human scale a web resembling a fishing net could catch a passenger jet in flight. However, efforts to produce it for human use are proving to be difficult, given our lack of familiarity with the design logic of nature. Kevlar is manufactured by pouring petroleum-derived molecules into a pressurized vat of concen-trated sulfuric acid and boiling it at several hundred degrees Fahrenheit. It is then subjected to high pressures to extrude the fibers into alignment. The en-ergy input is extreme and the toxicity odious. The spider's process is rather less odious. She spins with input of only sunlight and water. Her web is woven in ambient temperatures. Moreover, there is no long-term toxicity in her wake (note that long-term effects have not been considered that important in the de-sign for industrial systems). In contrast, in addition to saving the lives of those under gunfire, Kevlar lives forever in our overflowing landfills.

Increasingly, activist stakeholders have forced business organizations to be concerned about the impact on the social and natural systems in which they are embedded. A broader concern for sustainable development, that is, organi-zations meeting the needs of the present generation without reducing the ca-pacity of future generations to meet their needs (WCED, 1987), has emerged (Gladwin and Kennelly, 1995). High-profile leaders of diverse for-profit organi-zations increasingly argue that concern for balancing financial capital with so-cial and environmental capital is core to competitive advantage (e.g., Sir John Browne of BP, Peter Woicke of International Finance Corporation/World Bank, Arthur Blank of Home Depot, and Bill Ford of Ford Motor Company). This concern has been referred to as managing the "triple bottom line," con-sidered a core business practice in the movement to sustainable development (Elkington, 1998). The momentum toward sustainable business practices, along with common sense, suggests that we may no longer have to afford the long-lived, damaging side effects of Kevlar-like systems, that is, those based on industrial premises. What then would it look like to attempt the difficult task of creating web-like systems, that is, those based on principles of interdepen-dence with natural systems?

A focus on clarifying the design principles of nature opens up new ways of designing our organizations, their products and processes in a way that allows management to design for the needs of the postindustrial twenty-first century. Ecological scientists (Robért et al., 1997), evolutionary psychologists (Cosmides and Tooby, 1992), environmental designers (McDonough, 1997), management thinkers (Bradbury and Clair, 1999; Gladwin and Kennelly, 1995; Roome, 1998), and environmental visionaries (Hawken et al., 1999) have come up with a number of overlapping principles drawn from the study of nature. Situating human activity in its broader context of the natural environment, all stress the importance of nature's ability to profoundly shape human activity in spite of our hubris-filled efforts to the contrary. Those concerned specifically with the redesign of products and processes note that nature succeeds (and has done quite well for a few billion years) because nature works as a system in which inputs, throughputs, and outputs are balanced so that there is no waste. This zero-waste process in which "waste is food" may be contrasted with the industrial era exploitation of natural resources, sometimes described as "take-make waste" (Anderson, 2000). A zero-waste, closed loop strategy, in contrast, is accomplished through self-regulating feedback cycles and dense interconnectedness in a system that thrives upon unimaginable (though increasingly threatened) diversity. Examples of zero-emission processes (see especially the work of the Zero Emissions Resource Institute led by Gunther Pauli) are increasing in the organizational world. At the highest level, the concept of interdependence has helped design for zero-waste among networks of organizations, for example, Denmark's early example of industrial ecology in which various factories are linked so that the waste products of one become the fuel input for another. Zero-waste also describes new products, such as the Xerox line of Docucom office machines (Bradbury, 2000). Greater realization of social interdependence may also explain the recent growth of organizational networks more generally.

What might design for interdependence mean for organizational life? It is this very question that I brought to a group of women executives.

IMPLICATIONS FOR REDESIGNING MANAGEMENT
RESEARCH AND PRACTICE: TOWARD INCREASED
PARTICIPATIVE INQUIRY AND PRACTICE

We took the original invitation to write something about "managing as designing" as an opportunity to convene women leaders in the world of sustainability for a conversation about how we might redesign organizations. We posed a

124 simple question about the possibility of redesigning the taken-for-granted nature of our organizations: *Is it possible that those who were excluded from the original design of organizational structures could offer input for the redesign of more sustainable organizational forms for future generations?* We wondered specifically about the role of gender because, while a vast majority of executives in the Fortune 1000 are men, a significant proportion of executives in positions to manage organizational sustainability are women.[1] We wondered what this unusual gender ratio might mean for business and for management educators. We wondered what design criteria these leaders might uniquely offer to the necessary task of organizational redesign for a postindustrial era. The convening point of inquiry for the dialogue with the executive women became *"how might women redesign our organizations for future generations?"*

WOMEN EXECUTIVES DESIGNING ORGANIZATIONS FOR OUR CHILDREN'S CHILDREN

We wanted productive conversations about how organizations might be redesigned. The "pay off" to being in these conversations would be insights shared, corroborated, and adopted. The meetings were designed around the choice-points for quality in action research (Bradbury and Reason, 2001) that emphasize a broader bandwidth of concerns than traditional social science research. Particular emphasis was placed on developing a process so that all participants felt heard. We also emphasized practical concerns and oriented the conversation to the concrete practices of the participants. Advice was asked for and offered on particular issues throughout.

The first author began to structure the conversations around three questions so that each participant would have a grasp of others' approaches:

– What image/vision compels you in the work of managing sustainable business practices?
– What points of leverage have you found for encouraging sustainable business practices?
– What leverage exists for you in this effort?

Based on the transcript of the conversation generated on these three topics, seven statements that articulated recurring themes were drawn up, along with a statement to test for completeness. In a follow-up conversation, each participant was invited to express agreement or disagreement with the statements. As usual, after hearing each other check in, listening to each other engendered more conversation and clarity about which issues are most salient to women executives in their efforts to design organizations for our children's children. Those emerged as:

1. My work to promote sustainable development is *service*, a *calling* (not ordinary work).

2. *My children, my own childhood, and family* in general are the most potent points of connection for me in motivating me to engage with this work.

3. Generating *a community of co-contributors* is crucial to making sustainability real (in organizations/institutions).

4. It is crucial that I bring, and *allow* others to bring, *mind* <u>and</u> *heart* to work on these issues.

5. I seek to consciously *integrate* "techno-knowledge," "business knowledge," and "people knowledge" in this work.

6. I am particularly open to and informed by *nontraditional, interdisciplinary,* more intuitive "ways of knowing" when I approach this work, especially in efforts to understand interdependence. Whole systems thinking, shamanism, tribal patterns are examples of what is useful.

7. I place a great deal of importance on generating "productive encounters" to enhance this work, for example, listening deeply, asking transformational questions.

Illustrating the heart of the dialogues, one woman shared a compelling image from the story "The Man Who Planted Trees." In this, she emphasized the concern for dense interconnectedness and web-like ways of organizing. She said:

> A man plants one hundred trees every single day; he creates forests; he transforms the place. From the acorns there are trees; from the trees the towns can grow back. With more green comes more good life. We're naturally drawn to the good, to the green. But is this a male story or what! A guy by himself with lots of acorns in his pants and he is sowing his wild acorns! (laughter) I'd have preferred a group! Individual heroics are not for me; I'd like to be part of a community doing this. So I ask, what are the acorns we should be planting if we are to redesign organizations?

We then proceeded by discussing the "so what?" In so doing, we chose to focus on the implementation and influence strategies used by the women to help bring about new organizational arrangements.

A core theme in the executives' strategies concerned coordinating learning and input from all salient stakeholders in organizations. Strategies included the creation of more multifunctional teams required to report regularly on particular key performance indicators, thereby including not just metrics but illustrative stories to develop more understanding in other parts of the organization. All suggestions in some way related to the importance of uncovering the voices of various stakeholders, which had often been fragmented or never heard. One participant brought this common concern alive with the novel suggestion of bringing children into organizational design work. "Who better

126   to be the stakeholders in our efforts to design organizations for our children's children?" She continued:

> Wouldn't it be terrific to let the leaders meet with the children of all their stakeholders? The older kids/teens would be best; that would include the children of customers, suppliers, and neighbors. We'd let these kids talk with the business leaders about the company so they could start to develop an understanding together. It would be a win-win in that the leaders would get some input to their strategy and visioning processes. I would have them do some projection and let them look over time, then pull back and listen to how it lands with the kids. There would be tremendous learning all around.

In these illustrations, as with many others not used here, we see concern for the whole system, for the nonlinear effects of organizing extended to include a population not normally considered important stakeholders. We see also a productive concern for diversity of input that can counteract what Shiva (1999) refers to as "monocultures of the mind" that increasingly prevail as the language of economics overtakes so much.

REFLECTION FOR NEXT STEPS

Diversity, feedback, and a systems approach were mentioned as core considerations for designing systems informed by nature that, in turn, allow our organizations to live within nature. These principals came alive in this preliminary research by convening an underrepresented group of women executives to think together about organizational impact, not only as systems that exist today in relation to other social and ecological system entities but also exist through many tomorrows as they affect the quality of life of our children.

Further work will move the dialogue out from the original group of women executives to allow for more cycles of action and reflection. Ongoing interest has meant that the group continues to meet. We are guided by a focus on what each participant is seeking to accomplish in terms of sustainable business practices in her company. We ask, "Where is the energy for this initiative? Where are the obstacles?" We acknowledge that in nature all change occurs while it is being inhibited (Maturana, 2000). Our dialogue therefore allows us to grapple with how to involve stakeholders in a way that allows for personal connection to the issues at stake. It forces participants to think about how sustainable business practices may appear welcome or unwelcome when viewed from the perspective of different stakeholders. The dialogue moves forward on a premise that nature grows something new in the presence of something that already exists (Senge and Carstadt, 2001). This means that we take seriously that we do not make change; rather, we help to foster change in a context presumed to have obstacles.

That there is a specifically gendered way of approaching issues of sustainability is, of course, an oversimplification. Encouraged by many productive encounters with our male colleagues (some of whom have joined us in conversation groups), we believe the issue is not so much about men's and women's approaches to organizational life as it is about a difference in aspirations for using executive "power." We can have power "over others" or see ourselves in relationships of interdependence. Women have traditionally chosen the latter in larger numbers than our male colleagues.

We are currently arranging for broader reflection on the business "nuts and bolts" of the implications of having so many women in leadership roles within the sustainability arena. Does this mean that more women should be hired? Does hiring more women marginalize women executives and sustainability issues even further? At the very least, we believe our dialogues are one small contribution to redesigning a new way of living and working in organizations as we create the postindustrial world the planet and its many stakeholders need.

CONCLUSION

Our paper is the product of an invitation to consider managing as designing. Noting the tendency of systems informed by industrial era logic to negate and abuse nature, we sought to begin a different journey to postindustrial design logic. This was an opportunity for executives to inquire into how business can be at home in a more sustainable world. Because organizations are human rather than machine-like artifacts, we cannot drive change, per se. We can, however, grow something new in the presence of the old. In so doing, we can aspire to a world that works for everyone, including our children's children.

NOTE

1. It is propitious to note the very large percentage of women participants in the nationwide Net Impact association. Net Impact is a network of MBA students and alumni "committed to using the power of business to create a better world." (See www.weatherhead.cwru.edu/netimpact for more information.) As in corporate life, so in management schools: we are seeing women taking leadership in arenas in which business acts as an agent of world benefit.

REFERENCES

Anderson, R. 2000. Climbing mount sustainability. In *Reflections: The SoL Journal*. 1 (4): 6–12. Published by MIT Press for the Society for Organizational Learning.

128   Benyus, J. 1997. *Biomimicry: Innovation inspired by nature.* New York: Morrow.

Bradbury, H. 2000. *STREAMLINE: The marriage of profit and principles.* A teaching case. Available by request from the author: Hilary@po.cwru.edu.

Bradbury, H., and J. Clair. 1999. Promoting sustainable organizations with Sweden's Natural Step. *Academy of Management Executive.* 13 (4): 63–74.

Bradbury, H., and P. Reason. 2001. Conclusion: Choice-points for quality in action research. In *The Handbook of Action Research,* edited by P. Reason and H. Bradbury. London and Thousand Oaks, CA: Sage Publications.

Cosmides, L., and J. Tooby. 1992. Cognitive adaptations for social exchange. In *The adapted mind,* edited by J. Barkow, L. Cosmides, and J. Tooby. New York: Oxford University Press.

Elkington, J. 1998. *Cannibals with forks.* Gabriola Island, BC, Canada: Conscientious Commerce/New Society Publishers.

Fuller, B. 1971. *Operating manual for spaceship earth.* New York: E. P. Dutton & Co.

Gladwin, T., and K. Kennelly. 1995. Shifting paradigms for sustainable development: Implications for management theory and research. *Academy of Management Review* 20:874–907.

Hawken, P., A. Lovins, and L. H. Lovins. 1999. *Natural capital: Creating the next industrial revolution.* Boston, New York: Little, Brown and Company.

Hock, D. 2000. The art of chaordic leadership. *Leader to Leader.* 15 (Winter): 20–26. This article is available on the Drucker Foundation Web site, http://leadertoleader.org/leaderbooks/l2l/winter2000/hock.html.

McDonough, W. A. 1997. A boat for Thoreau, environmental challenges to business. University of Virginia. Paper delivered at the Environmental Challenges to Business Conference.

Maturana, H. 2000. Commentary on becoming a sustainable species by Bunnell & Sonntag. In *Reflections: The SoL Journal.* 1 (4): 72. Published by MIT Press for the Society for Organizational Learning.

Robèrt, K. H., H. Daly, P. Hawken, and J. Holmberg. 1997. *International Journal of Sustainable Development.* 4: 79–92.

Roome, N., ed. 1998. *Sustainable strategies for industries.* Washington, DC: Island Press.

Senge, P., and G. Carstadt. 2001. Designing the next industrial revolution. Winter. *Sloan Management Review.*

Shiva, S. 1999. *Monocultures of the mind.* London: Zed Books.

World Commission on Environment and Development. 1987. *Our common future.* Oxford, England: Oxford University Press.

15

GROUNDLESSNESS, COMPASSION, AND ETHICS IN MANAGEMENT AND DESIGN

Joseph A. Goguen

ALTHOUGH DESIGN and management typically address quite different domains, they share some important qualities. Both are uncertain, creative, challenging, and rewarding. Moreover, both prominently involve ethical issues, and both have seen significant problems reduced to calculation, which is then handed off to computers.

This chapter first describes some tendencies to reduce issues in design and management to purely technical problems and some difficulties with such approaches. It then suggests that, although extreme reductionism remains sterile, semiformal approaches that take account of social processes can be valuable. As an example, a design method called algebraic semiotics is sketched, combining ideas from sociology and computer science. This article also argues against extreme relativism, which claims that all social phenomena and human values are equally valid. However, it is not claimed that merely denying both absolutism and relativism solves any hard problems in design or management. Instead, this middle way suggests that there are no definite foundations for either management or design. This in turn leads us to explore groundlessness, the lack of any definite foundation, and to the discovery that groundlessness can inspire compassion and ethics, an insight that could, I hope, promote some significant progress.

Joseph A. Goguen, *Department of Computer Science, University of California at San Diego.*

Much of the literature in both design and management seeks well-founded, replicable methods for solving problems, in the style of mathematics, physics, or (at least) engineering. However, the rapid evolution of fads and buzzwords and the ubiquity of spectacular failures (e.g., Enron and Windows, to take just one example from each area)[1] attest to the lack of significant progress. Two often cited obstacles are: giving precise formulations of real problems and giving realistic metrics for the adequacy of solutions. I suggest that, in general, these obstacles cannot be overcome, and that instead of seeking reductionist solutions, managers and designers should learn to live in the groundless world entailed by social reality, rather than in the stable, grounded world that appears to be promised by reductionist science. Although many specific problems can be reduced to predictable routine methods, management and design operate in open social environments, so that the larger and more important problems are not reducible. Philosophers like Heidegger and Nishitani have developed deep insights into the groundlessness of the human condition, and how to live with it, as discussed later in this chapter.

If reduction to formalism is rejected, there is still a strong tendency to ground practices like design and management in less formal concepts that are somehow considered more fundamental, such as individual, group, medium, interaction, coherence, or value (Goguen, 2002). But none of these are natural pregiven categories; each arises from particular ways of categorizing experience, achieved through collective work. I believe that extreme reductionist tendencies are harmful because they raise expectations that cannot be fulfilled, thus leading to disappointment and fueling further cycles of hope and fear. Designers seem to have done a better job of resisting such theories than managers, so that managers may be able to learn from them in this respect.

SEMIOTIC GROUNDS FOR DESIGN

It is widely accepted that certain aspects of design and management can be formalized. Although I have many years experience managing small research groups, I will concentrate on design, because my experience in user interface design within computer science seems more relevant. The problem here is to design a display that presents some given information and action affordances in a more or less "optimal" way.

Communication is always mediated by signs, which always occur in structured systems of related signs (Saussure, 1976). This insight is formalized in Goguen (1999) with the notion of "semiotic system," which is an axiomatic theory for a system of signs, including hierarchical "constructors" for signs, and measures of their relative importance within the sign system. Context, including the setting of a given sign, can be at least as important for meaning as the sign itself. In an extreme example, the sentence "Yes" can mean almost anything, given an appropriate context. This corresponds to the important insight (Peirce, 1965) that meaning is relational, not just denotational (i.e., functional); this is part of the point of Peirce's famous semiotic triangle.[2] In algebraic semiotics, certain aspects of context dependence can be handled by constructors that place signs within larger signs, so that the original signs become contextualized subsigns. However, human interpretation is still needed for signs to have meaning in any human sense. Moreover, human interpretation is needed in deploying the formalism of algebraic semiotics because it is intended to be used flexibly in much the same manner as musical notation is used in musical performance.

In design, it is often important to view some signs as transformations or representations of other signs. Therefore, it is valuable to study representation in a systematic way and, in particular, to consider what makes some representations better than others. Although transformations are fundamental in many areas of mathematics and its applications (e.g., linear transformations, i.e., matrices), such questions of representation seem not to have been previously studied in semiotics; however, they can be addressed by "semiotic morphisms" (Goguen, 1999). Just as semiotic systems are theories rather than models, so their morphisms translate from the language of one semiotic system to the language of another, instead of just translating the concrete signs in a model. This may seem indirect, but it has important advantages over more common approaches based on set theoretic models in that it is open in allowing multiple models, as well as in permitting new structure to be added at later times.

In many real-world examples, not everything can or should be preserved, so that semiotic morphisms must be partial. For example, the table of contents of a book preserves structure and the names of major parts, but completely fails to preserve content (which is what makes it useful). The extent of preservation gives a way to compare the quality of semiotic morphisms (Goguen, 1999). It is notable that semiotic spaces and semiotic morphisms are qualitative rather than quantitative, in that they concern structure, and their quality measures are partial orderings, rather than linear numerical scales. In addition, various qualitative design rules can be justified, for example, that it is better to preserve structure than content, if something must be sacrificed (Goguen, 1999). Design is the problem of massaging a source space, a target space, and a morphism to achieve suitable quality, subject to constraints. This formulation applies just as well to managing an organization as it does to designing a Web site.

132   Harvey Sacks's notion of "category system" (Sacks, 1972) in ethnomethodology[3] (Garfinkel, 1967; Sacks, 1992) is related to semiotic systems, though it is less formal. Previous work on the social nature of information (Goguen, 1997) also uses ideas from ethnomethodology, and can be seen as providing a philosophical and methodological foundation for algebraic semiotics that avoids the trap of Platonism. George Lakoff, Mark Johnson, and others have studied the structure of metaphor in detail, creating the flourishing new field called cognitive linguistics (Lakoff and Johnson, 1980; Turner, 1997). Gilles Fauconnier introduced the notion of conceptual space for representing the systems of related concepts involved in metaphors and, with Mark Turner, argues that the "blending" of conceptual spaces is key to understanding metaphor, as well as many other areas of human thought (Fauconnier and Turner, 1998). Here metaphor is seen as an emergent structure resulting from integrating several (usually at least three) conceptual spaces, as opposed to classical theories that posit a mapping from one conceptual space to another.[4] It seems likely that these ideas will be useful in management and design, because both require the careful blending of numerous, often very complex, conceptual spaces. Moreover, they can be formalized to a great extent within algebraic semiotics (Goguen, 1999).

GROUNDLESSNESS AND COEMERGENT ARISING

There appears to be a conflict between grounding design in a mathematical formalism like algebraic semiotics and claiming that design is groundless. This appearance arises from an implicitly assumed Platonism for mathematical modeling in general, and semiotics in particular, instead of positioning them in social reality, which is groundless due to its being constantly reconstructed through the work of its members. This ongoing reconstruction is an instance of the Buddhist notion of *pratityasamutpada*, which in Sanskrit is literally "dependent arising," often translated as codependence or coemergence. Found in the earliest teachings of the Buddha, and developed further by Nagarjuna, Vasubandhu, and others, coemergence is the notion that nothing exists by itself, but instead, everything is interdependent, or more precisely, everything arises together with other things. It is similar to the Western notion of "hermeneutic circle," which has ancient origins in classical Greece and various mystical traditions, but has been especially developed in more recent times by, for example, Schleiermacher and Heidegger.

Coemergence has the important consequence that no ground can be found for phenomena. The groundlessness of the human condition is discussed in depth by Nishitani (1982), who points out (following his teacher Heidegger) that much of the recent history of Western thought can be seen as a progressively refined questioning of absolutes. Among the responses to this questioning, two extremes are identified: nihilism, which is absolute relativity, the denial of any meaning; and absolutism, which is the denial of the questioning. Such absolutism may take the form of dogmatism, fundamentalism, or extreme reductionism. Moreover, there tends to be an unstable oscillation between these two extremes, a condition that Nishitani calls the "field of nihility"[5] and that appears similar to the oscillations in organizational communications noticed by Alex Citurs (Citurs, 2002; Boland, 2002), which perhaps also result from an ongoing fruitless search for a stable ground.

It should not be thought that groundlessness is a stable, fixed state; indeed, it makes even less sense to reify groundlessness than other things. Nor is it passive. All living systems are dynamic, constantly rebalancing their state in order to achieve equilibrium within their environment. A suggestive analogy is walking, which uses motion to compensate for a constant unbalance, always taking account of changes and irregularities in the environment; it seems that some form of oscillation is typical of healthy systems as well as unhealthy systems. Francisco Varela and Humberto Maturana have developed notions of autopoiesis and structural coupling to facilitate discussing such issues for biological systems (Varela et al., 1991), but these ideas also seem relevant to the management of organizations, which must also reconstruct themselves in order to survive.

Based on experience with Zen meditation, Nishitani says there is a "middle way" that avoids the extremes of both nihilism and absolutism, as well as the unstable oscillation between them, by accepting groundlessness as a basis for being. The experience of groundlessness, and a path based upon it, have been described in many religious traditions, using phrases such as "dark night of the soul" and "cloud of unknowing." Results of practicing this middle way are said to include openness, compassion, and harmony with nature; joy, strength, and peace are also said to result. This is advocated by Varela, Thompson, and Rosch (1991) as a fruitful approach to cognitive science. Here, I suggest it also makes sense as an approach to design and management, dwelling in neither relativism nor reductionism, and drawing energy and inspiration from silence. This relates to the "planetary thinking" advocated by Heidegger (1958), in that it involves a reexamination of the Western worldview, drawing on Eastern ideas, in order to achieve a worldview that is planetary in scope, takes better account of human nature, and overcomes some negative effects of our instrumental, technological, consumption-oriented culture.[6]

COMPASSION AND ETHICS

Groundlessness is completely different from nihilism and nihility; it opens a field of freedom and creativity, within which one can discover the true po-

134   tential of situations. The inner possibilities of groundlessness have been discussed in numerous traditions. A recent book by the Dalai Lama (1999), which reached number one on the *New York Times* best-selling business list, draws on Tibetan Buddhism, but its approach is not so different from that of Meister Eckehart, Maimonides, Rumi, Lao Tzu, and many others. A major argument of his book is that everyone wants to be happy and content and that an important way to achieve this is to live ethically, for example, to avoid harming others. Fortunately, everyone has an innate capacity for compassion, for feeling the condition of others, and this makes it possible to act in a humane way. This capacity may have a neural basis in the recently discovered mirror neurons (Rizzolatti et al., 1996), which, for primates, are known to respond to specific gestures in others and which might well be further developed in humans. In any case, it is clear that empathy and compassion are inhibited by preconceptions and prejudices, but arise naturally out of an authentically groundless state.

Empathy and compassion provide a solid ground for ethical behavior, which is completely different from pity, busy do-gooding, and righteous rule-following. Arguments against rule-based approaches to ethics are well known, (e.g., Johnson, 1993); they are similar to arguments against reductionist approaches to other areas, for instance, management and design. Rules can never anticipate the complexities of the human condition, and in any case require interpretation, and second-order rules (such as Kant's categorical imperative) require even more interpretation than first-order rules (e.g., "thou shalt not kill"). Although rules can certainly be very valuable as guidelines, as argued above with respect to design, the usual philosophical problems of reductionism arise when they are elevated to universal principles. A perhaps surprising result of Buddhist meditation experience is that rules are not necessary for ethical behavior; human nature is sufficient, once it has been sufficiently refined. Groundlessness is then the ground for authentic behavior, including genuine ethics, as well as effective and creative design and management; indeed, from this perspective, effective management and design cannot be separated from genuine ethical behavior.

NOTES

1. Although Windows is certainly a commercial success, most professional computer scientists consider it a technical design failure, due to its many bugs, its poor user interface, its bad security, and its greed-driven development philosophy.
2. Whereas Saussure defined a sign to consist of a signifier and a signified, Peirce

has a third element, called an *interpretant*, which relates the other two. Interpretants 135
are often taken to include the social context and the person doing the interpretation.

3. Ethnomethodology is a perspective on sociology that is notoriously resistant to definition, but very briefly, one might say that it is concerned with the methods and concepts that members use to make sense of their interactions. Ethnomethodology denies that there is any preexisting ground of social or cultural reality that determines social interaction. Much recent work has taken different directions from those of the founder, Harold Garfinkel (1967), such as detailed analyses of the construction of conversation (Sacks, 1992).

4. Max Black, building on work of Ivor Richards, moved beyond Aristotle in considering metaphor a complex and emergent nondirectional relation between two domains, rather than a simple fixed mapping (Black, 1962). Although he was right about the complex and emergent character of metaphor, Black appears to have been wrong about nondirectionality, and his work also lacks the precision needed to put it in the same league as modern cognitive linguistic theories.

5. Actually, this phrase was chosen by the translator Jan Van Bragt; a better English translation of the underlying Buddhist notion would be "relative emptiness," as opposed to the deeper and more familiar notion of (absolute) emptiness (*sunyata* in Sanskrit), for which this article has used the term "groundlessness."

6. Heidegger (1977) gives a powerful and very influential discussion of the dark side of technology, and Thompson (1986) gives a thoughtful discussion of the philosophical context of planetary thinking in Heidegger (1958) and its relation to Nishitani (1982).

REFERENCES

Black, M. 1962. *Models and metaphor: Studies in language and philosophy*. Ithaca, NY: Cornell University Press.

Boland, R. J. 2002. Position paper. In *Advance Papers, Second Workshop on Distributed Collective Practice*. University of California at San Diego.

Citurs, A. 2002. *Changes in team communication patterns: Learning during project problem/crisis resolution phases—An interpretative perspective*. PhD thesis, Weatherhead School of Management, Case Western Reserve University.

Dalai Lama. 1999. *Ethics for the new millennium*. New York: Riverhead Books.

Fauconnier, G., and M. Turner. 1998. Conceptual integration networks. *Cognitive Science*, 22: 133–87.

Garfinkel, H. 1967. *Studies in ethnomethodology*. Upper Saddle River, NJ: Prentice-Hall.

Goguen, J. 1997. Towards a social, ethical theory of information. In *Social Science Research, Technical Systems and Cooperative Work*, edited by G. Bowker, L. Gasser, L. Star, and W. Turner. Mahwah, NJ: Erlbaum, pp. 27–56.

———. 1999. An introduction to algebraic semiotics, with applications to user interface design. In *Computation for Metaphors, Analogy and Agents*, edited by C. Nehaniv. Lecture Notes in Artificial Intelligence, Volume 1562: 242–91.

———. 2002. Consciousness and the decline of cognitivism. In *Advance Papers, Second Workshop on Distributed Collective Practice*, edited by G. Bowker. University of California at San Diego.

136 ———. Information visualization and semiotic morphisms (http://www.cs.ucsd.edu/users/goguen/pps/vri2.ps); Information visualization and semiotic morphisms (http://www.cs.ucsd.edu/users/goguen/papers/sm/smm.html); and UC San Diego semiotic zoo (http://www.cs.ucsd.edu/users/goguen/zoo), all of which are linked from the page http://www.cs.ucsd.edu/users/goguen/new.html.

Heidegger, M. 1958. *The question of being.* Translated by William Kluback and Jean Wilde. New Haven, CT: Yale University Press.

———. 1962. *Being and time.* Translated by John Macquarrie and Edward Robinson. Oxford, UK: Blackwell Publisher Ltd.

———. 1977. *The question concerning technology and other essays.* Translated by William Lovitt. New York: Harper and Row.

Johnson, M. 1993. *Moral imagination: Implications of cognitive science for ethics.* Chicago: University of Chicago Press.

Lakoff, G., and M. Johnson. 1980. *Metaphors we live by.* Chicago: University of Chicago Press.

Nishitani, K. 1982. *Religion and nothingness.* Translated by Jan Van Bragt. Berkeley: University of California Press.

Peirce, C. S. 1965. *Collected papers of Charles Saunders Peirce.* 6 vols. Cambridge, MA: Harvard University Press. (See especially volume 2: *Elements of Logic.*)

Rizzolatti, G., L. Fadiga, V. Gallese, and L. Fogassi. 1996. Premotor cortex and the recognition of motor actions. *Cognitive Brain Research,* 3: 131–41.

Sacks, H. 1972. On the analyzability of stories by children. In *Directions in Sociolinguistics,* edited by J. Gumpertz and D. Hymes. New York: Holt, Rinehart and Winston, pp. 325–45

———. 1992. *Lectures on conversation.* Edited by Gail Jefferson. Oxford, UK: Blackwell Publisher Ltd.

Saussure, F. 1976. *Course in general linguistics.* Translated by Roy Harris. London: Duckworth.

Thompson, E. 1986. Planetary thinking/planetary building: An essay on Martin Heidegger and Nishitani Keiji. *Philosophy East and West,* 36: 235–52.

Turner, M. 1997. *The literary mind.* New York: Oxford University Press.

Varela, F., E. Thompson, and E. Rosch. 1991. *The embodied mind.* Cambridge, MA: MIT Press.

16

THE FRICTION OF OUR SURROUNDINGS

Miriam R. Levin

THE PROTO-SOCIAL scientists of the Enlightenment wanted nothing more than to build harmoniously functioning societies fitted to the highly competitive, growth economies of Western nations. They made the power to control social relations through communication an engine of progress toward this organizational goal of modernization. And most importantly, they analyzed how communications and, thus, the human activities that constitute the glue of a culture in motion could be controlled through the design of specially designated spaces. As a result, since the late eighteenth century, it has become axiomatic that communication is a physical process, with physiological and psychological associations, in which information in the form of physical stimuli is transmitted between things and people, between individuals, and between things. These stimuli traveling through space can elicit resistance from the bodies they touch or act like gears transmitting a certain direction to the movement of those bodies through frictional contact with them. Thus, the light rays from a blue dress that pleasantly strike the eye of the beholder, the waves of sound from a voice that grate the ear, the stone walls of a passage that constrict people's movements, the electrical impulses that send one part of a machine to turn against another in automatic machinery, are reduced to the same kind of quantifiable information, and the recipients' emotional and behavioral responses become standardized and predictable. Included as communications media are everything from human senses and organs to spoken and written language to painted or printed words and images to buildings and sculp-

Miriam R. Levin, *History Department, Case Western Reserve University*. I thank Professor Thomas Hughes for helpful comments and editorial suggestions.

138   ture, city plans, to roads, canals, and the postal service. With technological advances in long distance and broadcast communication through electrical and electronic signals, the telegraph, telephone, film, radio, television, and Internet were easily incorporated into this genre.

Just as significant as this materially-based conception of communication has been authorities' interest in designing optimum environments to coordinate human activities in ways most beneficial to the polity (Scott, 1998). Here Enlightenment belief in empirical science and in rationally operative nature focused the attention of authorities, architects, engineers, reformers—all those interested in designing an operative socio-technical system—on identifying a set of physical signs and signals, shapes, colors, forms, spatial arrangements, and so forth, that would harmonize social interactions through the continuous flow of communication (Habermas, 1984; Rabinow, 1997; Levin, 2000). In their terms, they aimed at creating a series of interconnected environments whose reified character would reform not only citizens (human nature) but social and economic relations into a mirror of nature. In essence, they sought dynamic interactions by designing buildings, streets, signage, rooms, whole systems of technologies that would push certain physiological and psychological buttons to move social exchanges in the right direction. These were artificially constructed, yet considered natural, that is, based on the same principles as cosmic and biological phenomena, in their modes of operation and the effects they produced.

As a result of Enlightenment reformers' efforts, people in Western nations now exist in an environment of ideas and things with which they communicate and that control them. The questions arise: Who is creating this environment? What are their motives? Is the resulting control of us authoritarian or democratic? In the formulations of Enlightenment reformers, the notion of control took on two different political meanings identified with two different models of productive social orders: one, the idea of the culture of control as a set of values, activities, and modes imposed by a central authority that leaves little or no room for individual initiative—a closed system; the other, the idea that control cultures should be designed to allow people some independence in productive decision making—an open system. In order to create the necessary habits, it was necessary to create a properly designed, finely woven membrane of material culture out of the raw physical matter of the earth to artificially provide a stimulating environment.

One major question these self-appointed social reformers raised and attempted to answer was: What is the optimal design that will allow communication media to coordinate human beings' activity and keep goods and information flowing? In the development of large socio-technical systems, the points where technology and human beings meet have become enormously important event centers where history occurs and historical change takes place on a variety of levels. The consumption-junction is one kind of event, but not the only point at which the design of the intersection is crucial (as 9/11 made clear). In the history of control through communication, it is the design of these interfaces in the communication system that matter most to those with power to control (Levin, 2000; Levin and Williams, 2003; *New York Times*, 2002).

Space only allows me to discuss the example of one architect-engineer from the Enlightenment period concerned with inaugurating a system of control through communication. That is Claude Nicolas Ledoux (1736–1806), architect to Louis XVI of France during a brief period when the crown made efforts to reorganize the state fiscal system and with it, the economic habits of those engaged in commerce and manufacturing. Under the auspices of the rationalizing state, the short-lived reforms suppressed internal tariffs and disbanded the guilds to allow free circulation of goods, people, and money within the country and to introduce rational modes of production intended to enable sustained economic growth. The problem Ledoux faced was how to design spaces that managed both the workers and the work process into new, efficiently flowing channels.

In the 1770s, Ledoux was given the assignment of designing and building the Royal Salt Works at Arc-et-Senan in the Franche-Comté, part of the monopoly that brought large revenues into state coffers. Ledoux was a man well read in the works of his time, and his work on this project for the crown was strongly influenced by Enlightenment ideas on control through communication. It was in fact an example of a mode of architecture he helped invent known as *architecture parlante* (literally, talking buildings), in which aesthetic form, building materials, and structural arrangements were designed to stimulate certain socially productive responses from people who came into contact with those spaces.

Originally planned as a full circle of structures, half to be devoted to housing for employees, as constructed, the salt works was a vast enclosed semicircle of buildings. The courtyard was entered in through a large stone gateway flanked by huge Doric columns set in the center of the arch. Carved in relief on the walls of the gate were images of flowing water—references to the salinated river waters evaporated off in huge caldrons located in two large sheds at the center. Opposite the gate and between the sheds was the administration building. The tallest structure in the complex, it allowed the director to supervise through surveillance and workers to understand the organization in which they were operating. But panopticism was only one facet of the reform-minded communication system Ledoux established at Arc-et-Senan (Foucault, 1995, pp. 195–228).

Ledoux's major design premise expresses his concern with the proper linkage between the moral and social forces of a community of people and the impact of the material structures on their behavioral energies. Using the language of Newtonian mechanics, Ledoux claimed, "We can be made virtuous or vicious, . . . by the friction of our surroundings" (Vidler, 1987, pl. 75). The momentum of harmonious motion set off from the built environment was the way to stimulate virtuous—that is to say, in the case of this state-owned salt processing plant—cooperative industrious behavior among those who worked there. The source of that harmonious sensation, the physical signals that produced it, was an aesthetic that combined Newton's solar system with an acetic neoclassicism. The production of dynamic balance among simplified, stoical, geometric forms marking out a circular space emulated the dynamically equilibrated Newtonian system and signified the nature of the centralized monarchical system—the source of all directed momentum. In this design, the appeal to science, natural order, unadorned building materials, and limited geometric forms objectified the subjective preferences and political choices of centralized authority.

Because of limited space to pursue my argument here, I ask readers to take a big mental and chronological leap and accept that continuities exist between Enlightenment and present ways of thinking about control through communication. The ambiguous character of power relationships established within these artificial environments reveal the problematic nature of the relationship between authority and personal responsibility in democratic societies. There are three dimensions to be considered here:

1. There is an expansive, or spatially extensive, dimension to the mode of communication. The link the mode of communication makes with each user implies the presence of organizing groups and forces existing in the world beyond the immediate environment that assume uniformity of response and set highly standardized parameters for every individual's existence without any physical laying on of hands.

2. There is an intimate, psychological, and physiological dimension to the connection the mode of communication attempts to make with each user, which gives the user the authority to decide whether and how to respond, which direction to steer his/her energies and desires.

3. There is a power dimension in which the loci for exercising power are not fixed, yet the parameters for actions are established by rulers, administrators, and other designers of social spaces.

This power dimension is the real sticking point of media design (and here I refer to the list found at the beginning of this essay), as it has come to be formulated in the twentieth century. Everywhere business and government leaders, along with engineers and manufacturers, make claims for communication systems and various modes of communication such as the World Wide Web as democratic. They, along with architects and builders, make frequent efforts to institute city and regional designs, museum and office building plans that will enable new habits of understanding and conduct for members of a globalizing society.

But nowhere is there an exploration of what, in fact, this claim to democracy means. For to say these media are democratic is really to say their design is based on some standardized, universalized notion of humans as sentient beings whose bodies and minds function in accordance with the same laws and who will, thus, respond individually in predictable, utilitarian ways to carefully designed environments. It is not to say that these media of communication empower individuals to exercise their will equally or even freely, nor that their scientific design recognizes and nurtures the ethical, moral, and spiritual qualities that are part of human identity (Taussig, 1993). The set of controlled spaces meant to move the populations of the west toward a more organized existence orchestrated at the individual level created the promise of democracy through egalitarian universalism of design norms, while simultaneously moving the locus of historical action into a realm of limited feelings, emotional reactions, and choices among a limited set of experiences.

We thus remain in a bind created by our eighteenth-century predecessors, so far as the democratic character of these systems of control through communication are concerned. The question of where power and authority lie remain obscured. What has changed is that each individual's illusion of control of his or her relationship with others through communication has grown while the moral foundations of those relationships have become almost irrelevant.

REFERENCES

Foucault, M. 1995. *Discipline and punish: The Birth of the prison*. New York: Vintage Books.

Habermas, J. 1984. *The theory of communicative action*, translated by Thomas McCarthy. Boston: Beacon Press.

Hughes, T. 2000. Introduction. In *Cultures of control*, edited by Miriam R. Levin. London, New York: Harwood, pp. 1–9.

Levin, M. R. 2000. Preface and Contexts of control. In *Cultures of control*, edited by Miriam R. Levin. London, New York: Harwood, pp. ix–xvi, 13–39.

Levin, M. R., and R. Williams. 2003. Forum: Reconsidering technology in the aftermath of September 11th. *History and Technology* 19:1 (January 2003), pp. 29–83.

142   *New York Times.* 2002. Holes in the system allowed sniper suspects to roam undetected, officials say. November 29, AI, A27.

Rabinow, P. 1996. *Essays on the anthropology of reason.* Princeton: Princeton University Press.

Scott, J. C. 1998. *Seeing like a state.* London and New Haven: Yale University Press.

Taussig, M. T. 1993. *Mimesis and alterity: A particular history of the senses.* New York: Routledge.

Vidler, A. 1987. *The writing of the walls: Architectural theory in the late enlightenment.* Princeton, NJ: Princeton Architectural Press, caption, plate 75.

Williams, R. 2000. Nature out of control. In *Cultures of control,* edited by Miriam R. Levin. London, New York: Harwood, pp. 40–68.

17

MANAGEMENT AND DESIGN

A Historical Reflection on
Possible Future Relations

Keith Hoskin

WHEN DICK BOLAND first drew my attention to *Design* as the overlooked term in Herbert Simon's management trinity of "Intelligence–Design–Choice," I immediately thought I knew why that was. Design is different, because it doesn't turn into its opposite. For in management, Intelligence becomes "Intelligent Systems" and so becomes Non-Intelligence, the unreflective application of whatever "the System" says. Choice becomes Decision, which then becomes Non-Decision, going with what the Net Present Value numbers say or the optimal option deriving from the Decision Tree's probability calculations. But although in the management world there is plenty of Bad Design, there is never Non-Design. Even anti-designs like Thriving on Chaos are strategies by design, vying to evoke beauty in the eye of the beholder.

But the slick contrast is too easy for two reasons. First, Simon's trinity largely works because Intelligence and Choice-as-Decision do not always and necessarily implode this way. But second, *why* doesn't Design turn into its opposite? I want to reflect on that question, hopefully to help us understand ways to better Management Design and, more particularly, how Frank Gehry's design practice may help us down such a route.

My reflection is a historical one about the form of today's powerful knowledge as "disciplinary" knowledge. Historically, a new and unprecedented "disciplinarity" appears to develop (Hoskin, 1993) from the 1760s, as students in elite European institutions are variously required to present written work for examination and numerical grading. New pedagogical spaces spring up, the seminar in Germany and the laboratory in France, whose graduates develop

Keith Hoskin, *Warwick Business School, University of Warwick.*

144   new-style "disciplinary knowledges," which can already in the 1790s be seen as
prefiguring modern knowledge concerns and modern methods of investiga-
tion. In France, natural history becomes biology, as Monge dissects the organism to discover its "organ-ization"; in Germany in the new field of philol-
ogy, Wolf investigates languages in their evolving difference. As populations
learn to learn under these practices, across institutionalized education from
kindergarten to graduate school, we increasingly inhabit a well-disciplined
world dominated by disciplinary expertise.

These doubly disciplinary features are writ small but consummately in the
modern forms of Intelligence and Choice-as-Decision, exemplified in Simon's
trinity. The IQ test has a "writerly" architectonic, where a set number of pretested questions, administered by strictly prescribed protocols, enable one's
"inner truth" to be established algorithmically as a "quotient." Intelligent Systems simply vary the theme, with more complex pretested architectonics and
more recursive reflexive question\answer circuits and calculations. Decision
Theory techniques follow the same pattern of a procedural architectonics, a
prescriptive examination of possibility (the increasingly IT-based scoping of
the future as variable-rich scenarios) and a translation of uncertainty (the un-
quantifiable) into (quantifiable) risk.

The same dynamics come together to produce the new construct of "management," as is clear from studying its genesis. Alfred Chandler (1977) showed
how it is the effective combination of a particular architectonic structure, the
line-and-staff hierarchy as captured in the organization chart (see Figure 17.1),
with a form of writerly examinatorial process, for example, planning, reporting, and financial and nonfinancial performance accounting. The resultant
"administrative coordination" is an American invention, perfected on the
railroads, which transforms the economic world, as oligopolies made up of
large managerial firms come to dominate markets, in the triumph of the "visible hand."

However, detailed archival research now shows (Hoskin and Macve, 2002)
that management's pioneers were not businessmen but graduates of the U.S.
Military Academy at West Point. West Point graduates firstly engineer single-
unit management at Alfred Chandler's initial site for such management, the
Springfield Armory, and they also turn out to be responsible for engineering
Chandler's second breakthrough, multi-unit management, on the U.S. railroads, specifically on the Western and Pennsylvania roads. Most significant
of all is one Herman Haupt (USMA, 1835), who as Superintendent of Transportation on the Pennsylvania from 1849 constructs a new kind of managerial regime that puts the writing, examining, and grading of financial and

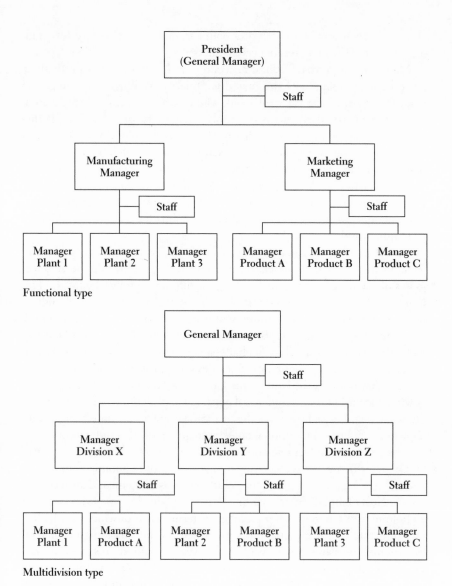

Functional type

Multidivision type

FIGURE 17.1 Some typical representations of the line and staff hierarchy as captured in organizational charts

146   "human" accounting at the heart of both organizational structure (or architectonics) *and* the processes of everyday activity.

Management is therefore not an economic invention but a particularly powerful manifestation of the new disciplinarity. Writing, examining, and grading enter business via West Point, where they were, from 1817 on, combined into a particularly intensive doubly disciplinary format by West Point's then superintendent, Sylvanus Thayer. He imposed the new French sci-tech knowledges, under a regime of daily examination and grading, in a new human accountability system that stretched across the student's career to determine graduation rank and prospects (Hoskin and Macve, 1988). The West Point management pioneers simply translated the practices under which they "learned to learn" into the business arena, enabling the transformation of the economic world.

How does all this relate to Design? First, Design can now be seen to be integral to all *three* of these other constructs, worming its way into the architectonics of each. At the same time, Design is different through being an older *technê*, with a long-established history, as in the masonic arts or shipbuilding, where calibrated forms of measurement were subordinate to the skilled master's "rule of thumb" or "eye." But as part of that earlier history, the old *technê* had begun encountering its own challenge (ultimately decisive) from a more writerly and calculative designing. Such designing first crystallizes in the work of Leon Battista Alberti, both in his famous *de Pictura* (c. 1435), which set down the techniques for geometrical perspective depiction, and in his later *de Statua* (c. 1450), which presents the first known system for translating the dimensions of a three-dimensional object into geometrical coordinates.

One general architectonic consequence for ways of knowing was, as Walter Ong (1958) saw, the spatializing of logical relations epitomized in Ramist method (see Figure 17.2). An older, "cluttered" way of seeing is displaced by a new "logical method" where an initial term is explained/defined via visualized dichotomies into opposed/complementary terms, each of which can be further bifurcated until explanation is exhausted, in the unfolding of bilateral friction-free lines and nodes. As Ong observes, as method, this is a universal solvent, through which nothing cannot be explained. It is the architectonic visualization behind the Decision Tree. It is also, rotated through ninety degrees, the template of the organization chart.

Here is one reason why non-design is not an option, because design is already embedded in management's "logic of visualization." But there is a further twist to the Design tale. For writerly calculative, Design only finally supplants older artisanal ways as disciplinary learning/knowledge displaces old

P. RAMI DIALECTICA.
TABVLA GENERALIS.

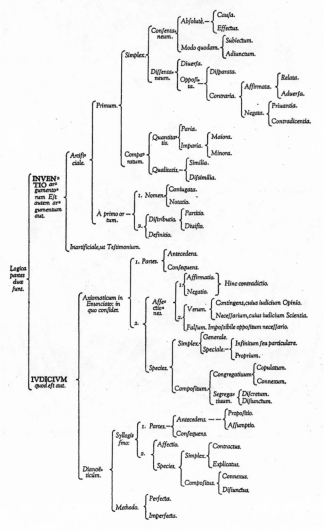

FIGURE 17.2   Exemplars of pre-Ramist and Ramist representations of the logic of knowledge. *Source*: P. Tartaret, Expositio super textu Logices Aristotelis (Paris, 1514). J. de Celaya, Expositio in prinum tractatum Summularum Magistri Petri Hispani (Paris, 1525).

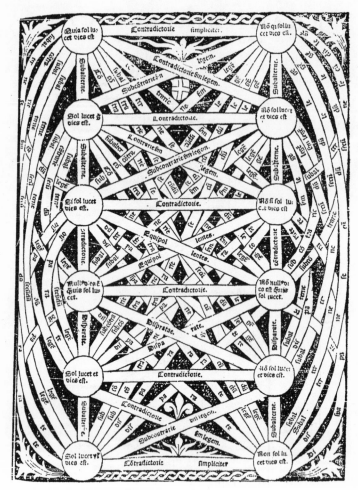

V. THE GEOMETRY OF THE MIND (CELAYA)

FIGURE 17.2 *(continued)*

master-apprentice models. In the field of bridge-building, the engineering historian Daniel Calhoun (1973) has suggested (ironically) that a new "intelligence" emerges as blueprints and calculations take over. He singles out the development of "counter-truss" bridging, something that occurs not in Europe, where design remains "statically indeterminate" and over-engineered, but in the United States, where in 1842 a "statically determinate" design was produced, enabling exact calculation of forces, using "simple trigonometrical methods and the principle of the parallelogram of forces to analyze the stresses

and strains in any truss that was compounded of triangular arrangements of
beams" (Calhoun, 1973: 297, 299). The design's author was Herman Haupt.

This conjunction, I now realize, enables us to reread the organization chart through a "counter-truss" lens, not as a friction-free visualization but as a capturing and stabilizing of contrary dynamics, where the staff function is the means through which the lines remain braced yet able to connect nodes.

But this is not the last word, as if we are left in an impasse, trapped under a repressive "disciplinary power," where management thinking and practice cannot escape this design model. Haupt discovered the *necessary* conditions for managerial organization, both in structure and in process, and he articulated the principle that at the base of both lies disciplinary practice — in this case, the new mix of financial and non-financial accounting, which he says, in the Pennsylvania's 1851 Annual Report is "assumed as the basis of the business organization." But we know that the ensuing system is not sufficient as a way of positively enabling management (in) practice.

Here Gehry's *designing practice*, in its refusal to accept that effective architectural outcomes require a slavish devotion to representational/perspectival design, may offer a new horizon, if we can acknowledge, as an endemic feature of disciplinarity, its liberating creative aspect. As Ong (again) observes, all modern expertise from romanticism to technology is similarly creative. The arts as much as the sciences excel from around 1800 in exploiting the "intellectual security" (1971: 278) made possible by what Ong describes as the "noetic abundance" of print knowledge, where word, number, picture, chart, and blueprint attain a graphic stability that means they can be "the same" for a globally dispersed expert community. As a sign of such security in art, Gombrich (1961) remarks on a shift in the practice of artistic composition — articulated by Cozens in 1790 and conspicuously adopted by Constable — away from drawing schematic figures in a (perspectively-gridded) field to letting lines and contours emerge freehand. Arguably, Gehry's designing practice marks the moment where architecture in turn discovers the "intellectual security" to move beyond perspectivalist/representationalist designing practice, while retaining (as management does via accounting) its necessary calculative constraints.

As such a breakthrough, it offers a new model and horizon for management designing that would refuse to allow the *necessary* features of org-chart design to be seen as sufficient. But such a transition is not simple. It requires from us intelligence and decision in support of this barely discernible new designing practice if we are to succeed in challenging our docile submission, at individual and organizational levels, to the well-internalized practices of writing, examining, and grading.

REFERENCES

Calhoun, D. 1973. *The intelligence of a people.* Princeton, NJ: Princeton University Press.

Chandler, A. 1977. *The visible hand.* Cambridge, MA: Harvard Belknap Press.

Gombrich, E. 1961. *Art and illusion: a study in the psychology of pictorial representation.* Princeton, NJ: Princeton University Press.

Hoskin, K. 1993. Education and the genesis of disciplinarity: The unexpected reversal. In *Knowledges: Historical and critical studies in disciplinarity,* edited by E. Messer-Davidow et al. Charlottesville: University of Virginia Press, 271–304.

Hoskin, K., and R. Macve. 1988. The genesis of accountability: The West Point connections. *Accounting, Organizations and Society,* 13(1): 37–73.

———. 2002. Pennsylvania ($)65,000? Paper presented at the Accounting, Business and Financial History Conference, Cardiff Business School, Wales.

Ong, W. 1958. *Ramus, method and the decay of dialogue.* Chicago: University of Chicago Press.

———. 1971. *Rhetoric, romance and technology.* Ithaca, NY: Cornell University Press.

III LEARNING FROM DESIGN PRACTICE

IN THIS SECTION, *we move from theoretical foundations to experiences of managing as designing and what can be learned from those experiences. Ina Wagner begins by presenting a long-term study of the work practices of architects, unpacking the implications for managers of some of the unique design methods and tools she encountered, including; "ways of seeing," "placeholders," and "persuasive artifacts." Fred Collopy then draws lessons from the work practice of Maya Lin as depicted in her book* Boundaries *and highlights the roles that tactile objects, writing, and drawing play for her in thinking through a design problem. Lucy Suchman counters this image of the individual designer and argues for the inevitability that design—whether Frank Gehry's or a manager's—is not the work of one person. It is almost always a distributed phenomenon that concerns ideas, objects, and people in circulation. Joe Paradiso builds on this image of distributed design by portraying the work practices at the MIT Media Lab and other design idea centers with which he is associated. He emphasizes the role of collections of diverse artifacts and the making of demos as elements in toolkits used by such groups in order to stimulate and guide collaborative design processes. Julia Grant then brings the discussion of practice back toward the sense of "thrownness" introduced by Karl Weick as she recounts her own experience in design and highlights the entrenched context of previous designs that a designer must navigate.*

Po Chung continues Julia Grant's focus on the individual and characterizes two ideal types of manager that he encountered in his role as cofounder of DHL International—the drivers and the designers. Peter Coughlan and Ilya Prokopoff, of the design firm IDEO, follow by recounting their experiences with corporate clients who approach them for help in moving all their managers toward being designers.

Jeanne Liedtka then shifts attention to the larger-scale question of corporate strategy formation and describes her experiences in working with managers to approach strategizing as a design problem. Betty Vandenbosch and Kevin Gallagher expand on this theme by exploring how constraints serve a valuable and generative role in management problem solving when it is approached as a design process.

Then follow four reports on projects in which collaborative design plays a significant role. Paul Kaiser discusses the importance of collaboration in the context of his design projects with Merce Cunningham, John Cage, and others. Alan Preston follows with a summary of lessons learned from the redesign of the Australian tax system, using Richard Buchanan's interaction design process. Sten Jönsson adds to these lessons by reporting on his longitudinal study of a design project for a platform car between Volvo and Mitsubishi. Finally, Kalle Lyytinen reviews the history of large-scale collaborative design in complex software projects, pointing out how little we have learned in our research over the last fifteen years and how much research we still have to do. The design stuff that managers and software developers deal with is composed of both multiple, diverse elements and their interacting ontologies, for which we have not developed an adequate research base.

18

"OPEN PLANNING"

Reflection on Methods and Innovative
Work Practices in Architecture

Ina Wagner

ARCHITECTS' WORK practices are a source of inspiration for thinking about "managing as designing." Architects are no longer in a position to define and control every single detail of a large building project. They are faced with an increasing number of stakeholders who have the expertise and power to make decisions—among them, the client, numerous specialists, authorities, the general contractor, and future users. As part of long-term fieldwork in an architectural office,[1] we have looked at how architects respond to this erosion of their former generalist role. Our observations suggest that the art of designing consists of mediations and interventions in highly conceptual, complex, and cooperative processes. Architects must learn how to carry conviction for the architectural concept and how to enlist the perspectives of multiple others. There is a need for methods and innovative work practices.

We use the term *open planning* for capturing some of these methods. Apart from the necessity to involve and mobilize the competence and cooperation of many others in the planning process, there are several additional reasons for maintaining openness: complexity, which implies the impossibility to define and fix the design details in a step-by-step process; the desire to expand the solution space and to see things differently; and the evolving and, in parts, unpredictable nature of the social use of a building or city. We work with a series of concepts and metaphors for describing the open planning approach (Wagner and Lainer 2003):

Ina Wagner, *Department of Computer Science, Institute for Technology Assessment and Design, Vienna University of Technology, Austria.*

– Mobilizing resources — the "art of seeing"
– Re-programming and the quality of the "different view"
– Working with placeholders — meandering
– The art of developing "persuasive artifacts"

MOBILIZING RESOURCES—THE "ART OF SEEING"

Openness is not an end in itself. One of the main motivations behind it is the need to expand the solution space for a design. Inspirational and experiential resources play an important role in this process. Architects are working with inspirations from many different aesthetic and scientific discourses — from the fine arts and the theater to biology and mathematics. Although some architects use pictorial material for generating and expressing their ideas, others prefer poetry and metaphorical text; yet others build their designs on (historical) research, the assembling of facts into "datascapes."

Fieldwork observations show how engaging in an immersive mass of material may support intensity in design situations. Architects draw inspiration from surprising, unexpected combinations of objects, such as images, books, CDs, and other objects of everyday life. While focusing on a project, they need to feel connected with the world outside and maintain a "window" to its range of opinions and interruptions — the site of the project, street life in front of the door, people, or a significant place in the city. At the same time, the limited space of the office may provide stimulating perspectives, with things and spaces overlayering each other — what we term *creative density* (Figure 18.1a).

Inspiration always emerges within a context. Objects or a place are not inspirational as such but may be so in connection with a project, idea, or particular task. They become a reference for thinking through a concept they might trigger or help shape: "What provides inspiration is not the object as such, the source, but what I can do with it, how I can manipulate it. If you work with a painting by Ernst Caramelle, it has nothing to do with urbanism, only if you start doing things" (RL) (Figure 18.1b).

Inspirations often arise from the transient and ephemeral way in which objects, people, and ambience are encountered, their peripheral presence in the back of one's mind. For many architects, inspiration can come from immediate events, assembled or ad hoc, such as film, video, and fashion photography, which are important resources for the work of imagining and conceptualizing (Figure 18.1c).

Architects' "art of seeing" is expressed in and supported by the diversity of representations they create. The material they produce is of different degrees of abstraction, different scale, and materiality—text, diagrams, comics, video, sketches, rough "sketch" models, virtual (3D) models, or CAD drawings. The diversity of design artifacts increases their possibilities for evaluating the design, as each representation helps make particular aspects of a design visible.

RE-PROGRAMMING AND THE QUALITY OF THE "DIFFERENT VIEW"

Creative work requires the possibility to transform and re-program—to explore solutions and contexts, to shift perspectives, to carry out experiments, to present and perform, to have time and space for free play and daydreaming, and to generate a "different view." The different view rests on the architect's ability to perceive the novel within the familiar, to discover relations between seemingly incongruent objects and notions—to relate the unrelatable. One architect expresses this idea in the following way: "to train yourself to, for example, when sitting on the train, change the color of the passing landscape, cut edges into the mountains, transform treetops into glass" (RL).

An example from the arts is a Janet Cardiff installation. She equips visitors of a building or part of the city with a CD Walkman or small video recorder. While following the artist's directions, they become involved in the stories they watch and listen to. Voices, footsteps, music, the sound of a car, or gunshots make up a fictional soundtrack overlayering the actual indoor or outdoor space (Biagioli 2000). Many architectural projects build on re-programming, changing familiar images of the city, the landscape, or objects of everyday life. The situationists developed a method—*dérive*—for creating a different view on the city, emulating the attitude of the *flâneur* and adding to it an analytical dimension (e.g., Arvidson 1995). Atmospheres, smells, materials, ambiences are registered and translated into maps of the city.

As part of their training, architectural students create different contexts for viewing their models—for example, against an alpine panorama, in the desert, or in the light of the setting sun. They project different textures and images onto them. One student, while working on a project about the beach, started seeing beaches everywhere, for example, where the sunlight was reflected on the road. These constant changes of context helped her think differently about beaches. Other examples we have encountered in our research include casting a collection of branches and leaves into bright metal to use as the façade of a building. Here, the architect envisioned a shimmering surface, using the metaphor of "industrialization and the re-interpretation of nature." In

FIGURE 18.1a

FIGURE 18.1b

FIGURE 18.1C
Inspirational resources: (a) Creative density—Friederike Mayröcker's workplace. *Source*: Friederike Mayröcker, photograph by Öhner/Kraller Wien, taken from Work@Culture, in Inszenierung von Arbeit, ed. Herbert Lachmeyer, Eleonora Louis, and Ritter Verlag, p. 196 (Klagenfurt: Büro, 1999). (b) Inspiration from art—Ernst Caramelle. *Source*: Ernst Caramelle, Image Bank, Catalogue for the exhibition in the BAWAG Foundation 7.9–25.11.2001, p. 27. (c) Short-time events, fast, assembled ad hoc—film and fashion photography as resources. *Source*: Ina Wagner

developing a new view, architects may take their designs into unfamiliar surroundings, such as a garden, or project pictures of the design onto unusual surfaces, such as colored cloth, to simulate new materials.

WORKING WITH PLACEHOLDERS—MEANDERING

Concretizing a design requires evoking the main concepts, thinking through
them, and gradually exploring the feasibility of various solutions on different levels of detail. This is a process that rarely proceeds in a linear, step-by-
step mode. It artfully oscillates between pre-scribing and de-scribing, fixing
and opening, between details and the whole, between precision and fuzziness.
This is what we describe as "meandering." A crucial aspect of this meandering movement is to be able to work with "floating concepts" and to maintain things at different stages of incompletion. Floating concepts help keep a
sense of things being tentative and incomplete. They define bandwidths for
development.

For example, in an urban planning study, the architects used the metaphor
of "diving in and cutting out" to describe the need for breaking up and structuring a set of layered elements in the design. The metaphor served as a guiding image for their work, without prescribing how it was to be accomplished.

The oscillating, which we describe as meandering, asks for a conceptual
shift from working with fixed elements or solutions to working with placeholders and to look at specifications as partial and preliminary. A placeholder
stands for something that might be there but is still in formation. It underpins
the passage from possibility to actuality that is the work of design.

Working with placeholders is a method for representing relatively complex
systems before they have taken shape. Placeholders facilitate communicating about something that has not been specified in detail. They enable people
to focus on the concept, rather than on a particular material, product, or
constructive solution. The images in Figure 18.2 were used as a placeholder
for the material for the façade of a building—they represent "glass of an irreg-
ular textile appearance onto which light will be projected."

THE ART OF DEVELOPING "PERSUASIVE ARTIFACTS"

Architects work with a great diversity of artifacts. These artifacts are not just
vehicles of information. They describe the building-in-design on multiple levels of detail, completeness, and technicality, using different visual languages,
and they play a wide variety of integrative roles in architects' cooperative work
(Schmidt and Wagner 2002).

FIGURE 18.2   Placeholders for a building façade. *Source*: Ina Wagner

An essential part of planning is the production of communication objects — "persuasive artifacts" — that carry conviction for the design of a particular solution, invite others into a dialogue, stimulate their imagination, and facilitate and accommodate their contributions (Latour 1986).

Architects' persuasive artifacts may combine metaphorical or descriptive text with images or sketches or use the specific sensual qualities of materials. Figure 18.3 shows three artifacts used to convey the notion of movie theaters "as stones that dip into water — above the surface of a rough, rocky quality, below precious stones that glitter in water — silver, gold, ruby, emerald" — in different visual languages. Characteristically, "persuasive artifacts" are underspecified. This makes them open to extensions, modifications, and novel interpretations. They help create a common understanding of a design idea or task; talk about a design in a rich, metaphorical way, supported by images to be pointed at and referred to; imagine qualities of space and appearance; and act as reminders of design principles, approach, method, open questions, and so forth. (Wagner 2000).

FIGURE 18.3   Persuasive artifacts depicting movie theaters. *Source:* Ina Wagner

Openness as a prerequisite of good design has been advocated before, often inspired by the work of Schoen (1983). It responds to the need for designers to expand the solution space of their work, on the one hand, and to cope with the impossibility of "controlling" users' detailed implementation and appropriation of a design on the other hand. Our condensed description is grounded in fieldwork on architects' work practices. It resonates in many ways with the conceptualizations of managing as designing in this book.

Among the metaphors from other disciplines and practices that come close to our notion of open planning is the music metaphor. Composers use simple symbols for expressing their ideas and "they rely on the reflexivity of the people who perform and listen to their music to fill the details" (Youngjin Yoo, see Chapter 31). This is evocative of working with floating concepts and placeholders for something which might be there but is still in formation. Working with incomplete and preliminary specifications enables designers to respond to the multiplicities of parameters and social worlds and their diverse perspectives on a building or organization. Lucy Suchman expresses this when talking about prototypes (which act as placeholders in the process of system design) as part of a dynamic assemblage of interests, fantasies, and practical actions, out of which new sociomaterial arrangements arise (see Chapter 20). Organizational theorists use the notion of cultural blueprints as shaping organization building but not necessarily determining the practices and artifacts that people develop (e.g., Guillén 1994).

The term *reconfiguration*, as used by Yrjö Engeström, corresponds to what the architects mean by re-programming—to use one's imagination to see familiar things differently. Engeström describes managing as designing as the "reconfigurative production of visions and articulative production of decisions" (see Chapter 10). Reconfiguring (or re-programming) may bring about a radical break with grown practices, but more often it helps work out small changes that make a difference for people's possibilities to read, appropriate, inhabit a space, or for organization.

Architects shape their environments so that they have a diversity of possibilities of seeing the design. Seeing and acting differently requires improvisation, argues Claudio Ciborra. Improvisation has to do with actors' emotions—moods, which he characterizes as "so ephemeral, sometimes superficial and unexplained, but they precede, or better ground, any mental representation of the situation and the action strategy." The architects' experiences of inspiration, and of contexts and moments that help them re-program and generate a "different view," are good examples of the role of mood in improvisation,

162 which for Ciborra is at the core of innovation (Ciborra 2002). Just think about making a simple door very deep — it all of a sudden becomes a library, an in-between space for spontaneous encounters, a place for a sink. These transformations are to do with the architects' spontaneous associations, a flow of images that is highly contingent, and emotional choices. However, "improvisation as mood" is not enough. The door as library needs to be detailed, fitted into the overall design, negotiated with multiple others, and may in the end develop into something entirely different.

For this work of aligning, we argue, architects as well as managers need, among other things: creative density — an environment rich in resources that may help open up an unfruitful venue; placeholders, which facilitate working with something that has not yet been specified in detail and allow temporary "fixations"; a diversity of representations of a design and, in particular, persuasive artifacts that invite others into a dialogue, enlisting their cooperation.

NOTE

1. The concepts and examples presented in this paper are based on a long-term cooperation with architect Rüdiger Lainer (quoted as RL). Quotes in this paper are from fieldwork in his office in the context of various projects (among them Esprit Project DESARTE http://www.media.tuwien.ac.at/desarte/index.html), from observing the work of architectural students in his master class at the Academy of Fine Arts (as part of IST–Project ATELIER http://atelier.k3.mah.se/home/default.asp), and from interviews with several architects about their work.

REFERENCES

Arvidson, E. 1995. Cognitive mapping and class politics: Towards a nondeterminist image of the city. *Rethinking Marxism* 8.2: 8–23.
Biagioli, M. 2000. Janet Cardiff — The missing voice. *Artfocus Magazine*, 68/8, Spring.
Ciborra, C. 2002. *The labyrinths of information: Challenging the wisdom of systems.* Oxford: Oxford University Press.
Guillén, M. F. 1994. *Models of management: Work, authority, and organization in a comparative perspective.* Chicago: University of Chicago Press.
Latour, B. 1986. Visualization and cognition: Thinking with eyes and hands. *Knowledge and Society: Studies in the Sociology of Culture Past and Present*, pp. 1–40.
Schmidt, K., and I. Wagner. 2002. Coordinative artifacts in architectural practice. *Proceedings COOP' 2002 Fifth International Conference on the Design of Cooperative Systems*, Saint-Raphael, France, June 4–7, pp. 257–74.

Schoen, D. 1983. *The reflective practitioner*. New York: Basic Books.

Wagner, I. 2000. "Persuasive artifacts" in architectural design and planning. *Proceedings of CoDesigning 2000*, Nottingham, September 11-13, pp. 379–90.

Wagner, I., and R. Lainer. 2003. Designing a visual 3D interface—A reflection on methods. ACM *Interactions Magazine*, November/December, pp. 13–19.

19

"I Think with My Hands"

On Balancing the Analytical
and Intuitive in Designing

Fred Collopy

MAYA LIN'S book *Boundaries* provides a rich, self-reflective assessment of design. In it, she reflects upon her sources of inspiration; the roles that sketches, models, and narrative writing play in her designs; and the effects of scale, names, and feelings on the resulting works. Her descriptions of her projects are filled with observations about what she does and how she does it. Like most personal narratives, it contains a mix of well-developed insight, big ideas and small ones, and the occasional contradiction.

Having read the book when it first came out, I returned to *Boundaries* a second time with a simple question—What can we learn from Maya Lin's design process? Covering two decades of work by a prolific and creative artist and architect, the book has an amazing scope. It is at once didactic and personal. It is filled with ideas that read at first like intuitive flashes, but that taken together reveal a complex structure. Indeed, the book is like her work. "My work is in part trying to mimic natural formations in the earth, complex but seemingly very simple. It is something I seek out in everything I do" (6:02–03).

In order to better grasp the underlying ideas and structures presented in *Boundaries*, I decided to represent some of its main themes in a concept map (Figure 19.1). The map I show here is obviously just one of many possible representations of the book. Inevitably, such an exercise focuses attention on some aspects at the expense of others. But it has allowed me to better see and reflect upon some very powerful structures, or intuitions, at work in Ms. Lin's approach to designing.

Fred Collopy, *Weatherhead School of Management, Case Western Reserve University*.

My first attempts at a map were done with magic markers on large sheets of butcher's paper. I started by putting down some of the big ideas that permeate the book, such as the importance of models and of writing and the role of intuitive gestures. I then drew links between ideas on the basis of text from the book. I decided that each link should be supported. Often the links were supported numerous places in the book, but I chose a typical expression in order to make the connections vivid.

Several categories emerged as I drew and redrew versions of the map. One had to do with large-scale movements that Ms. Lin makes through the design process. A second related to her use of analytic tools and research; a third, to the importance of the intuitive. I gave each of the three distinctive shading and added the notion of a balance between the analytic and intuitive directly to the map.

As I explored the concepts on the map, I decided that if there is a central theme that permeates *Boundaries*, it is related to this balancing the intuitive and the analytical. As Ms. Lin so clearly puts it, "My creative process balances analytic study, based very much on research, with, in the end, a purely intuitive gesture" (3:09). Perhaps nowhere is the balance more evident than in the creation of her Wexner Center piece, *Groundswell*. After many months of preparation, she personally guided and shook the large buckets of glass suspended from a crane to create mounds of color. She wanted to focus the piece's final form through the gestures of a specific moment in time.

This need to have her hands on her work is at the center of my map of her design process. She puts it best herself when she asserts "I think with my hands" (3:09). It is in her work with models that her ideas take shape. But those same ideas are shaped by her analytic study and research as well.

Ms. Lin's use of her hands in thinking echoes a sentiment expressed by Joe Paradiso in Chapter 21 of this volume. "We learn with our hands — although one can study and understand a concept through literature and diagrams, physically engaging with an actual object produces a deeper understanding; it stimulates the kind of intuition that is often critical to a designer." I think this may well prove to be one of the most fertile contributions of design thinking to management, the balancing of what have been essentially cognitive work practices with an increased reliance on our hands. New models, manipulated with new kinds of interfaces, will one day replace, or dramatically supplement, our current reliance on abstract thought and numerical analysis.

There are other lessons in Maya Lin's ways of working. Perhaps the most common question students ask when trying to create something novel is "how should I begin?" Ms. Lin offers two alternatives. One is by writing ("the purest of art forms" [2:05]). The other is through analytic study based on research.

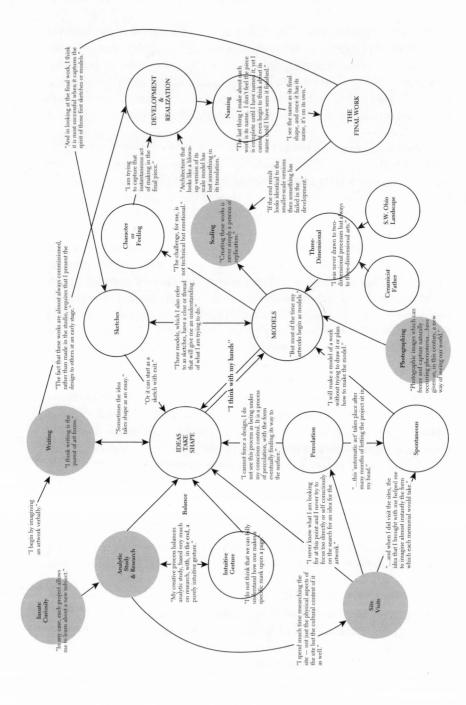

FIGURE 19.1   The balance of the intuitive and analytic in Maya Lin's design process.

Then an allowance for time at the site and percolation create the conditions in which an idea takes shape.

The use of models is one area where decision thinking and design thinking converge. Managers make frequent use of models, most often spreadsheet models. The use of models for decision making differs from what we see in the way that both Gehry and Lin talk about their models. Models are a center of gravity in Ms. Lin's work as they are in Mr. Gehry's. Both of them frequently insist that the model is not the thing being designed. For Lin, the models are all about capturing the spirit of a piece. Indeed, if the final architecture looks identical to the smaller-scale versions "something has failed in the development" (3:13).

As you examine the map, it becomes clear that you could, if you wanted to, view Ms. Lin's work processes in terms of a stage model. There seem to be four stages. Ideas take shape, models are created, the piece is developed and results in the final work. But it is not really that simple. For some pieces, the ideas come into being through the models. And the final work is not really the end. Though she declares "once it has its name, it's on its own" (3:13), we see evidence that Ms. Lin continues to appraise and learn from each piece. So, if there is a stage model at work here, it is not a tidy one.

In Herbert Simon's earliest writing about design, he viewed the space in which designs are located as essentially unbounded. Lin does the same. At the time of a site visit, she says "I never know what I am looking for at this point and I never try to focus too directly or self consciously on an idea for the artwork" (3:07). As Simon's understanding of bounded rationality developed, his view of design seems to have narrowed. Lin's success suggests that a more open search might offer fresh prospects to those who dare enter it.

A balance like that which Lin seeks in her work is also described by Karl Gerstner in the essay "Art = Design," in which he argues that image — in the philosophical sense — is the opposite of concept. "Concepts are abstract, particles of discursive thought, of logic; images are visible, intuitive entities of dreams and visions" (2001, p. 8). This is very like the tension Lin addresses in *Boundaries*, though she uses the language of analytic study and intuitive gesture. Throughout her work, she engages in processes that attempt to cross a boundary that separates concept from image. Gerstner refers to this higher-level integration, which is composed of both image and concept, as intellectual observation, or visualized thought, and notes that Immanuel Kant considered it direct access to "the real basis of nature." Kant considered it beyond the ability of the human to comprehend this basis. But works like those produced by Maya Lin provide a glimpse.

Gerstner, K. 2001. *Karl Gerstner: Review of 5 × 10 Years of Graphic Design etc.*, edited by Manfred Kroplien. Stuttgart: Hatje Cantz Verlag.

Lin, M. 2000. *Boundaries*. New York: Simon and Schuster.

20

DECENTERING THE MANAGER/DESIGNER

Lucy Suchman

AS FORMS of ordering, management and design are similarly oriented to the creation of sociomaterial arrangements within, or with which, others can act. Discussions of the formation of both management and design disciplines typically include an acknowledgement of their basis in the ordering practices of everyday life, followed by an account of their professionalization in the context of twentieth century desires for expansions of scale in organization and production (see, for example, Clegg and Palmer 1996; Yates 1989). A correlate of this process is that managing and designing come to be more and more the exclusive province of those with credentials to do so, at the same time that discourses of organizing and making things become correspondingly more esoteric. Moreover, with the proliferation of mediating technologies designed to meet requirements of scale (processes, procedures, standards, and the like), management and design disciplines become increasingly removed from the specific sites and practices that constitute their objects. At the same time, managing and designing are no less dependent on lived experience as their basis for action. It follows that, insofar as professional management and design practices take place in relatively insulated environments and privilege the technical knowledge and professional relations of the manager/designer, they necessarily rely on imaginary, underspecified conceptions of the worker/user.

The greater the distance — geographic, economic, cultural, experiential — between the life worlds of professional managers and designers and those persons and places who are their objects, the greater the need for *in situ* configuration work to fill the gap. In the case of both management initiatives and

Lucy Suchman, *Department of Sociology, Lancaster University.*

170   information systems design, this work involves appropriating something created elsewhere so as to incorporate it into a local environment and set of practices. The question is not whether that work will need to be done, but with what ease or difficulty. The trope of "invisible work" is one attempt to recognize the plethora of everyday ordering practices that are obscured in professional discourses of management and design (see, for example, Nardi and Engeström 1999; Shapin 1989; Star 1991; Suchman and Jordan 1989).

What would it mean, then, to reconfigure management and design discourses so that the inevitable reworkings involved in implementation or use would be seen not as design failures or user resistances, but as realizations of the design? One key move is to shift from a view of the manager/designer as the *origin* of change, or of new things, to an understanding of the manager/ designer as involved in the *circulation* of ideas and objects. Combined with an appreciation for the ways in which circulating ideas and objects are refracted in distinctive — even sometimes unique — ways through particular persons, this shift provides the basis for a decentering of the manager/designer, and an associated reconfiguring of management and design as collective practice.

To develop this idea more concretely, we can turn to recent efforts to develop critical, practice-based forms of participatory or cooperative design. A persistent trouble for professional designers of computer-based systems is the reported failure of their products to deliver on promised benefits, either to the economy of organizations or to the working practices of organization members. A common characterization of the source of this trouble is that designers' distance from the objects of their work results in an inadequate understanding of "user needs," taken as more and less precisely stated requirements for what a given system should do. Much ink has been spilled in the professional literature on this topic, and proposals abound for the introduction of processes, methods, and schemes of assessment developed to evaluate and improve upon existing design practice.

Experiments in various forms of cooperative design have aimed to close the distance between professional design and use by establishing collaborative working relations among relevant actors. Critical discussion in the field of information systems development questions the prevailing conception of the technology user as a passive recipient of an already-made, fixed, and stable object. Local appropriation is understood as less a question of receiving something already made and incorporating it into a new site of use, than of co-constructing useful and useable new social and material arrangements. Design-in-use, including the varying degrees of lay and professional customization work typical of any actual technology implementation, comprises the generative practices out of which new technologies are made.

While much of the literature on user involvement and system prototyping follows traditional lines in offering normative models for organizing professional conduct, the more radical initiatives involve a reorientation as well away from methods of formal analysis as core resources for system design. Various literary devices continue to have their uses, but the center of gravity shifts from the production of system specifications and various other abstract renderings of system functionality, to the prototype and associated practices as directly embodying the design. General methods of prescriptive representation are displaced by specific projects under this strategy, based in and contributing to reports on a repertoire of techniques, along with reflections on the significance of past experiences for future work.

A second shift toward a more radical reconstruction of traditional design practice turns on basic assumptions regarding the status of "user needs." For many if not most advocates, prototyping represents a strategy for "uncovering" user needs, taken as already existing but somehow latent, unarticulated, or even unrecognized by practitioners themselves. The project then is to elicit these preexisting attributes from the prospective user, to represent them precisely, and thereby to make them available for use by professional system designers. An alternative position is that prototyping practice simultaneously recovers and invents work requirements and technological possibilities, that each make sense in relation to the other. This alternative can be viewed as a form of *enactment* rather than representation, where the developing relation between use practices and new technological possibilities is realized in the artifact and associated reconceptualizations, rather than in any self-standing representational forms. The prototype, conventionally taken as a mediating artifact in designer-user interactions, is seen instead as constituted in and inseparable from those interactions. For the designer, the question is always, and reiteratively: What have we got at this point, and what can we say about it and do with it, vis-à-vis the circumstances at hand? This is not to say that there is no constancy to the artifact. Rather, it is the reiteration of these questions and the construction of satisfactory answers to them that create the continuity.

Insofar as an approach based on cooperative, iterative prototyping seems nonviable for all projects of professional management and design, the question I would pose is why? A central issue here is clearly one of scale. Frequently, approaches accepted as viable locally are at the same time assumed to be nonviable as things "scale up." Here again, distance from the object of managerial and design work is posited as inevitable, necessitating the introduction of various mediating technologies. But what if we approached increases in scale not as a matter of shifting the action of small-scale projects out onto technologies of project management and design, so much as a process of

172   proliferation? The strategy here would be to develop small-scale, experimental projects *combined with* planning for their progressive working together. "Working together" in this sense would involve reiterating aspects of successful projects enacted in one location in new settings, with requisite forms of customization and with attention to areas of useful standardization. Although elements of this process are already to be found, there are few examples of sustained commitment to a model of exploratory prototyping that repeats over an extended period of time, while effectively facilitating the extension of useful results across space. It would be the work of facilitation and extension, among other things, that would comprise the focus of management.

A poststructuralist approach to thinking about organization proposes that traditional preoccupations with order might fruitfully give way to an interest in practices of *ordering* (see, for example, Law 1994, p. 2). The move is from a view of objects and actions as pre-established and normatively determined in their significance, to an appreciation for the enacted, irreducibly relational constitution of material and social orders. At the same time, objects and actions are realized within culturally and historically reiterated fields of possibility, which afford the familiar ground of everyday experience. The implication is that ordering is ongoing, and that what appear as stable social and material features of a familiar landscape are the effects of practices reiterated over time and space. Management and design, as paradigmatic practices of order production, are leading candidates for reconceptualization under this view. These reconceptualizations orient us away from the designing manager as a singular and central actor, to managing and design as ongoing, collective achievements of differently located, mutually consequential persons and things.

REFERENCES

Clegg, S., and G. Palmer. 1996. Introduction: Producing management knowledge. In *The Politics of Management Knowledge*, edited by S. Clegg and G. Palmer. London: Sage, pp. 1–18.

Law, J. 1994. *Organizing modernity*. Oxford, UK and Cambridge, MA: Blackwell.

Miller, D., and D. Slater. 2000. *The Internet: An ethnographic approach*. Oxford, UK: Berg.

Nardi, B., and Y. Engeström, eds. 1999. "A web on the wind: The structure of invisible work." Special issue of *ComputerSupported cooperative work: The journal of collaborative computing*, Vol. 8, Nos. 1–2.

Shapin, S. 1989. The invisible technician. *American Scientist* 77: 554–63.

Star, S. L. 1991. Invisible work and silenced dialogues in knowledge representation.

In *Women, Work and Computerization*, edited by I. Eriksson, B. Kitchenham, and K. Tijdens. Amsterdam: North Holland, pp. 81–92.

Suchman, L., and B. Jordan. 1989. Computerization and women's knowledge. In *Women, Work and Computerization*, edited by K. Tijdens, M. Jennings, I. Wagner, and M. Weggelaar. Amsterdam: North Holland, pp. 153–60.

Yates, J. 1989. *Control through communication: The rise of system in American management*. Baltimore and London: Johns Hopkins.

21

From Tangibles to Toolkits and Chaos to Convection

Management and Innovation at Leading
Design Organizations and Idea Labs

Joseph A. Paradiso

ONE OF the first things one notices at leading design firms is the way they have many artifacts scattered about, from which designers can evolve new ideas and design concepts. Not only their own products, but also interesting designs from competitors are displayed and made available to pick up and examine. IDEO, for example, has a full-time staff member in charge of acquiring and curating this gizmo collection; new devices are continually collected, announced through publications and online lists, and made available at a central location (purposefully located in an area of heavy traffic flow) for their designers to examine and even check out as one would a library book. When in search of an idea or solution to a problem, I've found stockrooms serve a similar purpose: wandering through aisles stocked with different kinds of items and materials (the more categories the better) often provokes several ideas, frequently unrelated to the original purpose of the items on display. One unfortunate side effect to the rise of Internet retail is the shrinking and eradication of corporate and university stockrooms; the hidden cost in lost ideas isn't easily calculable.

Perhaps there is an analog to this "artifact" concept in the world of management via case studies. The tangible nature of the designer's artifacts, however, provides a major difference. Being able to pick up and manipulate these items with your hands and to feel and observe the way they work engages something very primal. We learn with our hands. Although one can study and understand a concept through literature and diagrams, physically engaging

Joseph A. Paradiso, *Media Lab, Massachusetts Institute of Technology.*

with an actual object produces a deeper understanding—it stimulates the kind of intuition that is often critical to a designer.

A major trend in human–computer interaction research is termed *Tangible Interfaces* (Ishii and Ullmer, 1997). The goal of this movement is to change the dominant means of interacting with information, moving away from today's graphical user interface (GUI), where we manipulate visual abstractions projected onto a flat screen. Proponents at the Tangible frontier are trying to move the computer interface into physical objects that can be more naturally manipulated. Information is then represented through some kind of physical abstraction; the data or concepts connected to the object are then explored through physical manipulation, much as the way the designer handles artifacts to obtain a deeper understanding of principle and aesthetic. It comes as no surprise that some of the best practitioners in this field are also designers, or have strong empathy with design principles. One can perhaps conceive of tangible toolkits for management processes, enabling physical exploration of organizational dynamics, a company's fiscal or logistical status, and so on. As tangible interfaces provide a means through which information can become physical, this paradigm could offer managers a means of tactilely exploring possibilities, much as in the way a designer engages with artifacts.

Many varieties of tangible interfaces have been developed by Hiroshi Ishii and his Tangible Media Group (see http://www.media.mit.edu/tangible) at the MIT Media Lab. Some of these projects explore information manipulation relevant to management applications (Arner, 2003). One example is the SenseTable (Patten et al., 2001), a desk-sized surface that is able to identify and track a set of pucks horizontally, vertically, and rotationally. Each puck also hosts a local control of some sort (e.g., a knob). The pucks can be dynamically bound to information that can be explored by moving them about the table and manipulating their local control. An overhead projection onto the table defines a dynamic, visual input-output space, immersing the user in the presentation of the data and its manipulation options. Other relevant examples are the Tangible Query Interfaces (Ullmer, 2002), designed by Brygg Ullmer. These are a set of compact electronic "widgets," each of which have a set of local controls and co-located display that allow people to physically express and manipulate queries into databases and large information aggregates. These devices can be used independently or docked in any combination to a graphical base station, allowing finer exploration of their associated information.

Toolkits, in general, have another purpose that is especially appropriate for innovative organizations such as design labs. They coherently encompass a set of capabilities, enabling people unfamiliar with the underlying technology or set of concepts upon which the toolkit is based to rapidly assimilate the nec-

176   essary principles and basic experience needed to begin applying them in their work. Toolkits can include anything that's relevant, ranging from physical objects through electronics hardware to software. Toolkits go beyond the collections of artifacts that design labs curate; they enable designers to engage with the principles driving the devices and to assimilate them rapidly. Studies of corporate innovation (Von Hippel and Katz, 2002) have recognized the importance of toolkits for stimulating the creative process. Oftentimes, the breakthroughs come when the tools are used in unintended ways. One of the main challenges in technology innovation is to determine what the "killer app" will be for a particular development; history abounds with quotes from inventors expounding on what their invention will enable, only to be dead wrong when their brainchild succeeds for an entirely different reason.

Much as in the way that design houses tend to encompass talent spanning many different specialties, the MIT Media Lab is home to an extremely diverse set of people who hail from very different backgrounds, ranging from art and design to physics and engineering. Much as how the scattered artifacts in the designers' collection or the diverse items on the shelf of a stockroom can stimulate innovation, the mix of backgrounds, expertise, and goals deriving from such a hyperdiverse group can produce frequent jolts that keep the participants on an edge. People who survive in such an environment naturally move to the boundaries between disciplines where new fields of inquiry can sprout.

Several components are important to keep such environments together. At the Media Lab, toolkits play part of this role. A group can encapsulate a sliver of its expertise into a toolkit, which can then be used by others for entirely different (and quite unanticipated) applications. Think of the Media Lab as a pot on the stove: the toolkits are the transportation mechanism for a convective process of learning and communication. Devices produced by the engineering groups propagate up to the content groups, where they are pushed into unanticipated niches. These applications filter back, inspiring the inventors and stimulating them to innovate further, and the process begins anew. Of course, the flow doesn't need to begin with engineering—just as artists can be inspired by a piece of technology, the technologists can be inspired by content. The important thing is that a process exists by which knowledge and innovation can be transported across intellectual boundaries.

Other factors, such as the emphasis on "demos," play important roles in breaking disciplinary barriers at the Media Lab, which is very much a "show me" environment. It is mandatory that students produce some kind of encapsulated "demonstration" of their research. This need not be anything like a final product (and is generally far from this), but it must somehow embody the core principles of their research. The goal is to enable them to powerfully and simply convey their directions, concepts, and results to a general audience, including our industrial sponsors and other visitors. Demos, however, also serve an important internal function in enabling groups arising from different disciplines to easily show their work to one another and spread concepts—they are very much a common language in conveying concepts to different groups and crossing the art/technology boundary.

Perhaps the most important factor in keeping an organization like the Media Lab mixed is our students. Although I've used the term "artist" and "technologist" as separate quantities in this text, each individual is a weighted vector sum of both, some more one way than the other. We tend to bring in students who are somewhere in the middle, able to understand something of each perspective. Even in the cases where they are firmly at one end or the other, their colleagues in the middle serve as conduits, infecting them with artistic outlook or technical concepts. Although students belong to particular research groups, their social structures respect no group boundary. They freely associate with one another and, of course, talk about their work. Keeping open minds, they'll take what they've seen in one group (again, often by catching the demo), establish an impromptu collaboration with a colleague elsewhere, and produce a cross-genre hybrid that's quite unanticipated. Many of our best projects get started that way. Further insight on how the Media Lab operates can be found in Haase (2000).

Interdisciplinary organizations, in particular, are by nature unstable. They can dissolve along several pathways as they grow and evolve. One is a drift toward specialization. Even though the physicists first hired into a nascent interdisciplinary team can talk with the musicians and graphics artists (after all, that's why they came in the first place), the physicists that they hire may be less inclined to cross boundaries, and the physicists that they hire get even more specialized. In the best of cases, this is due to a success: a part of the interdisciplinary group has indeed invented a new discipline and splits off to explore it full-tilt. In a less positive scenario, the split is due to a communication breakdown resulting from organizational drift.

It has been said (Gladwell, 2000) that the maximum size of a functional organization is roughly 150 people; if it gets much larger, they lose familiarity with one another and no longer function as a group. Interdisciplinary organizations may have even stricter quotas; in order to relate, they need to understand each other across wide conceptual gulfs. Providing effective management mechanisms to dynamically tune and adjust these organizations such that they optimally innovate is a challenge that becomes ever more important as these "idea factories" propagate and grow.

178 REFERENCES

Arner, F. 2003. It only looks like child's play. *Business Week*, Number 3856, November 3, pp. 86–89.

Gladwell, M. 2000. *The tipping point*. Boston: Little Brown & Company.

Haase, K. 2000. Why the Media Lab works—A personal view. *IBM Systems Journal*, 39:3&4, pp. 419–31.

Ishii, H., and B. Ullmer. 1997. Tangible bits: Towards seamless interfaces between people, bits and atoms. *Proceedings of the CHI '97 Conference on Human Factors in Computing Systems*. New York: ACM Press, pp. 234–41.

Patten, J., H. Ishii, J. Hines, and G. Pangaro. 2001. Sensetable: A wireless object tracking platform for tangible user interfaces. *Proceedings of Conference on Human Factors in Computing Systems (CHI '01)*. New York: ACM Press, pp. 253–60.

Ullmer, B. 2002. *Tangible interfaces for manipulating aggregates of digital information*. PhD thesis, Media Lab, Massachusetts Institute of Technology.

Von Hippel, E. and R. Katz. 2002. Shifting innovation to users via toolkits. *Management Science*. 48(7): 821–33.

22

(RE)DESIGN IN MANAGEMENT

Julia Grant

THE TASK of design in management faces some constraints distinct from those of the artist. The artist-designer faces a blank canvas, an uncarved block of marble, or some other fresh medium that awaits the creative process. The outcome of that design process has as its beginning unformed raw materials. Thus, it can become what the designer imagines, limited only by the characteristics of the medium and the creator. The designer may face limitations inherent in imagination and ability, but the effects of these will be specific to that designer, affecting only what she wishes to accomplish within the chosen medium.

The typical manager-designer does not have the same luxury. While she still must select an arena for action, comparable to the selection of the medium for the artist, that arena is not raw material, nor is it blank. The potential within the management context is rarely so pristine because a manager is usually working with a context that already has form. There is already a company in existence. There are people who work within it, who have been busily creating their own designs. There are physical and organizational structures dedicated to whatever has been created to date. Thus, at a minimum, existing structures must be redesigned simultaneously with the creation of a new design. Or, at an extreme, something must be destroyed before something new can be created. While the manager, like the artist, may also be hampered in her efforts by imagination and ability, she bears the additional burden of the preexisting, or simultaneous, creative efforts of others.

Julia Grant, *Weatherhead School of Management, Case Western Reserve University.*

FIGURE 22.1   Philip Johnson's *Turning Point*

To illustrate the task distinction, first imagine Michelangelo facing un-carved marble and creating *La Pietà*. Next, in contrast, imagine Philip John-son facing the completed work *La Pietà* and trying to create from it his sculp-ture, *Turning Point* (illustrated in Figure 22.1).

This rather extreme example illustrates the potential constraints we would place upon the artist-designer if we imposed on her creative process the prior outcome of someone else's process. We may be able to envision a (miniature) *Turning Point* within *La Pietà*, but we cannot create the sculpture as Johnson originally envisioned it. Or we can imagine deciding that the conversion of *La Pietà* into *Turning Point* requires blowing to bits the original sculpture. When this occurs, what we have accomplished is the creation of an empty space within which another block of sculpture medium can be placed and formed.

Michelangelo or other members of the art appreciation community will object to the destruction of *La Pietà* to create a space for *Turning Point*. In an existing company, other managers will object to the destruction of existing or-ganizational/managerial design because of their investment in it. But Sculp-tor Johnson is free to move down the road to an empty space. In management, only the entrepreneur has this opportunity, this freedom to relocate to a new, untouched space. And this, perhaps, is what makes that entrepreneurial role so attractive. The entrepreneur is free to design from the ground up, truly creating anew, without being constrained by the prior organizational/managerial creations of others. The entrepreneur essentially does find an open space, a previously uncharted territory, and designs her own creation, for better or for worse.

A diagram presented by Jurgen Faust in Chapter 32 illustrates the movement from chaos to design. As shapes emerge from the chaotic particulate mass, a design becomes more definite, more concrete, and with that transformation, possibilities that may have existed in the original state are no longer available. The entrepreneur has the advantage of the wider set of possibilities, in contrast to the manager within the existing firm where shapes have already formed. Thus, the process of design in management, outside of the entrepreneurial context, must confront the problem of creating some version of chaos within an existing context, rather than within a void. The prior investment of other human beings in their own, previously created designs leads to a stubborn tenacity in existing organizational, managerial, or operational structures because these structures incorporate commitment, investment, and human emotion, all of which must be reckoned with as part of the (re)design process.

In nonentrepreneurial management, the absence of existing design will occur only in extreme cases. For example, the event of bankruptcy creates the possibility, the space for a potentially new design. The experiences of managers who take on the challenge of turning around a failed or failing business provide another example of the changed range of possibilities. Perhaps old management can be cleared out, but a continued culture and infrastructure create constraints from which the purely entrepreneurial manager is free.

Absent destruction, the field of management is not essentially a fertile one for new design. Youngjin Yoo has written on the potential need for destroying current structures within another context, that of educational institutions. Quoting on his Web site from his World Management Conference address about institutional innovation within universities for e-learning, he says, "In many cases we are bound by our own imaginations. In order to seize these opportunities, we should destruct institutional structures and develop a 'controlled chaos' for new learning models." An example from education that contrasts the difficulties inherent in redesign, compared to design, has been illustrated within the Weatherhead School of Management. Over the past ten years, departments have successfully *designed entirely new* master's degrees, at least one of which was, in fact, quite innovative and creative. Yet within the *existing* MBA program, several energetic efforts to *redesign* the current curriculum have met stiff resistance, resulting in only marginal changes, with little meaningful new effects. What has been accomplished in this existing arena to date is comparable to reconfiguring a fold in a garment of *La Pietà*—a significant change to many eyes, but well short of the creation of a fundamentally different statue and meaning.

If the contrast to sculpture or painting is too extreme, perhaps architectural design provides a potentially fruitful comparison. This design context can inform the concept of design in management because it must address constraints comparable to those faced by managers. As Frank Gehry designed the Peter B. Lewis Building for the Weatherhead School of Management, he had conversations with the school's community about the specific needs to be met in order to accomplish the goals of the institution that would inhabit the space being designed. These needs necessarily had an impact on what sort of building could or could not be designed. Case Western Reserve University specified the plot of ground on which the building would sit, creating a space constraint that the architect had to honor. As construction progressed, additional constraints were created as a result of early decisions in the construction process itself, and those constraints affected subsequent design decisions and the resulting space. This interactive scenario is far from the blank canvas that a painter might face.

Such architectural efforts have differing outcomes. At one extreme, the Gehry design process on his own home has reportedly recreated the entire structure. Although the original infrastructure surely created constraints, as did the size of the plot of ground on which the house sits, the original builder/architect of the house was not on the scene to object as walls were moved and surfaces changed. If no one would object to the resculpting of *La Pietà* into a cubist representation, one might accomplish an analogous sculptural achievement.

At another extreme are the outcomes of architectural designs that resulted in expansion and/or renovation to the Cleveland Museum of Art and to Severance Hall. In each of those two cases, the architect was faced with a massive structure, much of the original of which would ultimately remain unchanged. The outcomes of those two design processes illustrate different types of redesign. In the instance of the Severance Hall renovation, completed at the close of the twentieth century, it is difficult to determine where the new structure begins and the old one ends. This redesign process was so informed and influenced by the original structures that the resulting building looks as if it has always appeared just as it is. There is little visible evidence of violence done to the original design.

The 1970s expansion of the Museum of Art, on the other hand, is purely utilitarian. There is no apparent attempt to match or even to blend the addition to the original classical architecture. The purpose of this redesign process seems to have been to add display galleries, and this goal was accomplished. But the new space has been built on additional, adjoining ground, rather than being integrated into the original structure, thus avoiding any claim to a seamlessly redesigned building.

Each of these architectural redesign projects has been affected by the original design in different ways, and each has been constrained, or not, differently. These examples can be applied to the managerial application of the design process. The goal for management is to understand how to "create" the destruction and/or space that must precede pervasive new (re)design. Is the management project closer to an unconstrained redesign, such as Gehry's house? The turnaround manager's field of action is similar to this. Or must the redesigned entity or project contain or reflect more of existing management structures? The manager in an ongoing organization faces this situation. Thus, an important part of the manager's role is to understand the difficulties and the constraints faced in managing as designing within organizations and to open the opportunities and spaces for new design similar to those enjoyed by an artist. This facilitation responsibility is inherent in the need to provide or create the space, the blank canvas, the uncut marble, to allow others to create new designs.

The truly enlightened manager will understand that this responsibility means that her own old designs may require modification or destruction to facilitate new ones. It will not be enough for those at lower levels of an organization to understand the concept of design in management if they are never empowered, never given the space to use it. Those with the power to enable new creative spaces within the management context must be the ones who embrace design.

23

Drivers Versus Designers as an Organization's Building Philosophy

Po Chung

MY THOUGHTS on the importance and connectivity of the elements of design and leadership in building an organization have been developed over the years as I successfully made the transition from an entrepreneur and cofounder of one of the most global of all global companies, DHL World Wide Express, to a professional CEO, leading the DHL network in 225 countries and political territories. In the first fifteen years of our existence, we were able to open a new country every five weeks and a new city every eight days, without making any acquisitions. We did it with an appropriate design in philosophy, culture, and corporate lifestyle. We were lucky to come up with enough appropriate designs, and we were smart enough to quickly separate the good ones from the bad ones. Thus, we ended up with an eclectic collection of appropriate designs for the nature of our business and the nature of our global and local resources.

DHL started as and continues to be an entrepreneurial company. However, along the way, our leadership teams had to make the transition from being pure entrepreneurs to professional leaders. Over this period of time, we found that four imperative skills emerged that enabled our founding entrepreneurs to make this transition: analytical skills, human skills, pathfinding skills, and design skills. I define these skills as follows:

> – Analytical skill: the ability to look at a complex set of data and alternatives and make the most appropriate choice(s).

Po Chung, *Chairman Emeritus and Cofounder, DHL International.* The author thanks Leonard Lane, an Executive Doctor of Management student at Case Western Reserve University, for contributing to this paper.

- Human skill: the ability to get appropriate tasks done through and with other people.
- Pathfinding skill: the ability to find the best way between where you are and where the company needs to be, to survive in the long term.
- Design skill: the ability to create appropriate makeshift short-term and durable long-term designs on corporate philosophy, corporate lifestyle, integrity, management structure, people training, operations, finance, product design, strategic review, and so on.

For the lasting and successful founder(s) of a company who make(s) the transition from entrepreneur to professional leadership, there is nothing more important than the design skill. Before I talk about the design skill of the founder(s) and the rest of the organization, I would like to talk about the importance of the overall design theme and style — the DNA — of every design in the new company. It is important to point out here that if the DNA is appropriate for its business, its environment, and its customers, the company will survive. Even when the founder or the founding team have superior analytical ability, if their philosophy and style (derived from practical skills, street smarts, and intuition) are inappropriate for their business, environment, and customers, the company will not survive.

This brings me to the analogy of drivers versus designers in relation to the growth of a company. Generally, I have found that there are drivers of cars and designers of cars and, by analogy, of organizations. In the business world, my experience is that drivers outnumber designers by fifty to one. This is an important point to understand, especially as we think about entrepreneurial organizations. A company starts out with both kinds of managers. In the beginning of successful companies, the designer-managers are usually in charge. The designers are people who can reduce everything to its basic form, explain it to others, and lead others to ask better questions. The designers take the time to understand the big picture and the context (the vision) in which decisions need to be made. They also understand how the internal guts of the business operate (turning the vision into reality). Many times the designers were not seen as exciting people because who wanted to listen to descriptions of the virtue of new rain tires or the power of a new exhaust system? Thus, partway into the development of a company, the driver-managers usually take over. Why does this happen? It happens because in a roomful of people (the growing corporate organization) drivers usually outshine the designers. They can tell good racing stories and make wonderful presentations. They do this because they are trained by driving schools — the business schools of this world — that provide them with analytical and communication tools, but not with street smarts, intuition, and philosophy. Designers are not very exciting because they talk about the basic stuff that makes the war stories possible. Who cares about logistics and supply chain management when you can listen to someone regale you with the art of the deal? These ruling managers are drivers by nature because they have been put into a management position, have some superficial understanding of the system, and therefore feel qualified to take the car (the business unit) out for a spin. They can negotiate corners beautifully, stop the car on a dime, and know when to get coolant, fuel, and lubricants. They can even talk superficially about the engine, the power train, the electrical system, the suspension system, the steering system, and the exhaust system; however, they do not have an in-depth understanding of any of these systems.

Flawed business models/designs happen because the racing team allowed these drivers, who were born on third base and thought they had just hit a triple, to start changing the system of the car. Inevitably, these cars (companies) will lose their race. Drivers can be trained by driving schools — the business schools of this world — however, designers are developed by years of apprenticeship. That is why, if we look at successful companies, we will find they promote from within because these people understand and have designed the appropriate system for the organization and its customers.

Let me give you an example of letting the driver take the car out for a spin. Suppose a company is designed to have an intense focus on the customer that is delivered at the country level, and regional offices are designed to be small and only play a coordinating support role. To reinforce this design principle, the company developed a bonus system in which everyone in the region had the same scheme, that is, regional management and country management. Everyone had one objective, which was to make the country as efficient and profitable as possible. It was a system that aligned regional management with the overall unit of profitability and aligned the country with a singular focus on the customer. When the drivers took over the corporate positions and regional positions, they wanted to expand their roles and make more money. Therefore, they needed to invent additional reasons for their existence to achieve this personal goal. Their method to achieve their own personal goals was to change their bonus system to include *their own personal objective*, thus allowing a significant portion of their bonus to be tied to *their own objectives*, not those of the countries. Because real work was done at the country level and statistics and so forth are tracked at the country level, regional management was constantly asking country management for resources to work on their own regional projects, thus taking valuable time away from the real focus, the customers. This eventually led to regional management taking an attitude that they knew more about the business than the people in the countries.

When this happens, you have people who have to justify their existence telling people who do not have to worry about their jobs what to do. When this happens, you have people who do not have enough to do, creating more work for people who already had too much to do. When this happens, you have people who are removed from the business telling people who are doing the business what to do. When this happens, you have high-level managers micromanaging. When this happens, senior people take away the fun part of the business, which was deciding what is best for the organizational unit, and leave the boring part to the organizational units' managers, who are implementing other people's decisions. When this happens, good people leave. When this happens, an entrepreneurial organization begins to die a slow, painful death. This is what happens when the drivers do not understand the operating system of the vehicle they are driving.

How do we build the design philosophy and skill into our way of doing business, developing designers rather than drivers? We begin by encouraging leaders at all levels to help create large degrees of freedom for all our employees. We found that the most appropriate way for the founders to create the greatest degrees of freedom possible in the organization is to:

- Preach the importance of the function of design as part of the work of any leader.
- Explain the principles of design in everything—the whats and the hows.
- Teach the DNAs of the company, including the strategies and critical success factors.
- Explain how the DNA and principles only apply at the ten-thousand-foot level. Below ten thousand feet, the principle of appropriateness takes over. When a system or service is adapted at the ground level, it should be appropriate to the culture, law, mentality, and attitude of the company. This means that design is also problem solving and problem solving is design.
- Give your people the chance to make mistakes in designing and learn by "trying" and error.
- Allow employees to think instead of just repeating the rules of the elders.

The higher you are in a company and the earlier you join a company, the more opportunity you have to participate in the design of the organization. The reason is simple. When there are more tasks than people, you can simply take the initiative to grab the task and do it. With the right philosophy, practical skills, street smarts, and intuition, you will grow a company of designers-cum-drivers who will give you a sustainable competitive advantage over the pure drivers.

24

Managing Change, by Design

Peter Coughlan and Ilya Prokopoff

WE READ everywhere about rapid and constant change and, therefore, the increasing unpredictability of the future. And yet, we have seen little in the way of tools and methods to manage that change effectively and proactively. The tools of traditional business planning start with the assumptions that maintaining the current state is the best strategy and that incremental growth is a satisfactory outcome. What if we can no longer base our future business on what has happened in the past? This essay suggests that organizations might look to tools from the field of design. These tools can help business managers both to get in touch with their customers' (and other stakeholders') unarticulated needs and desires and to intentionally imagine and create futures based on the one thing that seems to remain relatively stable even in times of great change — human behavior. When made a part of an organization's work processes and competencies, the tools enable the organization to embrace change as a normal part of managing their business.

A STORY TO ILLUSTRATE OUR POINT

A recent healthcare client of ours was engaged in long-range planning activities that included the introduction of a multistory patient care tower (to be completed in seven years). Shortly after finalizing their plans for the building, one of the hospital's core specialty groups severed ties to the hospital in order to open up an integrated service facility literally across the street from where this new tower was to be erected. This move, coupled with a drop in the cost

Peter Coughlan, *IDEO*. Ilya Prokopoff, *IDEO*.

of core medical technology, procedural changes that dramatically reduced the required length of stay in a hospital, and shifts in consumer demand and expectations about how care could be delivered, suddenly rendered obsolete any plans based on the hospital's past.

Looking at alternative data from what managers are typically exposed to, they might have seen that the drivers behind this change were evolving requirements for patient care — for example, competitive pressures, technology, and human resource issues. However, the data that management had at their disposal — customer survey and employee satisfaction data — indicated general satisfaction with the services provided by the hospital. The data did not reveal what problems, if any, customers had with the current services, or what they might have preferred if given a choice of services. No amount of examining the past could have prepared hospital leadership for this dramatic turn of events. What could management have looked at to make a better guess about their future? And once it understood its present condition, how could the hospital have come up with an appropriate plan for getting to the future?

TOOLS FOR CHANGE

Below, we describe three tools in the designer's toolbox that we have found effective in helping businesses to manage change. These tools include contextual observation, human-centered frameworks, and rapid prototyping.

Contextual Observation

Effective design (whether incremental or radical) begins with a clear understanding of the problem to be solved. In order to help formulate problem statements, designers look to people's behavior for the data they need. Specifically, designers use observational research methodologies to reveal latent needs that can form the basis of change initiatives. They do this by going out and looking at people engaged in everyday activity. Designers observe, take pictures, ask questions about the here and now. They discover what people specifically like and dislike about their work or play, what pictures they have in their heads about how a process works, how they have invented ways to work around a particular problem, and what ritualistic behavior they engage in during a given activity. In short, they look at what is commonplace and familiar, and they reveal the ways in which it is unique, allowing them to break through existing assumptions and acceptance of things as "the way it's always been done" so that new opportunities for change can be explored.

Some common methods we use to help our clients "see the familiar in unfamiliar ways" include:

- mock journeys, in which we simulate the experience of a customer, or someone else for whom we are designing
- shadowing those involved in a process to note their everyday behaviors, use of tools, communication patterns, and so forth
- expert walk-throughs to quickly understand complex processes
- spatial observations, to absorb the atmosphere of a location, observe behavioral patterns, and look for evidence of everyday workarounds or innovations that may indicate unmet needs
- day-in-the-life surveys to get stakeholders to take note of their own surroundings and behavior

We are always surprised by how difficult it is for managers, who typically have extensive quantitative and qualitative data at their disposal, to "see" their reality because the data have been stripped of the emotional content that forms the basis for the most compelling change initiatives. Giving people a different way of seeing that reality helps them to articulate their unmet needs or desires. For our healthcare client, getting them to shadow a day-in-the-life of a doctor, or to walk in the gown of a patient, gave them a much clearer sense of what was and wasn't working in the system. Seeing data captured from everyday reality (as opposed to data captured from a satisfaction survey) helped them to understand the vast number of opportunities to create new services or to improve existing ones, to retain customers and doctors alike.

Human-centered Frameworks

System-level problems are hard problems to solve. In organizations of any size, people often complain that the organization has "a life of its own," that "change is impossible" in spite of the fact that people can usually identify what is not working. The reason for this is simple: although most systems have evolved over time from something small and simple to something larger and more complex, their growth has not typically been managed in a holistic way. The design of the system is no longer contained in the head of a single individual or group — rather, it is emergent across multiple individuals or groups. Incompatibilities or even conflicts are no one person's or department's responsibility. It is simply that different parts of the same system have been optimized for their own local goals, resulting in silos that are hard or impossible to stitch together seamlessly.

Designers create frameworks so that they can simplify and unify design opportunities in order to conceive of possible futures and make sure that all the parts and pieces that compose these futures are coordinated with one another. Frameworks are powerful because they can be used to generate a coordinated set of ideas or opportunities and later to evaluate the degree to which a current set of offerings satisfies user needs and reflects an organization's intentional view of the future.

Frameworks reintroduce a holistic viewpoint to an organization and allow them to refocus on their reason for being: to provide value to customers, employees, and other stakeholders. For our healthcare client, we developed a framework that consisted of a "patient journey" that helped them to understand that the patient views their experience as a contiguous process, unaware of how the organization is structured to deliver care. For example, patients do not understand why, each time they move to a new location in the hospital, they are asked the same set of questions. From a hospital perspective, redundancy of information collection ensures accuracy and safety (and reflects the reality of nonintegrated IT systems). However, from a patient's perspective, it creates an experience laden with frustration and lack of trust.

Rapid Prototyping

Rapid prototyping helps people to experience a possible future in tangible ways. These include rough physical prototypes of products or environments, or enactments of processes and service experiences, as well as the internal infrastructure and business plans that will be required to deliver them. It allows a very low-risk way of quickly exploring multiple directions before committing resources to the best one. Prototyping is commonly used in design development to explore details of how a product, service, or experience will be manifest. It externalizes the project team's thinking, allowing for quicker convergence and more useful feedback from stakeholders. This feedback is based in the reality of an experience, rather than in an interpretation of a description of that same experience.

When organizations go about developing their strategies, they typically define both the problem statement and a proposed solution at the same time, as a means for getting approval and resources to move forward. Rapid prototyping gives an organization license to explore hunches or directions that may in turn give more clarity to the problem statement. It also helps organizations to continue to be mindful of the possibilities of creating systemic solutions.

Faced with the challenge of improving the dining experience at the hospital, our healthcare client used rapid prototyping to quickly explore ideas that allowed patients and family members to eat whenever they wanted to. One of the ideas that came out of this exploration was a concept for a mobile minibar that could be ordered and stocked appropriately. In the process of testing this idea, the team discovered and resolved issues around ordering, fulfilling, and maintaining the minibar. They discovered that this particular solution affected multiple parts of the system, from patient room design to admissions processes to food service design. A simple prototype allowed the hospital to surface these issues and solve for them all at the same time, resulting in a more unified experience for patients.

INTEGRATING DESIGN AND BUSINESS THINKING

Increasingly, our client organizations come to us expressing a wish to be "more innovative." We interpret this as a request to be better able to face change. While design continues to be seen as a specialized expertise, we have found that the tools of design are learnable and applicable to challenges that business managers face every day. When we couple design *process* experts (with no vested interest in perpetuating the current way of doing things) with business *content* experts (who are looking for ways to think differently about their area of expertise), we create a capacity to envision and realize futures that are both desirable for people and viable for organizations. The challenge remains for business schools to find ways of integrating design thinking into their curricula and for design schools to expand the purview of design to include not only products, services, and experiences, but the organizational means by which they are created and supported.

25

DESIGN THINKING

*The Role of Hypotheses Generation
and Testing*

Jeanne Liedtka

I WILL link design thinking to strategic thinking in business by focusing on the role of hypothesis generation and testing in design thinking and the relevance of such an approach to business practice. In doing so, I pay particular attention to the tension between scientific and artistic thinking in both design and strategy.

DESIGN THEORY

Serious attention to the design process itself is a fairly recent phenomenon. Vladimir Bazjanac (1974) argues that it began in the middle of the twentieth century in tandem with and influenced by developments in the fields of mathematics and systems science:

> All early models of the design process have one thing in common: they all view the design process as a sequence of well defined activities and are all based on the assumption that the ideas and principles of the scientific method can be applied to it. (pp. 5–6)

These early models of design, with their emphasis on "systematic procedures and prescribed techniques," were immediately criticized for the linearity of their processes and for their lack of appreciation for the complexity of design problems.

Rittel (1972) first called attention to what he described as the "wicked nature" of design problems (borrowing the term from Karl Popper). Such problems, Rittel asserted, are ill suited for linear techniques. Wicked problems are

Jeanne Liedtka, *Darden, University of Virginia.*

194   characterized by their level of interconnectedness, by the presence of ampli-
fying loops that produce unintended consequences when interfered with, by
the presence of tradeoffs and conflict among stakeholders, and by the nature
of their constraints. Each formulation of the problem, of which there are many
possible, corresponds to a different solution. Because no one is "optimal," potential solutions are neither true nor false, only good or bad. Strategy is a matter of choice rather than truth. Thus, all solutions are "contestable."

Rittel saw design as a process of argumentation. Through argumentation,
whether as part of a group or solely within the designer's own mind, the designer gained insights, broadened his or her Weltanschauung, and continually
refined the definition of the problem and its attendant solution. Thus, the design process came to be seen as fundamentally concerned with learning and
the search for emergent opportunities, rather than with optimization.

THE ROLE OF HYPOTHESES IN THE DESIGN PROCESS

Hypotheses play a central role in design thinking. Cross (1995), in reviewing a
wide range of studies of design processes in action, notes, "It becomes clear
from these studies that architects, engineers, and other designers adopt a
problem-solving strategy based on generating and testing potential solutions"
(p. 109). Schon (1974) describes design as "a shaping process" in which the situation "talks back" continually and "each move is a local experiment which
contributes to the global experiment of reframing the problem." (p. 94). Thus,
his designer begins by generating a series of creative "what if" hypotheses, selecting the most promising one for further inquiry. This inquiry takes the form
of a more evaluative "if then" sequence, in which the logical implications of
that particular hypothesis are more fully explored and tested. The scientific
method then, with its emphasis on cycles of hypothesis generating and testing
and the acquisition of new information to continually open up new possibilities, remains central to design thinking.

Yet, the nature of "wicked problems," as Rittel points out, makes such trial-
and-error learning problematic. He makes this point from the perspective of
architecture—a building, once constructed, cannot be easily changed. Thus,
design is successful when it creates a virtual world, a "learning laboratory,"
where such mental experiments can be conducted risk free and where invest-
ments in early choices can be minimized. As Schon (1974) points out:

> Virtual worlds are contexts for experiment within which practitioners can suspend
> or control some of the everyday impediments to rigorous reflection-in-action. They
> are representative worlds of practice in the double sense of "practice." And practice
> in the construction, maintenance, and use of virtual worlds develops the capacity
> for reflection-in-action which we call artistry. (p. 162)

Contemporary design theorists, however, have been especially attentive to the areas in which design and science diverge. Buchanan (1992) reprises Herbert Simon's (1969) assertion that the most fundamental difference between the two is that design thinking deals primarily with what *does not yet exist*; scientists deal with explaining what *is*. That scientists *discover* the laws that govern today's reality, but designers *invent* a different future is a common theme in these writings. Designers are, of course, interested in explanations of current reality to the extent that such understanding is essential to the process of executing the new design successfully, but the emphasis remains on the future. Thus, while both methods of thinking are hypothesis-driven, the *design* hypothesis differs from the *scientific* hypothesis. Rather than using traditional reasoning modes of induction or deduction, March (1976) argues that design thinking is *abductive*:

> Science investigates extant forms. Design initiates novel forms. A scientific hypothesis is not the same thing as a design hypothesis . . . . A speculative design cannot be determined logically, because the mode of reasoning involved is essentially abductive. (15, 19)

Abductive reasoning uses the logic of conjecture. Cross borrows from philosopher C. S. Peirce this elaboration of the differences among the modes: "Deduction proves that something must be; induction shows that something actually is operative; abduction merely suggests that something may be." (p. 110). Thus, a capacity for creative visualization — the magician-like ability to "conjure" an image of a future reality that does not exist today — is central to design.[1]

Arnheim (1993) asserts that the image "unfolds" in the mind of the designer as the design process progresses. And that it is, in fact, the unfolding nature of the image that makes creative design possible:

> As long as the guiding image is still developing it remains tentative, generic, vague. This vagueness, however, is by no means a negative quality. Rather it has the positive quality of a topological shape. As distinguished from geometric shapes, a topological shape stands for a whole range of possibilities without being tangibly committed to any one of them. Being undefined in its specifics, it admits distortions and deviations. Its pregnancy is what the designer requires in the search for a final shape. (p. 71)

Thus, the designer begins with what Arnheim calls "a center, an axis, a direction," from which the design takes on increasing levels of detail and sophistication as it unfolds.

The world of business mirrors the world of design in differing from the natural sciences in some important ways. As we have noted, the scientific method seeks to uncover and describe what *is,* while the aim of design is often to envision what *might be,* but is not yet. Applied to the business context, such design thinking seeks to create new possibilities and to choose among them, not merely to solve problems. As such, it is more concerned with purpose than with generalizable "laws" and more dependent upon context than "truth." In this way, design thinking may be more *art*— centrally preoccupied with the process of the design of the artificial — than *science,* the discovery of the "natural."

In business, the wicked nature of strategic problems calls for elements of both our scientific and artistic methods. Because the possibilities for problem definition and solution are unbounded, good hypothesis generation is critical. Because the solution represents invented choice, rather than discovered truth, its contestability affords a major role to argumentation. "Making the case" becomes critical, and the compelling logic coming out of the data-based hypothesis testing process is key. Explaining what *is,* although not the goal of design, is an essential step in developing confidence that the design action taken will actually accomplish the desired purpose. Learning, and the attendant modification of mental models, is necessary for acceptance and implementation. Ultimately, one of the great advantages in applying design thinking to business practice is that it forces us to incorporate both the art *and* the science of hypotheses generation and testing.

NOTE

1. It should be noted that creativity clearly also plays a role in the scientific method. It is, however, creativity in search of alternative explanations, rather than the image of a different future.

REFERENCES

Arnheim, R. 1993. Sketching and the psychology of designing. *Design Issues* 9(2): 15–19.

Bazjanac, V. 1974. Architectural design theory: Models of the design process. In *Basic questions of design theory,* edited by W. Spillers. New York: American Elsevier, pp. 3–20.

Buchanan, R. 1992. Introduction. In *The idea of design,* edited by V. Margolin and R. Buchanan. Cambridge, MA: MIT Press, pp. 10–16.

Cross, N. 1995. Discovering design ability. In *Discovering design,* edited by R. Buchanan and V. Margolin. Chicago: University of Chicago Press, pp. 105–20.

March, L. 1976. The Logic of Design. In *The architecture of form*, edited by L. March. Cambridge, MA: Cambridge University Press.

Rittel, H. 1972. On the planning crisis: Systems analysis of the first and second generations. *Bedrift Sokonomen* 8: 309–96.

Schon, D. 1974. *The reflective practitioner: How professionals think in action*. New York: Basic Books.

Simon, H. 1969. *The sciences of the artificial*. Cambridge, MA: MIT Press.

26

THE ROLE OF CONSTRAINTS

Betty Vandenbosch and Kevin Gallagher

CONSTRAINTS ARE limitations on action. They set boundaries on solutions. Yet, those boundaries have the potential to inspire. Many creativity techniques purport to free people from the constraints they place upon themselves, but in doing so, they set new boundaries within which to reflect. For example, in one creativity technique, participants are asked to think through an analogy or metaphor. Rather than thinking about employees' resistance to change, they think about children's resistance to vegetables. In another, they reverse the problem. Rather than trying to come up with ways to reduce expenses, they list ways to increase them. In both techniques, the idea is to open up people's minds to new ways of thinking about the problem by posing another problem with its own constraints and limitations. Altering our understanding of constraints removes the terror of a blank page. It offers us opportunities for learning about constraints and reinterpreting their meaning. It provides a starting point for exploring possibilities. However, starting from a different place is not the only way to manage constraints.

IDENTIFYING AND EXPLORING CONSTRAINTS

Many design disciplines recognize and accept constraints as fundamental to their processes. Although architects may work very hard to circumvent local planning laws, they recognize that a key component of their skill is their ability to provide creative solutions for their clients' programs, taking many limi-

Betty Vandenbosch, *Weatherhead School of Management, Case Western Reserve University*. Kevin Gallagher, *College of Business, Florida State University*.

tations into consideration. Engineers accept the physical limits of nature. Writers work within the tradition of their chosen literary genres. Poets write haiku or sonnets. An op-ed piece is fifteen hundred words long. Adherence to constraints requires designers to be more creative rather than less, often enabling brilliance or beauty to emerge.

In *The Design of Everyday Things,* Norman (1990) praises constraints and demonstrates how they make it easier for people to use unfamiliar objects. If the bolt only fits into one nut, that's probably the nut it belongs in. Narrowing enables effective design by reducing the potential for error and clarifying the possibilities for action.

In *Zen and the Art of Motorcycle Maintenance,* Pirsig (1974) describes how Phaedrus, the author's alter ego, helped students think of something to write. Rather than open up their options, he closed them down. He had one student write about the upper left-hand brick on the front of the Opera House in Bozeman, Montana. He had others write about their thumbs and one side of a coin. Narrowing enabled expansiveness by providing a starting point and a focus for creating.

LEARNING AS ACTIVELY ADDRESSING CONSTRAINTS

A focus on constraints does not imply acquiescence to them. Rather, it implies sufficient identification and understanding to make choices. What are the constraints? Should they be accepted? Should they be negotiated? Should they be resisted? Should they be ignored? Do they matter? Answers to these questions are only made possible with adequate understanding. Understanding is an outgrowth of learning, which emerges from the interaction of a stimulus and the mind of the learner. Hence, an ability to learn is fundamental to the capacity to focus on and explore the role of constraints.

For most cognitive theorists, individual learning falls along a continuum — from reproductive thought to productive thought (Maier 1945), from assimilation to accommodation (Piaget 1954), from accretion to structuring (Norman 1982), from exploitation to exploration (March 1991).

For example, Maier (1945) describes two strategies for problem solving: reproductive and productive thought. Reproductive thought occurs when people encounter familiar situations. They tend to apply previously successful strategies to deal with them. When they tackle a situation that does not correspond to the rules in their repertoires, they engage in productive thought and develop new rules to deal with it. Productive thought, and in Maier's opinion, learning, occurs when problems, or most of their elements, are new. Learning happens when people are forced to restructure and reshape previous experiences in order to deal with the current situation.

Jean Piaget (1954) describes individual learning as a process of adaptation. Adaptation takes place when an organism is changed as a result of interacting with its environment so that further interactions benefit the organism. Adaptation consists of two interrelated components: assimilation and accommodation. Assimilation is the process by which the elements of the environment are changed in accord with, and are incorporated into, the organism. In accommodation, the organism must adjust itself to environmental elements. Piaget claims both processes interact with each other and uses the analogy of food consumption to describe how they do so. The mouth changes the shape of the food by chewing it in order to assimilate it into the body, but at the same time, the mouth itself changes shape to accommodate the food. In the case of information processing, assimilation incorporates information into existing cognitive structures, while accommodation rearranges, redefines, or develops understanding to interpret and incorporate new or contradictory information (Flavell 1963).

NEGOTIATING THE MEANING OF CONSTRAINTS

Learning is first and foremost the ability to negotiate new meanings.

Wenger 1998, p. 22

Appropriating Wenger's language, an individual can negotiate personal meaning along a continuum from reproductive to productive thought or from accommodation to assimilation. The negotiation of the meaning of constraints fits into the same continuum. Constraints can be challenged or accepted. Even the acknowledgement of what constitutes a constraint is negotiated by the individual. For example, someone from Los Angeles or New York has a vastly different understanding of how much traffic constitutes a constraint than does someone from Boise or Crawford. The negotiation of the meaning of constraints is thereby antecedent to the choices afforded along this same continuum. Constraints can be accepted or challenged, adopted or explored.

How organizations deal with regulatory constraints provides an illustration of the negotiation of meaning that is possible. When an organization faces a regulatory constraint, it has several options. It can attempt to get a variance for the particular situation, it can accept the constraint as it stands, it can lobby to have the constraint changed, or it can work around it. Organizations regularly get tax abatements to locate in particular states or municipalities. The law defining how many containers of what dimensions a long-haul truck may pull has changed several times over the last quarter century, solely because of lobbying by organizations that haul freight or have freight to haul. Urban developers have worked around building height restrictions by creating a market for air rights. Recently, the tool manufacturer Stanley Works decided to move its headquarters to Barbados to avoid American taxes on foreign income. Unfortunately, it ran into another constraint—public opinion.

IMPLICATIONS FOR MANAGEMENT

Although learning is first and foremost an individual activity, the organizational milieu affects the nature and degree of learning it affords. For the most part, constraints are not the purview of individuals. Their meaning and import are explored by groups of people—the sponsor, the users, and the IT department; the client, the stakeholders, and the consultants; or the government, the engineers, and the company's managers. If the organizational environment encourages or demands the exploration of constraints, and provides the time and impetus to do so, it may be that constraints become explicit and well-understood, rather than unspoken and possibly overlooked.

Unlike those in the design disciplines, managers rarely explore constraints. Instead, they expend energy to work around or eliminate them. They talk endlessly about thinking outside the box, rather than taking the time to confront the box. By investigating how other disciplines understand and work with constraints, we may be able to provide insight into how managers might become more attentive to them and learn how to work with them. For example, architects expend a great deal of effort developing the program for a building, making themselves familiar with the building code of the municipality within which they build. Engineers are constantly mindful of the constraints of the materials they use and the laws of nature. Just as they are modeled in linear or integer programming, constraints form a space from which the design must emerge.

Eliyahu Goldratt (1990) believes that in every organization there is a single constraint that inhibits the organization from meeting its goals. He exhorts organizations to find that constraint and then determine how to release it. He also encourages organizations to focus only on the constraint, and not the resources that are not constrained. The Stanley Works example demonstrates the fallacy in this approach. It is very hard to determine the limiting constraint and which constraint deserves the most attention.

In management, the vast majority of constraints are socially constructed, but that doesn't render them any less real or immutable. A constraint can be the willingness with which an individual appropriates new or modified tasks. It can be the date by which a project has to be completed. It can be the government regulation that prohibits an organization from selling an insurance product. Although these are probably more negotiable than the law of gravity,

202   it is an understanding of the degree to which their meanings are negotiable and what options there are for dealing with them that determines the constraint space.

Unlike those found in the physical disciplines, managers' constraints are a dynamic unfolding discovery. Managers cannot always know at the outset of a project those constraints that will be the project's undoing; sometimes constraints develop as a project progresses. For example, users' resistance to a new system may be the result of poorly negotiated expectations. The recursion inherent in designing solutions and finding problems or opportunities is manifested in dealing with constraints—what deals with one set of constraints may raise another. Those managers who have the insight and patience to recognize and accommodate or assimilate constraints dynamically may well be the managers who succeed most often.

We propose that managers can learn from those who confront constraints in other disciplines. They can learn how engineers, architects, physicists, and artists identify and negotiate the meanings of constraints and how they decide to challenge them, accept them, or leverage them in the design process. By learning from other disciplines, we may develop new mechanisms to help managers think of their work as designing around and through the constraints they inevitably face.

REFERENCES

Flavell, J. H. 1963. *The developmental psychology of Jean Piaget.* New York: VanNostrand.

Goldratt, E. 1990. *The theory of constraints.* New York: North River Press Publishing.

Maier, N. R. F. 1945. Reasoning in humans: III. The mechanisms of equivalent stimuli and of reasoning. *Journal of Experimental Psychology* 35: 349–60.

March, J. G. 1991. Exploration and exploitation in organizational learning. *Organization Science* 2(1): 71–87.

Norman, D. A. 1982. *Learning and memory.* San Francisco: W.H. Freeman & Co.

———. 1990. *The design of everyday things,* New York: Doubleday.

Piaget, J. 1954. *The construction of reality in the child.* New York: Basic Books.

Pirsig, R. M. 1974. *Zen and the art of motorcycle maintenance.* New York: William Morrow.

Wenger, E. 1998. *Communities of practice: Learning, meaning and identity,* Cambridge, England: Cambridge University Press.

27

On the Design of Creative Collaboration

Paul Kaiser

STRUCTURE

A group's communications structure replicates itself in the structure of
the works they create together.

Conway's Law

This loose paraphrase (and possible misreading) of Conway's Law, which
I came upon ten years ago in the classic *Mythical Man-Month* handbook,
struck me with the force of a revelation at the time and has been borne out
ever since (triumphantly or disastrously) in the course of my many artistic
collaborations.

Again and again I've seen that when communication breaks down between
people creating something together, what they end up with is as distorted and
misshapen as the pattern of their interchanges. This pattern is itself a kind of
involuntary design, and in it you can make out the disproportioning effects of
distance, incomprehension, and ego.

CAGE/CUNNINGHAM

A paradoxical and extreme solution to Conway's Law clarifies the communications structure by annulling it. In the approach devised by avant-garde performance artists John Cage and Merce Cunningham in the early 1950s and
still used by Cunningham to this day, the choreographer, composer, and visual

Paul Kaiser, *Digital Artist.*

artist all create their parts of a dance in complete independence right up to the very last minute, uniting their work only at its premiere on the stage.

Ostensibly, their reason for adopting such an off-center approach was to escape the limiting preconceptions of the conscious mind. Just as important, I believe, was a second unstated motive: to avoid any clashes of ego. When you consider that Cage and Cunningham often worked with visual artists of such renown as Robert Rauschenberg, Jasper Johns, and Andy Warhol—none of whom were known to be shrinking violets accustomed to taking direction from others—you see that this Zen-like approach of collaborating through noncollaboration has additional merits!

All this was confirmed in my own collaboration with Cunningham, when Shelley Eshkar and I designed the visual décor in the form of digital projections for a dance entitled BIPED (1999). The random juxtapositions of projections, dance, and music made for the most wonderful counterpoint, which has since been much acclaimed. The only personal and artistic antagonisms we encountered were with the lighting designer, whose role was not properly defined in this scheme and who therefore tried unsuccessfully to augment our projections with his lighting.

The Cage/Cunningham model may be too extreme for many cases, but rather than reject it out of hand, it's often possible to modify it to your needs. In creating the groundbreaking opera Einstein on the Beach, theater artist Robert Wilson and composer Philip Glass devised an overall structure of acts, durations, and themes together, but then proceeded to work out their parts independently. Thus, although neither music nor staging had to subordinate itself to illustrating the other, they both addressed and embodied the same overarching ideas.

MIND READING

At the other extreme comes a form of collaboration bordering on mind reading. This demands close proximity, intense communication, and patient tolerance for anarchy, and it functions best after years of working together.

I have enjoyed two or three such collaborations and find they've always provided an odd spectacle to anyone witnessing them from outside. Our comments and suggestions to each other can be oblique and even downright rude —why make the effort of forming a complete explanatory sentence or paragraph, when the first few words will do, or even a grunt or upraised eyebrow? If, in the event of disagreement, it ever comes down to a question of who's in charge, the answer is a little unnerving: it's the piece itself that gives us our orders, telling us how to bring it into being. We don't always understand these

orders, it would seem, so no matter how elaborately we may have worked out
our plans and designs, we cast them aside in a flash if we sense they have
derailed.

CONCEPTUAL BLINDNESS

People cling to their own ideas. When they create something new, they'd like
their own ideas to prevail. Although some of this may be put down to ego, there
may be something else at work here, a kind of conceptual blindness. Possessed
by their own vision of the world, they simply can't see any other way of looking at it.

I mean this literally. And to make this literal truth plain to see, I created a
piece for San Francisco's Exploratorium Museum called *Inkblot Projections*. A
Rorschach-like inkblot comes easily enough if you splatter ink on a piece of
paper, and then blot it by folding it in half to form a bisymmetrical abstraction.
When you hold up the resulting image, you and everyone around you will always start seeing things in it. The trick is, you won't be seeing the same things.
Where you see a mother's face, someone else sees a lunar landscape, while another sees a merry-go-round, and a third a Petri dish — the variations are amazing. But more so is the fact that once you've interpreted the image your way,
it's really hard to make it out the way someone else has, even if he or she explains it to you. You are conceptually blind to this new composition because
you've already composed it yourself; before you can start to see it anew, you
have to decompose it back down to its abstract elements.

In *Inkblot Projections*, animation aids you in this de- and re-composition.
For each of five inkblots, five different voices guide you through distinct ways
of interpreting that image, with the corresponding blots highlighting in the
simplest possible way as they're mentioned. What results is a fantastic symphony of contrasting voices, stories, and visions.

All of which illustrates another aspect of collaboration, the only point of
which is to create what you could not conceivably envision yourself.

INTERACTION

Typically, one thinks of collaboration as being between human beings. But I
believe that in a slightly different sense you also collaborate with your materials, onto which you do not simply impose your vision, but rather discover it
there. To take a stock example, Michelangelo felt he *found* his forms in his
stone, then set them free in his sculptures.

Setting forms free brings to mind a striking experience of mine. For an in-

206   stallation piece called *Loops* (2001), a collaboration that started out among people—Shelley Eshkar, Marc Downie, and myself—eventually turned into a collaboration with the software simulation we had created together.

Here's how it worked. Having motion-captured the intricate dance of Merce Cunningham's hands, we had a data set of forty-eight points (twenty-four for each forearm) that tracked their position in time and space. Building on Downie's artificial intelligence and real-time graphics research at MIT's Media Lab, we gave each of these points a limited sort of autonomy and intention. For example, each point could decide from moment to moment what kind of hierarchy it should join—should it connect to other points according to the anatomy of the hand, or should it instead link to corresponding points on the other hand, forming a sort of cat's cradle?

These and a myriad other decisions gave rise to an emergent structure that was never the same from one run to the next. For our part, we could keep refining that structure as we elaborated our artwork, but this refinement was more in the nature of tuning than of sculpting.

The responsive and even intelligent quality of our "material" (i.e., the program itself) deepened my sense of tools and materials as active collaborating agents. Who can doubt that this sort of man/machine collaboration will only intensify in the future?

WORDS

Talking something into existence is my phrase for how projects come about. This talking may simply be talking to myself, or rather to my selves, because there seems to be a lively process of mental interlocution as questions are put to and answers provided by different parts of my mind. Or it may start as a conversation between collaborators, who act in a similar way. In either case, the project gains solidity and momentum just through this magic of description. Before long, we start treating the project as a real thing, even if we have taken no practical steps toward its realization.

Its first material existence is likely to be only a little less insubstantial, for it usually emerges as visual conjecture in the form of sketches and notes on paper or whiteboard. These tend to spark still more ideas creatively, but they also serve another function: that of persuasion. For a project needs to become real not only to its creators, but also to others outside that close circle, such as the potential supporters or audience. The proverbial napkin sketch sometimes does the trick, but more often, these notes and sketches must be elaborated into a pitch or a proposal or even into publicity. Which can turn us over to the flip side of this process, which is:

Talking something to death. Although this phrase usually means to prolong the discussion of something past any point of possible action (certainly a danger even in creative work), here I mean it in a somewhat different sense. Such a thing as a grant proposal usually demands a greater certainty and exactitude than is really present yet, and so, despite the best of intentions, it helps bring about a pompous insincerity that can kill the underlying creative impulse.

Worse, it can even bypass that creative impulse altogether, as one sees all too often in works created only to look good on paper. The caption and illustration in the catalog, Web site, or newspaper play a far greater role in the project's perceived success than the actual experience it engenders. As Shelley Eshkar has pointed out to me, the very method employed in art and design schools — the "crit," or critique — provides inadvertent training for this kind of sham because it's the student's performance in explaining and presenting his or her work that often speaks louder than the work itself. "Speaks" is the right verb here because by this point, it's all a matter of words, even though many of the best works are practically mute.

STANDARDS

So how do you design creative collaborations? How do you foster them in institutions? What objective criteria or standards could and should be created?

I don't know. For all the reasons above, I'm dubious of any ironclad standards. I remember a conversation with a gifted Berkeley professor, who told me that demand for entry into his PhD research team was so competitive that they selected only those candidates with the highest academic records and the test scores to match. I pointed out that such criteria would have excluded many a worthy soul, including Albert Einstein.

It was Einstein who once cautioned us to make things "as simple as possible, but not simpler." So as we look into designing management systems, we might articulate some general principles or guidelines without precluding all sorts of exceptions and special cases. The most powerful creative collaborations have been pretty idiosyncratic, and though they have sometimes coalesced into productive institutions (as in the Bauhaus and the Black Mountain schools), these have tended to last but a short time and, what's more, to have resisted many efforts to recreate or reproduce them elsewhere.

But if creativity tends to be anarchic, its great virtue is that it can spring up in the most unexpected places, even from what seems to be barren soil. We just have to keep our eyes open so that when we see it, we recognize and encourage it.

28

DESIGNING THE AUSTRALIAN TAX SYSTEM

Alan Preston

THE AUSTRALIAN tax system forms part of the human-made, rather than the natural, environment—hence, of its nature, it should be an intentionally designed artifact. It comprises a number of tax bases (for example, income tax, goods and services tax, fringe benefits tax, and excises) applied at the federal level of government (so excludes taxes levied by our states and territories).

Revenue authorities typically have a small number of core functions related to their respective tax systems: for the Australian Taxation Office (ATO), these functions have comprised revenue collection and protection, revenue distribution, tax law interpretation, and tax system design. "Tax design" as used here comprehends the design of tax policy, tax law, and supporting administration (for example, collection systems, tax forms, paper-, voice- and e-based information) to implement that policy.

BEGINNING THE INTEGRATED TAX DESIGN JOURNEY

Recent years have witnessed a spate of reforms to the tax system, putting pressure on our existing tax design capability. Responding to a review of Australia's business tax system (*Ralph Review*, 1998–99), the ATO initiated in December 1999 a project called Integrated Tax Design.

Professor Richard Buchanan (2001), serving as the project's chief design mentor, offered us the following starting point:

Design is
  a. the human power
  b. of conceiving, planning, and realizing

Alan Preston, *former Second Commissioner of Taxation, Australian Taxation Office.*

c. products that serve human beings

d. in the accomplishment of any individual or collective purpose.

His definition thereby focused us on the agency, purpose, outcome, and scope of design. We began to progressively develop our own substance to his notion of (paraphrasing somewhat) the architectonic art of design as a systematic discipline of integrative thinking, of deliberation preceding making (Buchanan, 1995b).

DESIGN AGENCY: HUMAN POWER

What did the element of agency mean for the Integrated Tax Design Project? We noted the Buchanan observation that "the essential humanism of design lies in the fact that human beings determine what the subject matter, processes and purposes of design shall be. These are not determined by nature, but by our decisions" (Buchanan, 1995b, p. 55).

We agreed very early on that managing as designing would stand or fall on our people — on our design culture, on the core competencies of staff, and on our capacity to operate with disciplined creativity in an environment the essential ambiguity of which demands skills of synthesis, not just of analysis.

So the rebuilding of our design culture has involved a range of initiatives with our people, including conferences, skilling programs, publication of how-to guides, and an emphasis on a collaborative, team-based design ethos.

DESIGN PURPOSE: CONCEIVING, PLANNING, AND REALIZING

The element of purpose has been a rich vein to mine in developing an integrated tax design capability. At a broad process level we found we lacked articulation of the end-to-end design process that must link policy formulation to its execution in both law design and administrative design. Without it, we had no prospect of managing the tax design practice well — or of leading the development of an integrated tax design (ITD) capability.

To that end, a key conceptual construct has been the ITD Process Framework (Figure 28.1). Colloquially referred to as "The Stacker," it sets the strategic context for each tax design project proceeding concurrently, each represented by a separate disk. Stacked vertically, the disks are supported by people, product, and process pillars and are concentrically arranged around a system-in-use axis representing the current state of the Australian tax system. The pillars and axis are embedded in a foundational base representing our constitutional system of government.

The process cycle to be followed by each tax design project (disk of The

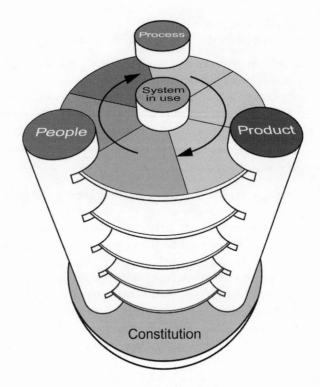

FIGURE 28.1   The ITD process framework ("The Stacker")

Stacker) is represented by a second foundational model known as "The Wheel" (Figure 28.2). The Wheel symbolizes the operational design capabilities — such as methodology, Quality Assurance (QA) processes, and decision gateways — to be applied in a generic way to each tax design project. It provides a simplified framework for design integration on the one hand and for progressively more detailed subdivision of process on the other. It comprises six overlapping stages — formulating intent, creating a design blueprint, designing products, building products, testing the user pathway, and implementing change — and expressly recognizes that tax design rarely follows a linear progression and is a process both multifaceted and inherently unpredictable.

In the Buchanan definition, design purpose also juxtaposes thought and action: conceiving and planning on the one hand and realizing, or making, on the other. Our existing fragmented, sequential design practices had combined with the dominant "doing" character of our culture to emphasize the making of individual products at the expense of forethought in design. Almost universally, design projects proceeded in the hands of separated subteams without

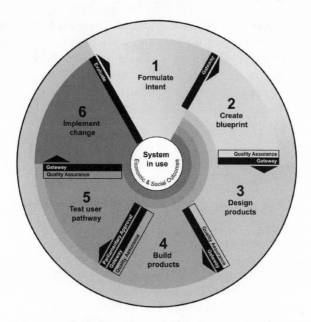

Interdisciplinary, user-centered, codesigned

FIGURE 28.2   The ITD process cycle ("The Wheel")

benefit of an overall design blueprint, critically reducing the scope for achieving coordinated design outcomes. A key contribution of the ITD Project, via The Wheel, has been to insist on the development of design blueprints following an initial clarification and sharing of policy intent and, at subsequent gateways in The Wheel, to require QA against those blueprints.

DESIGN OUTCOME: PRODUCTS THAT SERVE HUMAN BEINGS

The definitional element for design outcome created a strong resonance that has amplified itself throughout the ATO tax design practice. Design mediates policy intent and user needs via the making of products. In practice, we found that it was not only the nature of policy intent that we had not adequately understood: our understanding of both user needs and our product range and strategy was even more sorely deficient.

In concert with a long-standing dominance of the revenue collection and protection function, our tax design practice had been too inward-looking, too closed off from user needs, reinforcing community perceptions of an ATO-centric design practice.

Part of the response must be a much greater willingness to consult throughout the design process, and the current government has committed itself to that outcome in recently announced changes to tax design responsibilities. But an important part of the response must also be the incorporation of professional user-centered design competencies into our design practice. The ATO has made significant progress in this area through its "Listening to the Community" initiative.

DESIGN SCOPE: THE ACCOMPLISHMENT OF COLLECTIVE PURPOSE

The element of scope in the definition highlighted some thorny issues for the ITD capability. In particular, how should we define the collective purpose of the Australian tax system and how are we to measure its degree of accomplishment?

Regarding the first issue, Richard Buchanan (1995a, p. 10) observes that the design of complex systems or environments has evolved to reflect "more consciousness of the central idea, thought, or value that expresses the unity of any balanced and functioning whole."

To focus that consciousness, the ITD Project has defined the role of *pathway custodian* for major tax regimes that affect key groups of users. The pathway custodian is charged with capturing and holding the evolving vision for the defined group of users and ensuring that implementation takes place in accordance with the design blueprint and faithfully delivers on policy intent. Above all, the pathway custodian role deliberately emphasizes design leadership from a user's perspective.

As for the second issue, measuring the degree or quality of accomplishment of collective purpose in designing the tax system is no less challenging. Many hands are involved in both formulating and executing policy intent. The interactive nonlinearity between intent and execution further muddies the waters of tax system design. Since most design measures also involve delivery of numerous products across all our product families, in essence our search for quality must again focus on the unity of a balanced and functioning whole.

Although there is a long way to go on the quality front, we have instituted the mechanism of independent reviews of design implementation at appropriate stages of The Wheel, particularly to assess the quality of implementation of policy intent. As an accompanying measure, we have designated a senior leader to have an overarching design integration role, ensuring that all tax design projects are complying with the requirements of integrated tax design. We have also begun preliminary work on quality concepts specific to our individual product families (tax code, interpretation, information, transactional, and compliance).

MEASURING OUR PROGRESS

The Australian taxation system is not yet what could be described — in consistently positive terms — as an intentionally designed artifact. But an intent to see that outcome is hardening. The notion that there is a systematic and integrative discipline of design able to be harnessed to collective purpose is gaining hold. We have accepted that no off-the-shelf design solutions are possible — the ATO must fashion and sustain its own capability. Fledgling communities of practice around design leadership, design facilitation, information design, user research, and business process simulation are creating and sharing the knowledge on which that capability is being built. Furthermore, strong organizational impetus is being given to shifting the tenor of design from "inside out" to "outside in," resulting in products that are easier, cheaper, and more personalized for specific market segments. Richard Buchanan has noted that "design is continually evolving, and the range of . . . areas where design thinking may be applied continues to expand" (Buchanan, 1995b, pp. 25). In Australia, we are rather excited that one of the foundational systems in a democratic society has become a new area of application.

REFERENCES

Buchanan, R. 1995a. Wicked problems in design thinking. In *The idea of design: A design issues reader*, edited by V. Margolin and R. Buchanan. Cambridge, MA: MIT Press.
———. 1995b. Rhetoric, humanism and design. In *Discovering design*, edited by R. Buchanan and V. Margolin. Chicago: University of Chicago Press.
———. 2001. Design research and the new learning. *Design Issues* XVII, No. 4, Fall: 3–23.

29

Persuasive Artifacts

Sten Jönsson

HOW SHOULD one go about design work that involves many kinds of experts and more than one principal? Obviously, arguments for a design solution will have to appeal to multiple and contradictory values and there will be multiple communities to persuade. This is the situation in the car industry where new models are increasingly developed in alliances—if not between companies (the patterns of ownership are becoming increasingly interconnected), then between brands—and with increasing participation of specialized subcontractors. There will be too many voices and too few members who can help integrate the fragments into a persuasive "gestalt." The problem will grow with the increase in specialized knowledge applied to the task. The suggestion to work out a more detailed specification of the design task is not a solution because it would only move the problem one step away from the launch date. Because values change, early specification is likely to become obsolete before it is realized. A design of premium quality thus has to be worked out in dialogue with knowledgeable people. The "customer" does not seem to be a very good partner—except, maybe, in the case of architects, but even then, imagination is too limited. Frank O. Gehry told us that when professors were asked to describe their ideal future office in a new academic building, they invariably described their current office. And in the car industry, the saying among designers is "If you ask the customer, he will want to have last year's model!" How can a dialogue on premium design be maintained against such inhibiting, institutionalized structures? First, there is a need to jolt the participants out of their

Sten Jönsson, *Göteborg Research Institute, Göteborg University*.

ties to conventional standards, and then there is a need to keep the design process open to influences from the outside.

Frank Gehry talked about using *"schreck* models" for the purpose of getting people off track and inducing them to apply new perspectives. These *schreck* models are monsters that will force articulation of preferred dimensions that in turn can lead to further questions, thus starting a new dialogue. Ina Wagner, drawing on Latour, used the concept "persuasive artifacts" to denote communication objects that "carry conviction for the design of a particular solution, invite others into a dialogue, stimulate their imagination . . . ."

The problem with those persuasive artifacts that we produce to do work for us is that we lose control over their meaning once we have made them public. This has been demonstrated by the latest development of speech act theory under the influence of Latour's ideas concerning "actants" (artifacts that act upon/with/for us). Early speech act theory (Austin, Searle) focused on whether the speaker had succeeded in producing the intended speech act. The norms and conventions of language posed certain requirements for an utterance to be understood as a promise. But critiques such as that of Derrida said the very presence of conventions can be used for deception. An "ironic wink" can turn the conventional meaning of an utterance upside down and thereby nullify it, but it will not reveal what the speaker is really up to. It will leave a zone of ambiguity to be penetrated by the hearer. This means that the speaker has lost control over the meaning of his or her own utterance. The speaker has created a communicative situation and the hearer goes to work making sense of it. Cooren (2000) uses Greimas's (1987) semio-narrative model to analyze how this is or can be done. The claim is that the hearer makes sense of an utterance by placing it in relation to a narrative form. If the utterance contributes to the narrative, it makes sense. The canonical form of a narrative has four phases:

- "Manipulation" (which initiates the narrative that somebody "has to do" or "wants to do" something)
- "Competence" (which makes the actor "able to do" or "know how to do" something)
- "Performance" (the act of "doing" something)
- "Sanction" (which recognizes a performance with, for instance, a reward)

An utterance can be fitted into any one of these phases and each phase can, in turn, have subnarratives. This canonical form is universal, but, in the particular instance, the hearer will select the narrative to use, and even if the speaker can influence the choice, there will always be the zone of ambiguity mentioned above. This is akin to what Bruner (1986) calls "subjunctivity," the

216   organizing property of a narrative to leave the meaning somewhat undetermined and to invite others to contribute.

Participation in the dialogue then means to participate in the coproduc-
tion of a narrative as an organization of differences that will give a reasonably
joint meaning to the project under discussion. A persuasive artifact induces
participants to embark on the mission to coproduce the narrative that makes
sense of that artifact!

OBSERVATIONS OF PREMIUM PRODUCT DESIGN IN CONTEXT

In our research we want to know how competent people accomplish what they
do in their area of competence. It is not likely that we can achieve this through
interviews. Direct observation is required in order to have a referent in interpretation and coding. This is the argument of ethnomethodologists like
Garfinkel (1967) and Sacks (1992). We do not want to test whether the product
developers work the way we think they should, according to our theories. We
also do not want to avoid being too influenced by our own theories when
we interpret or code the data we collected from the field. For these reasons, we
want to elicit the help of the participants themselves in interpretation. This
has been accomplished by first video recording project management meetings
and editing short sequences from the recorded meetings. These sequences
have been played back to participants individually with the question "What is
going on here?" Their comments have been audio recorded and transcribed.
These recordings, and the comments on them, provide the main basis for
identification of communication issues. A large number of interviews and
measures of work climate on three occasions over a three-year period provide
background information.

Here I choose to focus on the observed effects on communication in the
product development team of a contradiction between brand values: how
members deal with noise (a quality variable) caused by a priority being given
to "joy of driving." Space forces me to be brief.

After a series of strategic initiatives in the 1980s and 1990s oriented toward
intensified product development, Volvo decided to "upgrade" its portfolio of
car models to compete directly with the German cars. Hence the stress on
"premium." This meant that "joy of driving," "distinct and attractive design,"
and "ownership experience" were added to the previous set of core values
"safety, quality, and environment." Our study followed the installation of
turbo engines and low profile tires in the smaller S/V 40 models for 1998 and
the subsequent development aiming at the U.S. market in 1999. The problem
is that when you increase the "joy of driving" by increasing speed and "sporti-

ness" you also increase noise — road noise as well as wind noise. These consequences were expected, so there was a noise expert on the development team.
"Properties" was one of the functional managers in the project who gathered
in the Project Management Group (PMG) meeting for half a day every second week to follow up the status of the project and make decisions on proposed solutions to outstanding design problems. The project was located away
from Volvo headquarters in Holland at the joint venture production plant with
Mitsubishi. The context for the project was rather complex due to the fact that
the new car was built on Mitsubishi's Carisma platform (modified to reach
Volvo safety standards but still focused on common parts to gain economies of
scale) and that production was outsourced to the joint venture NedCar. The
reader may imagine the amount of negotiation with outside parties added to
this project on top of the traditional problems with interfering functional departments (cf. Womack et al. 1990) and with suppliers. Here we are focusing
on contradictions between brand values.

The PMG meetings are long, intensive meetings and the group is large,
about twenty-five people, because of the philosophy developed at Volvo to
achieve coordination by keeping many members well informed about all aspects of the project. The consequence is that meetings tend to become semi-
nars rather than decision-making occasions. The meetings may therefore be
inefficient, as most respondents complained. To reduce the problem, the project had a Technical Management Group (TMG) meeting on the afternoon
before the PMG meeting to take care of the more "seminar-like" issues.

Video-recorded episodes, some involving noise consequences, from the
PMG meetings have been replayed to participants individually, and their responses to the question "What is going on here?" have been audio-taped and
transcribed. The episode itself and about fifteen interpretations of it by participants have been analyzed. Two common factors emerge: (1) conflicts between core values initiate discussion on responsibility, and (2) these discussions tend to move members toward the periphery of the group. One such
episode is summarized here (forgive the brevity):

> The noise expert had driven his test car at high speed on the German autobahn and
> discovered a wind noise probably stemming from the trim molding around the
> windshield and/or sun roof. He had brought this quality problem up in yesterday's
> TMG meeting. The discussion there had focused on fixing the trim molding and
> that was the task of the "Exterior" lead engineer. In the PMG meeting, the project
> leader, who was not present at the TMG meeting, questioned whether this be-
> longed to the project. It was a problem for the Quality department because it was
> the geometry of the base car that was the root of the problem. The counterargument
> was that it was the high speed that caused the noise and it was strategic because cus-
> tomers buying the turbo version are likely to drive fast. Anyway, there was a simple

solution (that in fact had already been initiated by Quality) and that was to fix the trim molding better. Now Exterior was anxious to define the problem as a fixing-the-trim-molding. The noise expert commented that he felt let down by the project leader saying that when you bring up strategic issues like this one, people should take it seriously and initiate a proper study of the sources and not jump at simple solutions. People will not want to bring issues up if they are ignored like this (colleagues indicated that he should have known that Quality was already at work on this problem). It was concluded that the noise expert lost position in the team in this episode (centrifugal moves).

Other episodes, all with their unique situatedness have been analyzed to show how speakers lose or gain position in the team

Even if these situations are never clear-cut due to the complexity of the specific embeddedness of the project, I claim that a common factor, when the project deals with conflicts between brand values, is that member positions in the team shift. It is a matter of moving toward a more peripheral position because of failure to assume or not being given responsibility. In another set of episodes where the project faced constraints from the environment (cost reviews or time schedule changes), it was found that the team tended to band together in the fight for the integrity of the project and members who stood up for the project could gain position (centripetal moves).

There was little reference to the brand values (implicitly taken for granted) in argumentation, but there were these gains and losses in position (or social capital). This agrees with a theory of membership work as presented by Munro (1996), which consists of two aspects: identity work and alignment.

In order to be a (competent) member of the team, we have to have a role in the team as a constructive contributor that is recognized by the others. We work out an identity in the context of the team and measure our success in terms of centrality in the group. Then we are trusted to speak on behalf of the group and make binding commitments. A member who loses face will be under observation. This seems to be a strong driving force in premium product design projects. The tool for this gaining of membership is demonstration of commitment to the common quest by the presentation of artifacts and arguments that are "aligned" to that quest.

A first requirement for this to happen is that the common quest is articulated and the aligning member has an opportunity to contribute. The articulated common quest is a narrative under construction. It provides the context (ground) against which the contemplated contribution (figure) is given meaning—by the proposer as well as by the members of the team. Another aspect of the articulated narrative is that it helps members avoid misunderstanding because they will work out "implicature" (Grice 1967) from this coproduced narrative. Sensemaking may thus start from common ground.

Manipulation	Competence	Performance	Sanction
• wanting to do	• being able to do	• doing	• recognition of
• having to do	• knowing how to do		performance

FIGURE 29.1   Canonical form of a narrative schema (Cooren 2000)

It remains to account for how the narrative is coproduced by team members, and the first requirement is to abandon the speaker's intention as the starting point. The speaker goes "public" with a speech act and is exposed to the risk of "misinterpretation." Cooren (2000) points to the fact that utterances are actions in the sense that they have narrative form. He adopts the semio-narrative theory of Greimas (1987) to provide a canonical form of a narrative and adds the idea of "actant" (Callon 1986). Utterances of two kinds are required — utterances describing *a state* and those describing *doing* — to arrive at a canonical form of a narrative schema as depicted in Figure 29.1.

This schema depicts speech acts as action cast in a narrative, project shape. When we understand each other's speech acts in this way, it is only natural that we shape our contributions to the exchange in alignment with, or in opposition to, that narrative. An utterance produces a communicative situation that links people together, via an object (the text), that is, somebody is addressing somebody else. This link is formed when the text does something to the recipient. In this way, the recipient *attributes* what the text is giving to her by relating the text to other texts in forming a reasonable interpretation (never certain). These production/attribution dimensions determine the types of transformations that are implied. To each of these types of acts can be coupled ideal conditions of satisfaction (like sincerity). Next, we turn to rhetoric to identify the two strategies (liaison and dissociation) we use to make people accept our discursive objects, how we make our artifacts persuasive.

Through rhetorical devices (or silent rhetoric like a binding contract), my narrative may get inserted in your narrative, and I will give a contribution to your project if you accept such an insertion. Such a mechanism is possible if we can mobilize the missing link, the instrument that is used in accomplishing the narrative. Here Cooren (2000) has already laid the groundwork by separating the text from the speaker and pointing to the text as "actant" (Callon 1986). If we look at the contribution (submission) to the project (mission) as an actant we can also see that it is quite possible to work under a mission (alignment) without being totally committed to all its goals (like the academic who submits a paper to a journal). If, however, a participant wants to link

220   his/her identity to the project (e.g., for career reasons) membership work is the central aspect. Then we could measure accomplishments in terms of position shifts in the team. Thus, we are likely to find varying degrees of identification with the project among participants in premium product development.

REFERENCES

Bruner, J. 1986. *Actual minds, possible worlds*. Cambridge, MA: Harvard University Press.

Callon, M. 1986. Some elements of a sociology of translation: The domestication of the scallops and the fisherman of St. Brieuc Bay. In *Power, action and belief*, edited by J. Law. London: Routledge & Kegan Paul, pp. 196–233.

Cooren, F. 2000. *The organizing property of communication*. Amsterdam/Philadelphia: Benjamins.

Garfinkel, H. 1967. *Studies in ethnomethodology*. Englewood Cliffs, NJ: Prentice-Hall.

Greimas, A. J. 1987. *On meaning. Selected writings in semiotic theory*. London: Francis Pinter.

Grice, P. 1967/1989. *Studies in the way of words*. Cambridge, MA: Harvard University Press.

Munro, R. 1996. Alignment and identity work: The study of accounts and accountability. In *Accountability: power, ethos, and the technologies of managing*, edited by R. Munro and J. Mouritsen. London: International Thomson Business Press.

Sacks, H. 1992. *Lectures on conversation*. Vols. I–II, edited by G. Jefferson. Oxford: Blackwell.

Womack, J. P., D. T. Jones, and D. Roos. 1990. *The machine that changed the world*. New York: Macmillan.

30

DESIGNING OF WHAT?
WHAT IS THE DESIGN STUFF MADE OF?

Kalle Lyytinen

DESIGN IS defined in *Webster's New World Dictionary* (1978) as "(1) to make preliminary sketches, sketch a pattern or an outline for; plan, (2) to plan, carry, esp. by artistic arrangement or skillful way, (3) to form plans in the mind, contrive, (4) to plan to do, purpose; intent, (5) to intend or set apart for some purpose." The definition carves out design as a human activity with the following elements: (a) it has an inherent purposefulness (items 4, 5); (b) it is cognitive and anticipatory in its content and oriented toward the future (items 3, 1); (c) it demands a certain level of proficiency in getting it done (item 2); and (d) it involves often, though not necessarily, a rational moment of analysis, reflection, and reasoning to develop its anticipation (item 5). The challenge — and the beauty — of the discourse about design is its generality. Any activity counts as design as long as it involves an intentional element and is not habitual adaptation; it orients us toward shaping a future world in the form of an artifact through cognitive engagement; it interacts with other artifacts, including sketches or patterns; it relies upon analytic procedures of tearing apart the artifact in its environment; and it demonstrates skillful accomplishment based on experience and/or theoretical (abstract) models. Such activities span a wide range from architecture, policy, management, computer engineering, software and industrial "design"[1] to graphics design, or even marketing campaigns. Most scholars in these disparate discourses would agree on some or all of the features that provide a family resemblance of design as a basis for thinking about and designing design. This brings together design discourses in or-

Kalle Lyytinen, *Weatherhead School of Management, Case Western Reserve University.*

der to find "patterns," to generalize across situations and styles, and to discuss the cognitive dimensions of design.

The relative importance of each of the listed elements of design varies from one context to another. Industrial design emphasizes a skillful and innovative interaction with artifacts, while computer engineering, software, or management discourses highlight in their own peculiar ways the importance of model-based cognitive reasoning and analytical processes. They also integrate design into a larger context of choice and evaluation (management) or production and/or construction of novel artifacts (computer engineering, software). Many breakthroughs in design are outcomes of questioning and challenging this view and bringing new angles and voices to the debate—for example, how much design is really anticipatory and how much is ongoing adaptation when situations talk "back," or to what extent does design embed intentional purpose at the start and to what extent is it narrated after the fact, and so on. This is all good as it enables us to share interpretations and ideas, learn from others' experiences, and expand our world. At the same time, increased digitalization and model-based cognition permeate all realms of human activity. This has radically improved anticipatory capabilities, broken down walls of complexity and uncertainty, and expanded terrains that can be "designed." For example, notions of organizational design have emerged only during the last thirty years although the actual organizing activity dates back to the first tribal societies. Likewise, the idea that knowledge "creation and dissemination" can be designed has only become *le mot du jour* during the last decade. In principle, it looks like everything *can* be designed and therefore *should* be designed.

In this short essay I will not argue against the sort of design imperialism included in the above analysis as some corners of postmodernism would do. Expansion of design space reflects the ethos of modernity and its very idea that reason forms a solid (and only) basis for organizing and improving the human condition.[2] Instead, I will engage in a much more modest analysis and play with the idea that design is not just one type of human activity, as may be falsely inferred from the above general characterization of design, but a family of activities with their distinct features. In fact, creating illusions of one idea of design is dangerous: it hides important differences in many interventions into the future world. Consequently, my main point is that design stuff (i.e., design ontology) can be and is *different*, and accordingly, the constraints, theories, and/or processes that design draws upon by necessity vary. The recognition of such differences is essential in understanding design and designing for design.

My discussion draws upon discourses around information system design. The reasons for choosing this area are twofold. First, I have been actively engaged in these discourses for nearly two decades (Hirschheim et al. 1995; Lyyti-nen 1987) and this short essay offers a novel occasion for reflection. Second, information system design is an interesting context to analyze design as it embraces both technical and social aspects of design and its design stuff is always up for grabs because no consensus exists among communities as to what counts as information system design. On the one hand, it forms an environment for symbolic intervention in the form of semiotic engineering — the design of signs that gets stored, transferred, and processed by the computer. On the other hand, it forms a physical/engineering intervention in the form of designing a computer system with specific functional and architectural features that interact with machine architecture, how much space and processing resources it deploys or how secure its service is.

Fifteen years ago I wrote a synthesis of theorizing about what information system design is in light of system development methods (Lyytinen 1987). In that paper, I pointed out that the question of what gets designed during system development was not settled within the community. The community offered a wide range of assumptions about what can or should be designed, and how the stuff to be designed was built up and made known. I pointed out that it was a very different question whether the design dealt with technical artifacts, such as computers and software, or the human behaviors, expectations, and work processes that surrounded them. The conclusion of my analysis was that information system design involved the creation of plans that intervene in all three design spaces. Most literature on information system design at that time had not recognized (1) the multiplicity of design stuff that composed system design; (2) that the critical issue in information system design is how these "ontologies" interact, depend on, and inform one another; and (3) that the need for simultaneous design of multiple ontologies implies that we need to expand our horizon of system design.

In relation to the first issue, the discourse of today has improved considerably, and I think there is currently no one who denies the need to integrate multiple ontologies in system design. The major debates center, rather, around the order in which different design elements are attacked. That is, should organizational design follow technical implementation or vice versa,[3] and what sort of design elements should be put in the foreground in specific situations? For example, when designing an Enterprise Resource Planning (ERP) system for a whole organization versus when developing a small application to support document sharing, the domains of design can be radically different.

The second issue is still debated and remains quite poorly articulated: How do our capabilities to conceive work and other social behaviors or our inherent language competence become translated and inscribed in the behaviors of a computer system so that communication and work is made possible? This "miracle" of system design, and its ramifications for how to think about system design, rarely enters into any academic or practical analyses of what happens during information system design. To use Wittgenstein's phrase, it is in front of our eyes all the time but we cannot see it. We rarely ask what design activities, artifacts, and anticipations make system design truly work. Clearly, this is not dependent solely on a solitary designer who skillfully puts together technical elements in a given design. It involves, in addition, a more diverse activity in which the design space is continuously cocreated through anticipations, theories, and imaginations of what can be or what is possible in our language, social order, and technological world. Such processes of imagining, shaping, and enacting different communities of world and social order are not, however, an active part of discourses that focus on information system design.

The third point relates to the design ontology in social spaces, if we take the social construction of reality seriously. The world of technology and technological design is a solitary world of control and individual creation: a designer skillfully shapes available elements within his or her technical grasp into an architecture that supports the desired functionality. Such activity can — in the Schönian way — talk back in that the functionality and the architecture are in a constant drift and become targets of reflection. This design world is driven by control, prediction, and the omnipotent capability of the designer to make it fit with his anticipations. In the realm of language and social order, the situation is different. The world is not controlled, but cocreated and negotiated, and it depends on the recursively organized knowledge of each others' beliefs of how things are, how they should be, what they mean, and how they work (Hirschheim et al. 1995). The issue, which we often evade, is: How can the designers design at all in the sense that we have defined above? Design in this context is not planned, sketched, and anticipated — it *emerges* from our capability to enter into a dialogue with multiple communities and our capability to exercise power in front of forces that resist change. Moreover, it demands skill and cognition, but in a very different way than normal design language. To me, no sufficient and clear way to address this dimension of design in information systems has yet to emerge. I will take two recent attempts, structuration theory and actor network theory, to clarify my point. Neither of these approaches nor their application in the information system context discusses the creation of a new design artifact in terms of design. Rather, they seek to understand the content, or the nature of *design outcomes as a socially constructed system of technical and social elements*, what these elements are, and how they are or can be related. Yet, they have implications for what information systems design is, which have not been spelled out in these debates. I do not find the current implications of these theories very reassuring for our understanding of design.

From the view of structuration theory, the whole idea of our capability to design "structures" or "modalities" is denied because at the end they emerge from recursively organized practices in which social structures are consumed and reproduced by individuals. Practices, on the other hand, establish the foundation of all social life, where we get things done. Hence, a designer in structuration theory can only design in two ways. First, he can create physical elements and other similar things in the world during technical design by exercising power. Then, by making these resources available to our practices by either appealing to us or by using force, they may become structured into our practices over time. Here design is a separate technical intervention and is clearly cut off from its linguistic and social dimensions (i.e., domains of signification and legitimation/power in Giddens's terms). Second, the system designer can become an active participant in the structuration processes by influencing and mobilizing stocks of knowledge, signification structures, and mechanisms of power, thus affecting how social and technical elements become structured in linguistic or legitimation domains. My reading of this side of design is that such activity takes place outside the first type of technical design because "signification" structures cannot be written or inscribed into the computer — they reside only in our heads. To me, this type of separation is problematic and leads to the situation where there is no way to think about how one simultaneously designs the social world, the language game, and its technical manifestation.

From the view of actor-network theory, design is about "inscription": we make the technical artifacts behave in ways that induce people to follow them and associate with them. This offers a nice metaphor of what information systems have to achieve in order to succeed as a form of technical design, linguistic change, and organizational intervention. Technical artifacts inscribe and must inscribe behaviors that lay a foundation for new social and linguistic behaviors in a sociotechnical network. In this sense, the idea of inscriptions, enrollments, and actor networks offers a novel way to think about what makes the miracle of system design possible. Yet, actor network theory remains unclear about how such design and anticipation actually takes place. How is it possible that the technical, the semiotic, and the social order become dependent and mutually enforcing elements in inscriptions and how do designers go on designing, anticipating, and sketching all these elements simultaneously?

I do not know how to come to grips with this challenge. Yet, I hope that the first step in addressing it is to think more carefully about vocabularies — as this

226   book calls us to do — in order to expand our design horizons by discussing the horizons of design. This may lead us to better understand the miracle of system design and to formulate approaches that are informed by new vocabularies. Such vocabularies can help overcome the divide between the technical and the social and describe design not as a singular technical activity, but as a joint weaving of the tapestries of thinking, communication, and acting supported by the diverse technologies that inscribe our behaviors.

NOTES

1. By "design," I mean the high-level design of artifacts that meets both functional and aesthetic requirements as exemplified in high-level design, fashion, or industrial design.

2. This does, however, imply that the reason should not be open to what constitutes reason and how this can be shaped by historical contingencies.

3. This is a hot issue that has been raised in relation to the implementation of Enterprise Resource Planning systems, which demand organizations change their structure and processes in order to exploit these systems effectively.

REFERENCES

Hirschheim R., H. Klein, and K. Lyytinen. 1995. *Information systems development and data modeling — conceptual and philosophical foundations.* Cambridge: Cambridge University Press.

Lyytinen, K. 1987. A taxonomic perspective of information system development: Theoretical constructs and recommendations. In *Critical issues in information systems development,* edited by R. Boland and R. Hirschheim. New York: John Wiley & Sons, pp. 3–41.

Webster's New World Dictionary, 2nd ed. 1978. Cleveland, OH: World Publishing Company.

IN THIS SECTION, *we look forward and consider ways in which a theory and practice of managing as designing can enrich and guide the future of management. Youngjin Yoo opens by exploring the analogy between music notation and knowledge work. He argues that the openness and incompleteness of music notation, as discussed by Nicholas Cook in Chapter 8 of this book, can teach managers about the power of heightened trust between those who plan and those who execute and can enable improved performance. Jurgen Faust then continues this borrowing from the arts and explores how a theory of sculpture by Joseph Beuys can be adapted to rethink organization as a process instead of as an object, showing how Herbert Simon's classic writing on organization can be reinterpreted through sculptural theory. Paul Eickmann, David Kolb, and Alice Kolb then report on their research on learning by artists, contrasting the different mix of learning styles they observed between artists and management students. They propose that managers rely too heavily on text in their learning and can benefit from exposure to learning styles that may at first be uncomfortable for them, such as demonstration, practice, production, and critique.*

Niels Dechow then directs our attention to changes required in our approach to organizational research, arguing that the observational grid that we impose on organizations when we study them misses the dynamics most important for understanding managing as designing. He proposes that research that appreciates the interplay of technology, vision, and narrative in networks of transition will open more productive avenues for research on managing as designing. Rikard Stankiewicz then provides a road map for research on the ways in which managers can shape a more appropriate design space, which, in turn, can shape more productive problem-solving processes. Bo Carlsson follows this line of thought and discusses how policies can be formed that facilitate com-

petent systems for engaging the increasingly complex, nondeterministic, evolving situations we face in today's economy.

Finally, Richard J. Boland Jr. and Fred Collopy draw on the workshop discussions and book chapters to present an initial vocabulary of design for managers. It is necessarily incomplete and intended as a starting point for a continuing effort by managers to become more aware of, more skillful with, and more concerned about the quality of their vocabulary for managing as designing. We are all trapped in our language, but we have the capacity to change our vocabulary and our practices. We hope that the chapters in this volume will serve as a beginning for making managing as designing the preferred way to approach our responsibilities as organizational actors.

31

THE LESS, THE BETTER, PERHAPS

Learning from Music Language

Youngjin Yoo

THE OTHER day, I was at Severance Hall, watching the Cleveland Orchestra perform a century-old piano concerto. This orchestra had never performed the piece before. It was incredibly rich in its texture and filled with emotions. I was struck by the extraordinary energy erupting out of the orchestra, filling the entire hall. When the composer composed the piece, he must have felt something. He might have even seen or heard something. And, he put his feelings and thoughts into the music. Yet, what were left behind were pieces of paper with a set of symbols and, perhaps a few words at the most. However, more than a century later, to a conductor and the members of the orchestra who performed the piano concerto, those limited words and restrained symbols were more than enough. More than enough to stir up their own imaginations, feelings, and thoughts. More than enough to touch and move people who filled the concert hall that night. Yet, the composer never spoke to anyone in the hall.

I have been studying and thinking about knowledge management and computer-mediated communication over the last ten years. I have studied desktop videoconferencing systems, groupware, and other modern computer and communication technologies. Many of the problems that I have studied share a common thread. That is, computer-mediated communication is often too constraining and is not rich enough for effective communication, coordination, and learning. As a result, we (technologists) build more and more tools, with more bandwidth, with more speed, and with richer media. We first

Youngjin Yoo, *Weatherhead School of Management, Case Western Reserve University.*

230   added audio channels, then video channels. We added multimedia graphics. We also added interactive data and application-sharing capabilities. Then,
we realized that we did not have enough bandwidth. So we wanted broadband Internet connections. Now, we want broadband wireless connection
everywhere. We invented e-mail. But, the responses from our colleagues and
friends via e-mail were simply not fast enough. So, we invented "instant" mes-
saging systems. We even have media "richness" theory. The richer and faster,
the better the world would be, we thought.

I first experimented with computer and communication networks for
teaching in 1995. Back then, we connected two classrooms, one in Maryland
and the other in Arizona, via two sets of 28.8kbps modems and 128kbps ISDN-
based videoconferencing. The modem connections were used to transmit professors' PowerPoint slides to the students at the other side. It was painfully slow.
We had to remove all the fancy background patterns that Microsoft programmers wanted us to use. The videoconferencing was slow. The image was
blurring. The sounds and the motions were usually out of sync. Back then, we
thought that once the technology became better and faster, more universities
and professors would do what we did as an experiment for real. Around that
time, someone even wrote an article entitled "Will the Internet Revolutionize
Business Education and Research?"

Now we have an impressive array of technology at our disposal. Connections are much faster. Our school is moving into a building with a "gigabit
switched network to the desktop." I don't have to remove nice background patterns from my PowerPoint slides any more. Students can see the videoconferencing from their desktop or laptop computers (soon, they may be even able
to walk down the street with their PDAs). Yet, there is still no sign of a revolution in business education and research to be found, at least not one due to the
technology.

A few years ago, I conducted a field study at a large global management
consulting firm for their use of "knowledge management systems." It was a
large repository of probably hundreds of thousands of documents created by
the consultants. Consultants of the firm all over the world could share the
"best practice" of the firm to solve their clients' problems. It was heralded as
an exemplary use of technology to manage organizational knowledge. To my
surprise, however, few consultants were actually using the systems in the field.
The reason was that they could access the systems only through the dial-up
connection and most of the files they wanted were too big to download via
dial-up. Therefore, many consultants simply did not access the systems unless
they were in their offices, which was very infrequent. They often used the systems to win the contracts, but rarely used them during the project. The man-

agement of the firm also talked about adding video clips to share "tacit" knowledge. They felt that documents were too constraining to share tacit knowledge. Today, the firm has access to a virtual private network with high bandwidth Internet access. I don't know whether they added tacit knowledge to their system using video clips of their experts. But, what I know is that the firm is still searching for the holy grail of technology for effective knowledge sharing, particularly valuable tacit knowledge.

Going back to my experience at Severance Hall, I have to wonder why management people (particularly those of us who love to apply technology to solve complex business problems) cannot do what musicians all over the world have been doing for centuries. Their symbols are deliberately limited and simple. Yet, musicians routinely communicate extremely complex sets of ideas and feelings — beauty, sorrow, death, and life — using these limited and simple symbols. I propose that the secret lies in the way they use the symbols. In music, symbols are not used simply to communicate ideas and knowledge. Instead, musical symbols are used to design a musical space in which performers and audience are effectively invited to participate. When an orchestra is performing a piece, they are not communicating with the composer through the notes. Rather, they are creating a musical space in which the audience is also invited to participate. They are invited to design their own spaces using their own imaginations. Composers do not communicate all of their thoughts and feelings through the symbols. Instead, they rely on the reflexivity of the people who perform and listen to their music to fill the details. Thus, the musical space shapes and is shaped by the people who design them, and the symbols are used to bring them together across time and distance. It is this notion of "design" of the space that shapes and is shaped by the actions of participants and the use of simple and limited symbols in the design of such space that I would like to emphasize in this essay.

Unlike composers, we technologists often try to provide more and finer details with better technology. We often forget that the technology that we design will be used by other people who can think. We design technology as if people are mere connectors of these intelligent tools. Thus, we use more symbols and symbols are getting more elaborate. Yet, we fail to effectively communicate.

For example, new e-learning tools are fast. We can put many things on a Web site. Our entire lecture can be captured via video and made available over the Internet. Yet, there is no evidence that e-learning is actually enhancing students' learning. Why? I would like to suggest that it is because our current e-learning tools are designed only as tools to *communicate* prepackaged contents, not as tools to *invite people to design and create* learning spaces. Many e-learning tools are designed as if there will be no teachers and no learners. Some of them are designed as if there are no learning processes, but only content. These tools treat knowledge as objects that can be created, packaged, and delivered to students. If our vision for e-learning includes only intelligent tools that connect "dummy" teachers and "dummy" learners, they will fail, even if the tools have the greatest and the latest features.

However, when we start thinking about learning spaces that shape and are shaped by teachers and learners, technology tools begin to have very different roles. Like musical symbols, they are used not only to communicate, but also to invite people to join the learning spaces that are made of both people and technology. Thus, it requires the simultaneous design of both technology and the learning process. When the technology is used to design such sociotechnical learning spaces, we will begin to see more *real* changes in our learning processes and outcomes. Will we still look for technology that is faster, better, and richer? Probably, yes. But probably for different reasons.

Let me conclude with an anecdotal example. PalmPilot's handwriting recognition system expects a lot from the users. In fact, it demands that people learn its "graffiti" system and get used to it. As a result, the designers of PalmPilot could keep it small enough to fit in a palm, yet very effective. Contrarily, Apple Computer's Newton attempted to learn everyone's different handwriting styles. As a result, it became complex and bulky and it failed. The designers of PalmPilot were able to design a man-machine system of PDA and used their simple tools to invite others to join, but Apple's designers were only designing the tools. PalmPilot's designers were able to trust their users and used simple tools; Apple's designers did not leave any room for the users.

Composers need to trust the people who will perform and listen to their music in order to re-create what they want to create to begin with. They always have to think about the people and their symbols together. After all, musical notes without people to perform them do not do anybody any good. Likewise, technologists will need to learn to design technology and organizational spaces simultaneously. For that, they will have to learn to trust the people who live and practice in organizational space first.

32

Purposes in Lieu of Goals, Enterprises in Lieu of Things

Jurgen Faust

THE DESIGN PROCESS

Does it make a difference whether we have a clear image of a design process or not? Does it have an impact whether we think of the management process as mechanical and spatial as opposed to organic and temporal? The design process envisioned here refers to the openness of an archetypal generating process. Design in a management environment in this sense has to be focused on the organization of the movement and not of the shape.

Although within the archetype we cannot define a goal, the design process has to have a purpose. The distinction between a goal and a purpose seems to me very important. A goal is a clearly defined target or the object of one's effort, and a purpose is an intention, which always implies openness and includes the concept of a "creative angle." It allows for changing the goal within the processes, without losing the momentum of direction. If we look over the designer's shoulder, we find two different directions: conceptualizing and constructing, or learning by doing and enhancing design through a dialogue. Everyday experiences usually show both aspects. In order to create some solidity in this fluid environment in the following metaphors, we will use a "theory of sculpture" to theorize, analyze, conceptualize, and understand the implications of actions within the realm of managing as designing.

Jurgen Faust, *Technology and Integrated Media Environment, Cleveland Institute of Art.*

234 "THE THEORY OF SCULPTURE, AS A METAPHOR
TO SHAPE DESIGN PROCESSES"

If we study art and design in an academic environment, we are introduced to a few color theories; only a few have ever heard about the fifty-four existing theories (Farbe, 1992). Even fewer know or read about a "theory of sculpture" as an analogue model for the three-dimensional world. Here we will refer to a theory developed by Joseph Beuys based on principles that alchemists used in the Middle Ages: sal (salt), sulfur, and mercury (Harlan, 1986; Harlan et al., 1984). Applying his model, I have enlarged it in order to describe the design artifacts that can be observed and constructed (Faust, 1996).

Such a theory (or model, image, metaphor, or whatever we call it) should be seen as the "map of the landscape" that helps us to find the way, but doesn't replace the need for good driving. Such a theory helps to establish conditions we are working with and within. It creates an abstract layer, which allows us to integrate the position of an observer of a second order, which is necessary if we are to surpass purely subjective reason (Luhmann, 1990). All the natural and artificial objects that we see or can potentially think of and construct are based on two types of evolutionary structures (generating processes) and an endless sum of in-between qualities, where we find aspects of both extremes (see Figure 32.1).

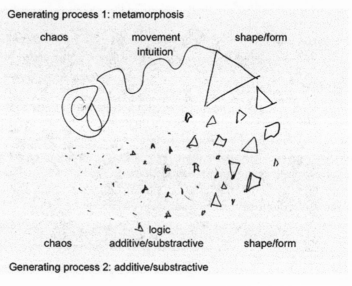

FIGURE 32.1   Two generating processes in a theory of sculpture

Generating Process 1

Objects and conditions, moldable and shapeable, are moving through meta-forms (metamorphosis), continuously changing a form without adding and subtracting material. Imagine a designer molding and shaping a wax or clay cube continuously into a sphere without adding or subtracting material.

Generating Process 2

In the opposite process, objects and conditions are changed through addition and subtraction in order to reach the state of a new shape, whether continuously or in steps. To get a sense for such a process, we can think about the cube again, but made out of stone or wood. Now we would have to add or subtract wood or stone in order to change its shape. Both processes form the basis for the theory.

Applicable terms:

chaos	movement	shape
gas	liquid	solid
mercury	sulfur	sal
birth	live	death
future	presence	past
nerve system	rhythmic system	metabolism

We usually know the purpose of a design assignment, but we don't know where and when it will end successfully. This is as valuable in a traditional design process as it is in the management area. We call a process successful if we achieve the goal, if we reach a state that successfully fulfills the parameters we defined with the problem. The beginning phase of the actual design process is quite a bit more difficult to describe because, in the beginning, everything is still intangible, it is still "up in the air." Referring to the Greek word for something that is not solid, we can call it *chaos*. With chaos and shape/form, we define the extremes, the two poles, which are connected through the two different qualities of movement (processes) as we see in Figure 32.1.

If we apply the two different processes in the realm of thinking we have an interesting metaphor for how we achieve categories: logically and intuitively. The logical way to create means deducting, adding (subtracting), or linking existing categories as we see it in Wittgenstein's early work (Wittgenstein, 1974). Or as Dewey states in one of his four senses of thought: "Each term leaves a deposit which is utilized in the next train. The stream or flow becomes a train, chain, or thread" (Dewey, 1991).

The intuitive process may appear more difficult: suddenly the idea, the concept appears as an *immediate apprehension or cognition*, "a note of inven-

236   tion" (*Merriam Webster's*), but we don't really know where it came from. It also happens unpredictably, when or where we didn't plan or expect it.

But a concept that integrates both, which relates to Bergson's contrast of intuition and intellect as a means by which we manipulate reality for purposes of action, can end with a category, with a form, which is defined or which can be defined (Bergson, 1992). This tangential notion about thinking is important because we should not use the theory as a fixed shape. Such a model should be molded and reshaped through application and shouldn't be a matrix that we put over a phenomenon we perceive. If we look at Figure 32.1, which symbolizes the theory, we have a metaphor to understand the difficulties in bringing designing and managing together. Analysis and adding and subtracting are the thinking processes that are appreciated in the science world. The art and design field is more driven by imagination, inspiration, and intuition. Each community is suspicious of the thinking process of the other, and we need people who are artists as well as scientists.

MANAGING AS DESIGNING

In the following discussion, we will translate this theory into the management field.

Chaos. Usually a new design assignment within an enterprise starts after a clear definition of the assignment and goal. If the manager-designer starts with the precondition of a clear achievable goal—for example, to make a certain amount of profit—the form/shape is clearly defined and the design assignment shifts. How to design a process to achieve a clearly defined goal is now the task. The manager-designer doesn't know the shape of the process. Such a moment has a chaotic and open structure. "Chaos" in that sense is the precondition for all generating processes: it is the moment in time when the ideas can and should compete. But we all know that chaos as a necessary condition for a creative process is for many designers and managers the biggest challenge on a personal and on a professional level. We usually try to prevent chaos through the application of forms and processes we already know. With the knowledge of such a theory, manager-designers could use chaos as an important strategic phase in achieving design quality. This presupposes a clear knowledge of the properties of chaos and how to use it to solve the assignment. I observed over many years, including settings where I was responsible for the process, that if we prevent chaos in the creative wellspring, we end up later with chaos in a place where we don't want to have it and where we don't need it.

Movement. If we organize the shape/form instead of the movement or the context for the movement, we organize extreme spatial and physical parameters, which will prevent a new solution. This is the "old concept" manager who knows and has the solution beforehand and uses meetings mainly to distribute information. The structure in such a case is "hard" and centralized. Design solutions, if they happen at all in such circumstances, happen in the mind of the manager before he enters the meeting room. If the manager-designer organizes the movement within an enterprise, he organizes and prepares the lively part of an organization. He cares about the conditions for supporting creative platforms; he cares about the rhythmic systems and processes that keep the enterprise together.

It may happen that in one of the "chaotic sessions" there is movement in thinking and in acting that travels in unexpected directions. But the reward can be high. Such processes maintain the vitality of an enterprise because the members of such an organization are included in the vision, mission, and goals. Such a manager as designer is a coach, who is able to organize the team and who knows how to position the best players within the team. Hierarchy in such a "post heroic" era, as Dirk Baecker (1994) stated, would include knowing where hierarchy is necessary and where it isn't. The stability of an enterprise immediately will grow with such a movement, like the stability of a bike rider who speeds up to a certain pace.

Form/Shape

The movement gets repeated, the new form is established and rhythm appears. After a certain amount of time, the shaping force in the first place ends up being the blocking energy, which prevents further movement—this phenomenon has an interesting and a problematic side. Nonprogrammed decisions have the tendency to end up as programmed decisions (Simon, 1960). This is not a pitfall, if we know it and if we use this phenomenon, because we need all three different layers (chaos, movement, and form) in an enterprise.

How can we best work, then, with the "over-forming over-aging" in an enterprise? It is a mystery if we don't know where the programmed decisions have to be and where the places for new subenterprises within the enterprise should be initiated in order to keep enough growth energy within the organism. We all know that sooner or later the entire organization will be in danger because of the inflexibility and dominance of its programmed decisions. The entity is not flexible enough anymore to adjust to changing conditions. Then the enterprise could break apart or dissolve and disappear.

We can read the developed theory horizontally and temporally (Figure 32.1) or we can read it vertically and spatially (Figure 32.2). I wouldn't favor one over the other, but I also understand that the dominance of the spatial conscious-ness is sometimes annoying and might keep us away from necessary progress (Boland, 2001). We must know, in the spirit of Jean Gebser, when and where spatial thinking is needed, which allows us to differentiate. But we also need to know where and when temporal, integrative thinking is necessary (Geb-ser, 1985).

If we think about the theory vertically and spatially, as in Herbert A. Si-mon's *The New Science of Management Decision*, we can realize that an entity like an enterprise has at least three different layers: "In the bottom layer, we have the basic work processes — in the case of a manufacturing organization, the processes that produce raw materials, manufacture the physical product, warehouse it, and ship it. In the middle layer, we have the programmed deci-sion-making processes, the processes that govern the day-to-day operation of the manufacturing and distribution system. In the top layer, we have the non-programmed decision-making processes, the processes that are required to de-sign and redesign the entire system, to provide it with its basic goals and ob-jectives, and to monitor its performance" (Simon, 1960).

Although I am excited by the similarity of Simon's description to my own work, I don't see the automation of programmed decision making as the last

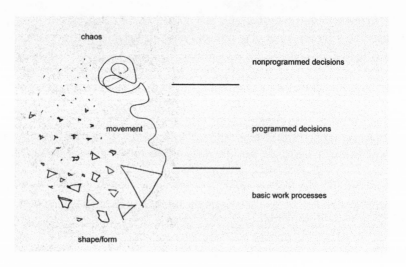

FIGURE 32.2   Degrees of structure in organizational processes

step (Simon, 1960, p. 34). We can hardly block the flow from chaos to form.
But in order to keep the enterprise alive, we have to maintain all three layers. In the top layer, ideas get developed, and this is where the chaos can happen. We also can call it the layer of the senses, the nerves. It's the spiritual part of a living being, where the future of the enterprise appears. The second layer, which connects the nonphysical with the physical, is the layer of movement. Here the repetitive, rhythmic, and programmed decisions feed, regulate, and carry the enterprise on a daily basis. It is the stream of fluid within a body. The third layer is the physical environment and it is always a product of the past. It hosts the enterprise and supports the rhythmic and the spiritual layer. The word *layer*, which itself connotes spatial dimensions, is misleading. These three layers are not separated; they are all interconnected and mutual, like in a living being.

My intuition says that an enterprise is a living being of the highest order, which has to be lively and flexible enough to change its form in order to achieve its purpose. Such an enterprise has to have senses to perceive and to think; it has to have rhythmic circulation processes and an adequate metabolism. Such a model has to include an entity that is bigger then the parts that belong to it. At this point, we discern a major difference between the traditional design process of an object and the design process envisioned here. The management design process contains a social community that has to be actively included in order to design the whole.

The management structures of the past were based on a system of metaphors abstracted from spatial and physical observations. These structures are objective and clearly definable because we can describe their place within a space. The "new" management design process is temporal and implies change whenever it is necessary. The concept of "roving leadership" (DePree, 1989) is an example of this design process. In the management design I propose, we perceive issues, context, and needs by focusing on organizing the movement of an organization and not the shape. Then we are designers and artists in the truest sense, working in a management studio located between human beings.

REFERENCES

Baecker, D. 1994. *Postheroisches management*. Berlin: Merve.
Bergson, H. 1992. *The creative mind*, translated by Mabelle Andison. New York: Carol Publishing Group.
Boland, R. J. Jr. 2001. The tyranny of space in organizational analysis. *Information and Organization* 11: 3–23.

240   DePree, M. 1989. *Leadership is an art*. New York: Bantam Doubleday Dell Publishing Group, Inc.

Dewey, J. 1991. *How we think*. Amherst, NY: Prometheus.

Farbe, I. 1992. *Eine Ideengeschichte der Farbe von Narciso Silvestrini und Ernst Peter Fischer*, Dielsdorf: Lichtdruck AG.

Faust, J. 1996. *Kulturdesign, Vom Objekt zum Prozess*. Schriften Kunstseminar Metzingen Freie Hochschule, Metzingen, Germany.

Gebser, J. 1985. *The ever-present origin*, translated by Noel Barstad and Algis Mickunas. Athens, OH: Ohio University Press.

Harlan, V. 1986. *Was ist Kunst? Werkstattgespräch mit Joseph Beuys*, Stuttgart: Achberger Verlag.

Harlan, V., R. Rappmann, and P. Schata. 1984. *Soziale plastik, materialien zu Joseph Beuys*. Achberg: Achberger Verlag.

Luhmann, N. 1990. *Fredericj D. Bunsen, Dirk Baecker, Unbeobachtbare Welt, Ueber Kunst und Architektur*, Haux: Bielefeld.

Merriam Webster's Collegiate Dictionary, Tenth Edition, Springfield, MA: G & C Merriam Company.

Simon, H. A. 1960. *The new science of management decision*. New York: Harper & Row.

Wittgenstein, L. 1974. *Tractatus Logico-Philosophicus*, translated by C. K. Ogden, with an introduction by B. Russell. London: Routledge and Kegan Paul. http://www.kfs.org/~jonathan/witt/tlph.html (accessed September 1, 2003).

33

Designing Learning

Paul Eickmann, Alice Kolb, and David Kolb

The rhythm of loss of integration with environment and recovery of union not only persists in man, but becomes conscious with him; its conditions are material out of which he forms purposes. Emotion is the conscious sign of a break, actual or impending. The discord is the occasion that induces reflection. Desire for restoration of the union converts mere emotion into interest in objects as conditions of realization of harmony. With the realization, material of reflection is incorporated into objects as their meaning. Since the artist cares in a peculiar way for the phase of experience in which union is achieved, he does not shun moments of resistance and tension. He rather cultivates them, not for their own sake but because of their potentialities, bringing to living consciousness an experience that is unified and total. In contrast with the person whose purpose is esthetic, the scientific man is interested in problems, in situations wherein tension between the matter of observation and of thought is marked. Of course he cares for their resolution. But he does not rest in it; he passes on to another problem using an attained solution only as a stepping stone on which to set on foot further inquires.

John Dewey, Art as Experience

IN THIS passage from his last book, John Dewey (1934) uses his concept of the experiential learning process to describe differences between artistic and scientific learning styles. In this essay, we will explore the differences between artistic and scientific education, comparing the learning styles of management students at the Weatherhead School of Management, as reported by Boyatzis

Paul Eickmann, *Cleveland Institute of Art*. Alice Kolb, *Experience Based Learning Systems*. David Kolb, *Weatherhead School of Management, Case Western Reserve University*.

242   and Mainemelis (2000) and BFA graduates from the Cleveland Institute of Art. We will examine learning to design as a learning space with potential as an educational process that integrates artistic and scientific learning.

COMPARING EDUCATION IN MANAGEMENT AND THE ARTS

Our observations of the way the educational process is conducted in art schools and management schools reveal some striking differences that in many ways illustrate Dewey's description of the artistic and scientific learning process. A first awareness of these differences came as we were preparing a learning style workshop for art students. We asked what readings should we give and Paul Eickmann said, "You know, for art students learning is not text driven." This stood in dramatic contrast with management education, which is almost entirely organized around texts that deliver an authoritative scientific discourse. The scientific basis of the management curriculum was established in 1959 by an influential Carnegie Foundation report that sought to improve the intellectual respectability of management education by grounding it in three scientific disciplines: economics, mathematics, and behavioral science.

The text-driven approach of management education contrasts with the experiential learning process of demonstration-practice-production-critique that is used in most art classes (Table 33.1). This process is repeated recursively in art education whereas management education is primarily discursive with each topic covered in a linear sequence with little recursive repetition. Management education focuses on telling whereas art education emphasizes showing. Management education tends to emphasize theory whereas art education emphasizes integration of theory and practice. Art education focuses on the learners' inside-out expression whereas management education spends more time on outside-in impression. Most of the time in management classes is spent conveying information with relatively little time spent on student performance, most of which occurs on tests and papers. In art classes, the majority of the time is spent on student expression of ideas and skills. Art education tends to be individualized with small classes and individual attention whereas management education is organized into large classes with limited individualized attention. An assistant dean at the Columbus College of Art and Design, who majored in music as an undergraduate and later got an MBA, contrasted the three hours a week he spent in individual tutorial with his mentor with the shock he experienced in entering a tiered MBA classroom of two hundred students. Finally, art education tends to be represented by faculty members with diverse learning styles whereas management education tends to favor specialized faculty members with a primarily abstract learning orientation.

TABLE 33.1
Comparison of Arts Education and Management Education

Arts Education	Management Education
Aesthetic	Scientific
Demo–practice–production–critique	Text driven
Recursive	Discursive
Theory and practice	Theory
Showing	Telling
Expression	Impression
Individualized	Batched
Diverse faculty	Abstract faculty

LEARNING STYLES AND THE LEARNING SPACE

Experiential learning theory builds on Dewey's concept of experiential learning integrating his model with other experiential learning theorists, Kurt Lewin, William James, Jean Piaget, and Paulo Freire. Experiential learning theory defines learning as "the process whereby knowledge is created through the transformation of experience." (Kolb 1984, p. 41). The learning model portrays two dialectically-related modes of grasping experience—Concrete Experience (feeling) and Abstract Conceptualization (thinking)—and two dialectically-related modes of transforming experience—Reflective Observation (reflecting) and Active Experimentation (acting). Individual learning styles are determined by an individual's preferred way of resolving these two dialectics. Integrated learning is a process involving a creative tension among the four learning modes that is responsive to contextual demands. This is portrayed as an idealized learning cycle or spiral where the learner "touches all the bases"—feeling, reflecting, thinking, and acting—in a recursive process that is responsive to the learning situation and what is being learned.

The Learning Style Inventory (LSI) is a simple self-assessment tool designed to help learners describe their preferred style of learning by ranking their preferences for feeling, thinking, acting, and reflecting. The dialectic poles of grasping experience via feeling or thinking and transforming experience via acting or reflecting define a two-dimensional learning space. Learners' scores on the LSI place them in one of nine distinct regions of the learning space, each of which is associated with a specific process of learning from experience. These regions are named for the points of the compass and are divided into specialized learning regions and integrative learning regions.

The learning process in specialized learning regions, NW, NE, SE, and SW, strongly emphasizes one pole of the feeling/thinking dialectic and one pole of the acting/reflecting dialectic. Individuals in the NW region learn pri-

244   marily through acting and feeling. In the NE region, learners emphasize
reflecting and feeling. In the SE region, learners emphasize reflecting and
thinking. In the SW region, individuals learn through thinking and acting.

In the integrative learning regions, N, E, S, W, and Central, the learning
process integrates the poles of one or both of the two dialectics. The learning
process in the N region integrates acting and reflecting in feeling. In the E region, the learning process integrates feeling and thinking in reflecting. In the
S region, learners integrate acting and reflecting in thinking. In the W region,
the learning process integrates feeling and thinking in action. In the C region,
learners have an integrative approach to learning that balances feeling, thinking, acting, and reflecting.

COMPARING LEARNING STYLES OF ART
AND MANAGEMENT STUDENTS

Tables 33.2 and 33.3 show how the learning styles of art and management students are distributed in the learning space. Art students are concentrated in
the feeling-oriented northern regions of the learning space whereas management students are concentrated in the thinking southern regions. Among art
students, 37.8 percent are in the north regions and 22.5 percent are in the
south. Among management students, 45.7 percent are in the south regions
with 21.2 percent in the north. There are more art students in the eastern regions than in the western regions (36.0 percent to 26.1 percent). There are
more management students in the western regions than in the eastern regions
(36.3 percent to 30.4 percent). Sixty-three percent of art students have integrating learning styles, compared to 56 percent of management students.
Among art students, the SW region is the least populated (1.8 percent) whereas
the least populated region for management students is the NE (5.1 percent).
Among management students, 10.2 percent are in the balancing C region and
14.4 percent of art students are there. Boyatzis and Mainemelis (2000) found
correlations between abstract learning styles and grades and GMAT, indicat-
ing a bias toward abstraction in evaluation and selection practices. For BFA
graduates, there was no relationship between grades and learning style.

LEARNING STYLES OF BFA GRADUATES IN DESIGN

The field of design is of particular interest for the idea of managing as designing because it involves integrating artistic imagination and scientific analysis.
A faculty member in the Design Department at the Art Academy of Cincin-
nati described the nature of design as follows: "In design, the subject is given

TABLE 33.2

Learning Styles of CIA BFA Graduates (N = 111)

NW Feeling—Acting 12.6%	N Feeling Acting—Reflecting 16.2%	NE Feeling—Reflecting 9.0%
W Acting Feeling—Thinking 11.7%	C Feeling Acting + Reflecting Thinking 14.4%	E Reflecting Feeling—Thinking 13.5%
SW Thinking—Acting 1.8%	S Thinking Acting—Reflecting 7.2%	SE Thinking—Reflecting 13.5%

TABLE 33.3

Learning Styles of MBA students (N = 1286)

NW Feeling—Acting 10.1%	N Feeling Acting—Reflecting 6%	NE Feeling—Reflecting 5.1%
W Acting Feeling—Thinking 13.5%	C Feeling Acting + Reflecting Thinking 10.2%	E Reflecting Feeling—Thinking 9.3%
SW Thinking—Acting 12.7%	S Thinking Acting—Reflecting 17%	SE Thinking—Reflecting 16%

to us. Our work is to take what is given and transform it into an idea that communicates the desired message in the most successful way." Thus, the design process requires integration of the designer's inside-out creative expression to given outside-in specifications and objectives. Such integration occurs in the dynamic process of integrating the feeling, thinking, acting, and reflecting modes of learning. Table 33.4 shows the learning style distribution of design majors. The design department has five areas of concentration: illustration, medical illustration, interior design, industrial design, and graphic design. The table indicates that 20.3 percent of design students are in the balancing

TABLE 33.4

Learning Styles of CIA BFA design graduates (N = 64)

NW Feeling—Acting 14.0%	N Feeling Acting—Reflecting 12.5%	NE Feeling—Reflecting 10.9%
W Acting Feeling—Thinking 7.8%	C Feeling Acting + Reflecting Thinking 20.3%	E Reflecting Feeling—Thinking 15.6%
SW Thinking—Acting 3.1%	S Thinking Acting—Reflecting 4.6%	SE Thinking—Reflecting 10.9%

Central region. Of the sixteen BFA graduates in the central region, thirteen are majoring in design, and 60.8 percent of design students have integrating learning styles.

If we take the stance of management education as design, we may be able to see that the artist's dilemma in coming up with the most inventive, insightful, and effective solution to the problems at hand is no different from the challenges managers face in their daily tasks. A shift to a more integrated learning environment may in fact improve the managers' ability to be creative and effective in solving problems and situations in various arenas.

IMPLICATIONS FOR EDUCATION

The concepts of learning space and learning style have important implications for designing educational systems that promote learning. As we have seen, each of the nine regions of the experiential learning space is associated with specific learning processes. The learning processes in each region are in turn most effective for the achievement of certain learning outcomes. For example, the feeling-oriented northern regions are most effective for learning interpersonal skills whereas the thinking-oriented southern regions are most effective for learning analytic and quantitative skills. An individual's learning style represents their preference for a particular region of the learning space, their home base, so to speak. To learn skills outside of their home region, learners need to move to other regions. This framework is useful for curriculum development, student development, and faculty development.

Curriculum development needs to address not only content objectives, but 247 also the learning processes that are most effective for learning the content. In management education for example, although the Carnegie report was successful in establishing a scientific basis for management education, beginning in the late 1980s, MBA programs received intense criticism for being too focused on abstract learning. MBA graduates were viewed as: "(1) too analytical, not practical and action oriented; (2) lacking interpersonal and in particular communication skills; (3) parochial, not global in their thinking and values; (4) having exceedingly high expectations about their first job after graduation . . . ; (5) not oriented toward information resources and systems; and (6) not working well in groups" (Boyatzis, Cowen, and Kolb 1995, p. 4). In response, many management schools have introduced learning programs that emphasize the northern and western regions of the learning space, such as executive mentoring, action learning, and team learning.

Students can be empowered to take responsibility for their own learning by understanding how they learn best and the skills necessary to learn in regions that are uncomfortable for them. Faculties also have learning style preferences for particular regions of the learning space, and most often they tend to teach the way they learn. Understanding the learning regions most suited to learning their course content and the individual learning styles of their students can help them recognize the need to teach in different ways that flexibly respond to course objectives and student learning needs.

REFERENCES

Boyatzis, R. E., S. S. Cowen, and D. A. Kolb. 1995. *Innovation in professional education*. San Francisco: Jossey-Bass.

Boyatzis, R. E., and C. Mainemelis. 2000. An empirical study of the pluralism of learning and adaptive styles in an MBA program. Paper presented at the annual meeting of the Academy of Management, Toronto.

Dewey, J. 1934. *Art as experience*. New York: Perigee.

Kolb, D. A. 1984. *Experiential learning: Experience as the source of learning and development*. New Jersey: Prentice-Hall.

Mainemelis, C., R. E. Boyatzis, and D. A. Kolb. 2002. Learning styles and adaptive flexibility: Testing experiential learning theory. *Management Learning* 33(1): 5–33.

34

THE MANAGING AS DESIGNING PROJECT CALLS FOR A REDESIGN OF THE RESEARCH SETTING!

Niels Dechow

IN THE era of scientific management our laboratory was set up in the factory. Our research was focused on the division of labor, and our studies were largely reinforced by mutually exclusive and collectively exhaustive constructs such as, for example, the form or the function of management as a thing—a noun. As a collective, these settings helped us in explaining management as a separate part of production. Since then, reality has changed in such ways that management increasingly is framed as an integrative art of production.

Why not use the managing as designing project to challenge our ways of "setting the scene for science"? No longer is the factory given as the laboratory for our research. We don't care much about the division of labor. Yet, it often seems as if research in management was taking place in the age of scientific management. Ongoing research still seems to cluster around two of the proven questions: What does *human* X do better or differently than Y? Does *technology* Z add value? Hallmark research in our field has been created on the basis of these questions. However, it seems increasingly difficult to employ these questions because, as a method of inquiry, they separate the social from the technical and thereby infer that each of them is endowed with "immutable content."

However, the challenge in the managing as designing project is not only the reframing of management from a separate science to a creative art integrated with production. The challenge in this project is that the reframing fun-

Niels Dechow, *Saïd Business School, University of Oxford.*

damentally requires us to consider the question: How do we design the research setting?

My goal is not to micro-scope a new set of questions for managerial research. On the contrary, my interest is in discussing the ways that our reframing of management from a thing to an activity should make us reflect on the
ways we macro-scope our research methodology. Three issues in particular
come to mind as important. The first one is concerned with the grid that we
use to structure our investigations and seek to explain management. The second issue is about the constructs that we use to *in*form the grid we lay out over
management. The third issue focuses on the way we read the results coming
out of this grid-work and seek to explore management.

The foundation for the following discussion is that society and technology
are intertwined. Technology is not purely a social construction — it doesn't disappear just because we decide it doesn't exist. Nevertheless, technology is constructed and construed in social spaces. Obviously, this worldview is construc-
tivist, and this means that my interest is to find out how designs come together
through a series of competence-tradings in a space that is given in time by our
present technical and social resources.

HOW DO WE DO THE GRID-WORKS?

When discussing good design, we often boil everything down to its form and
function and in this way we address how things work — the function of form
(in function). The purpose of the grid is to make the "things" explicit. The
purpose of our constructs should be to describe how these *things work* — interact and thereby exchange competences. Three forms through which managing as designing can be seen to function could be (A) Vision, (B) Narratives,
and (C) Technology.

When organizations implement new technologies, they often proceed on
the basis of a vision about how things should work and a narrative about how
things have worked in the past. Once configured, this technology enables organizational practice in certain ways, which in turn creates a space for a different or new narrative, which over time paves the way for new goals (visions)
and calls for a different technology — once knowledge about the capacity and
capabilities of the new/current technology has been appropriated.

The point really is that we need to allow our studies on management to focus on the ways that the three building blocks of technology, vision, and narrative are connected. Technologies are rarely implemented without a reference to a vision about the future and a narrative about the past, which is why
the form and function of management is always "in the making." The purpose

of the grid is to record the form in such ways that one can explicate its construct of technology, narrative, and vision.

On the basis of these thoughts about the grid-work, the next issue that we need to revisit—if we want to study managing as designing—is about the constructs by which we inform the grid for our research. As mentioned, the problem in our current research enterprise is that we cannot talk in competent ways about management as an activity because our traditional approach separates form from function (exemplified through archetype questions like: What does X do differently than Y? And how does technology Z add value?) Traditional scientific reasoning considers the form *or* function of management and polarizes reality into either-or situations—stories of success or failure. These black or white images are problematic because they tend to overlook the gray zone in which most activities happen.

IN WHAT WAY DO WE NEED TO BE ABLE TO STUDY THE FORM IN FUNCTION?

A brief discussion of some recent field research will illustrate a shortcoming among what is already known in practice, the axioms of research in that particular field, and the explanations that we so far have been able to establish. Enterprise Resource Planning (ERP) systems have been on the market for more than ten years. These packages are marketed as if it is possible to design the form and function of organizations by a few structuring tools that are labeled with flashy terms. Corporations worldwide have bought into this idea. Many of them however, have encountered severe difficulties in getting these systems to work and the rate of information systems failure is probably as significant as ever.[1] For a long time, the dominant thinking in this field has been driven by the socio-technical axiom: the goal of any information systems implementation is to optimize the technical and social systems, jointly. Yet, research has not been able to offer a sound explanation of how things work—in particular, when they don't work. On the contrary, it seems that the gap between practice and research is widening because it remains a characteristic of our research that we ascribe failure to either social or technical dysfunctions without being able to tell how things work in the gray zone where most of the designing activities take place. Rather than overcoming the limitations of traditional research, we have for a long time reinforced the habit of ascribing immutable content *to* the setting instead of learning *from* the setting how certain translations between technology, vision, and narrative at the same time produce and prohibit organizational competence.

In order to be able to study managing as designing (i.e., as a verb and not as

a noun), we need to design the research setting in such ways that we enable
ourselves to look at the ways in which agents seize, mold, and make particular
competences through certain combinations of technology, vision, and narratives. Instead of designing our research setting through constructs that force reality into our laboratories, we need constructs that allow us to understand the
field in which managers design their reality. The point therefore is to eliminate our constructs as much as possible in order to make room for the labels
by which practitioners organize their reality into a network of nodes.

The networking of technologies, visions, and narratives is one of the two
steps that we need to take in order to map their ongoing (designing) efforts.
The second step is to follow the translations that create motion through their
network and mobilize exchanges between its social and technical properties.
One question that addresses both steps is: How do things (actors and factors)
relate? This circular and reflexive question may appear naive. However, it
forces the researcher out of his or her laboratory and into the activity-based
space where managers design their reality in order to make things work.

WHEN STUDYING MANAGING AS DESIGNING, WHAT OUTCOMES SHOULD WE SEEK?

We need to be able to illustrate how management as an act of designing
constantly establishes and destroys "trading zones" between human and non-
human actors. There are two implications. One implication is that we need to
establish our explanations on the basis of an understanding of the ways that
practical outcomes are created through constant networking (of nodes). The
other implication is that we need to realize that network nodes are present only
because someone—by means of these nodes—is able to design a community
of practice that is endowed with certain competences. None of the nodes are
there because of some "immutable content" that otherwise would allow us to
draw simplified conclusions such as: technology X does or does not add value
to corporations!

Instead, we should seek to enable ourselves to illustrate management as a
real-time topology in which its path-creating and path-dependent course de-
forms the ways that it is possible to combine technologies, visions, and narratives. In doing so, we enable ourselves to explain in what ways the outcomes
that corporation X achieved with technology Y are different from the outcomes developed by corporation Z, and why this leads the two corporations to
create different sets of competences.

As mentioned above, the challenge for the managing as designing project
is not only to reframe management from a separate science to a creative art

252   integrated with production. The challenge in this project is that the reframing fundamentally requires us to consider the question: How do we design the research setting?

With this position statement, I propose three axioms. The first axiom is that in order to *explicate* managing as designing, we need to focus on the technologies, visions, and narratives (nodes) because these are important forms through which management functions. The second axiom is that in order to *explain* managing as designing, we need to focus on the networking of these technologies, visions, and narratives because none of these nodes have immutable content independently of each other. The third axiom is that in order to *explore* managing as designing, we need to focus on the trading zones that result from the networking because they, at the same time, both produce and prohibit organizational competences.

NOTE

1. Numerous articles and research reports document this issue, such as, for example, KPMG Management Consulting, 1997; Koch, 1997; Davenport, 1998; Deloitte Consulting, 1998; Hildebrand, 1998; Wagle, 1998; and PA Consulting, 1999.

REFERENCES

Avison, D.E., and G. Fitzgerald. 1995. *Information systems development: Methodologies, techniques and tools,* 2nd ed. New York: McGraw-Hill.
———. 1999. Information systems development. In *Rethinking management information systems,* edited by W. L. Currie and B. Galliers. New York: Oxford University Press.
Czarniawska, B. 1993. *Writing management—Organization theory as a literary genre.* New York: Oxford University Press.
Davenport, T. 1998. Putting the enterprise into the enterprise system—If you're not careful the dream of information integration can turn into a nightmare. *Harvard Business Review,* July–August: 121–31.
Deloitte Consulting. 1998. *ERP's second wave—Maximizing the value of ERP-enabled processes.* New York: Deloitte Consulting.
Hildebrand, C. 1998. Beware the weak links. *CIO Magazine,* August 15, www.cio.com/archive/enterprise/081598/_risk.html.
Koch, C. 1997. The big uneasy. *CIO Magazine,* October 15, www.cio.com/archive/101597_uneasy_content.html.
KPMG Consulting. 1997. *Profit-focused software for package implementation.* Research Report. London: KPMG Management Consulting.
Latour, B. 1987. *Science in action.* Cambridge MA: Harvard University Press.
———. 1993. *We have never been modern.* Cambridge MA: Harvard University Press.

————. 1999. *Pandora's hope—Essays on the reality of science studies*. Cambridge, MA: Harvard University Press.

Mumford, E. 1999. Routinisation, re-engineering, and socio-technical design: Changing ideas on the organization of work. In *Rethinking management information systems*, edited by W. L. Currie and B. Galliers. New York: Oxford University Press.

PA Consulting Group. 1999. *ValueMining—What happened to the business value of the ERP system?* PA Consulting Group—Research Report.

Penrose, E. 1995. *The theory of the growth of the firm*, 3rd ed. New York: Oxford University Press.

Preston, A. M. 1991. The "problem" in and of management information systems. *Accounting, Management and Information Technologies*, 1(1): 43–69.

Wagle, D. 1998. Too often it's made on faith, not good judgment. Will it cut costs? Common pitfalls in implementation. *McKinsey Quarterly*, 2: 131–38.

35

DESIGN AND DESIGNABILITY

Rikard Stankiewicz

THE FOLLOWING discussion of *designability* is based on my research on the relationship between the evolving structure of technical knowledge and the innovation and problem-solving processes in technology (Stankiewicz, 2000; 2002). These processes vary greatly across different fields of technology and over time. Much of that variation can be reduced to a single dimension formed by two polar types: the *design-driven* technologies, on the one hand, and the *discovery-driven* ones, on the other. Software development comes close to the first pole, while drug development best approximates the second. Most technologies, however, fall somewhere in between. Designability is a variable.

What then precisely is designability? And what are its determinants? Design occurs when *the process of conceiving/planning of an artifact/process is separated from its actual production/performance.* This in turn presupposes two things: (i) the process occurs at the symbolic level — it is virtual, and (ii) the symbolic expression of design can be "translated" into operations. Designability is measured by the degree to which these conditions are fulfilled. It depends primarily on the scope of the available knowledge base and the degree to which that base constitutes a well-articulated, socially-shared *design space.*

Formally, a design space is the combinatorial space generated by a set of *operants* — for example, components, unit operations, or routines. Operants in their turn can be defined as the structure-function (or process-function) rela-

Rikard Stankiewicz, *Lund University.*

tionships that are used in the designing and assembling of artifacts. Any technical object (artifact, system) is either an operant in its own right or a configuration of operants. Decomposing an artifact into its constituent operants, we will eventually arrive at a point where we cannot proceed any farther. The operants at this boundary are our "primitives."

In evolutionary terminology, the operants are the "techno-memes" at the core of technological inheritance. They are heterogeneous information packages in that they have both declarative and procedural dimensions. This information is encoded and transferred in a variety of ways and contains both coded (symbolic) and tacit elements. The degree of articulation and codification influences the ease with which operants can be transferred and symbolically manipulated. Equally importantly, operants can be embodied in artifacts and transferred in that form.

Design spaces shape problem-solving processes. They do so mainly by generating the domain of possibilities within which the search for technical solutions is undertaken. The richer and more finely grained the design space, the more precisely it can be used to map the corresponding "fitness landscape," and thus optimize the actors' ability to identify and articulate goals.

Design spaces undergo change over time. There is a large difference between the stone-and-bone space of the cavemen and the vast and highly differentiated space of, say, the modern electrical engineer. Analytically, one can distinguish two dimensions in that change:

– the expansion of spaces through the addition of new operants, and
– their progressive structuring and articulation.

The evolution of a design space involves sifting from the pool of individual and collective experience those elements that make good operants, that is, that *jointly* facilitate adaptive problem solving. In general, such operants might be expected to have certain characteristic properties, such as *replicability, stability*, and *reliability*. The *primitives* from which more complex operants are derived should be capable of generating a *fine-grained, hierarchically-structured, generic* design space with a multifunctional domain of applications. The systems to which they give rise should be characterized by *transparency, decomposability*, and *maintainability*. The operants should be capable of being described, represented, and manipulated *symbolically* to facilitate design process and to enable their *communication* and sharing in a large community of practitioners.

Even a relatively modest set of operants is capable of generating a vast design space. Different uses and application domains of the space are constantly discovered, particular artifact lineages emerge and evolve, and so on. Along

256   with such specific application knowledge, the user of a design space is likely to acquire a generic knowledge of the space — its *grammar*.

The accumulation and structuring of technological knowledge are similar in important ways to the growth and development of a *language*. This process can be found in both primitive and advanced design spaces. Indeed, the language metaphor occurs frequently in talk about technology — as in "libraries of peptides," "the language of architecture," "computer languages," "the mechanical alphabet," and so on. It suggests that the "memetic systems" of technology are *generative* cognitive systems, capable of applying "transformation rules" to combine a finite set of "building blocks" into an indefinite variety of messages/forms. Such systems are familiar in music, mathematics, linguistics, chemistry, molecular genetics, and so on. Indeed, they are essential to all truly complex evolutionary phenomena.

A well-developed design space is likely to be spanned by a *hierarchy* of design languages. This is reflected in the "top-down" strategy typical of design processes. The broad features of the artifact are first outlined and then used as constraints/specification for more detailed designs at a lower level, and so forth. For a relatively simple artifact produced by a single person, different languages are not required to describe the various stages in this process. But with increasing complexity, the responsibilities of overall design and detail are separated and require different skills and different languages. Thus, software engineers have had to develop a whole range of lower and higher design languages, from the simplest primitives of the binary digits up to a very general "metalanguage" that can be used to describe — and hence structure — almost *any* design space.

Now, what about the managerial design space? How does it compare with the technological spaces discussed above?

The organizational/institutional design space may be said to consist of behavioral patterns that can be assembled into larger clusters or systems. Most of these patterns are products of historical evolution; they have been, as it were, "discovered" in the course of social practice. However, the design space that they form differs sharply from that found in the mature technologies discussed above.

The behavioral patterns, that is, the organizational operants, tend to be highly specific, contextualized, and therefore hard to replicate. They usually are characterized by low stability and reliability. The organizational design space is "shallow" in the sense of lacking a well-integrated hierarchy of design levels and associated design languages. The systems to which it gives rise are opaque rather than transparent. They keep changing over time. They are organic in character and therefore are not easily decomposable. All of this means that the organizational design spaces are hard to analyze, codify, and represent symbolically. They do not easily give rise to a coherent design language — which is why the management sciences are rather less cumulative and successful than engineering ones. Such design languages as do develop in the management fields tend not to be widely shared and are generally short lived.

We are therefore forced to conclude that the organizational/institutional design spaces are relatively crude. They do not give rise to a high-level designability. Social technologies are much more like craft technologies than like engineering. They are empirical, that is, discovery driven. Their design practices are imitative rather than analytical. Social/organizational design could best be described as incomplete or "framing" rather than complete or final.

Framing design occurs when there is poor translatability of high-level of design languages into the low operational levels; that is, the primitives are complex, heterogeneous, dynamic, and unreliable. Framing designs are created in a high-level language but cannot be fully operationalized. At best, they define lower-level problems that are then solved through various forms of social "cut-and-try" experimentation. In other words, the design and implementation processes are not clearly differentiated.

Considering these limitations of socio-organizational design, one may well ask: Is managing as designing a realistic proposition? The answer to this question depends in large measure on how we assess the developmental trends. Is the designability of social systems increasing? I believe it is. There are many factors contributing to that increase. I should like to mention three of them.

First, there is the social dynamic itself. The speed and complexity of social change makes the traditional muddling-through approaches to organization increasingly ineffective and costly. Design is the means of rapid change and adaptation. We are therefore more willing to invest in enhanced designability of social systems and to collaborate to achieve it.

Secondly, our societies are becoming increasingly "technologized." To the extent that technologies are important mediators of social relations, the increased designability within technologies brings with it enhanced designability of the social systems themselves. This seems to be particularly true of the information and communication technologies.

Thirdly, information technologies are improving designability in all domains because they facilitate symbolic representations of complex systems. I think it would be interesting to develop the notion of social design as the process of consensus building and conflict resolution through the creation and use of shared representations of social systems. The notion of "framing design" as the focus of communicative interaction is worth pursuing.

Stankiewicz, R. 2000. The concept of "design space." In *Technological innovation as an evolutionary process*, edited by J. Ziman. Cambridge, UK: Cambridge University Press.

Stankiewicz, R. 2002. The cognitive dynamics of biotechnology and the evolution of its technological system. In *New technological systems in the bio-industry—An international study*, edited by Bo Carlsson. Boston, MA: Kluwer Academic Publishers.

36

Public Policy as a Form of Design

Bo Carlsson

I'd rather be vaguely right than precisely wrong.
John Maynard Keynes

THE PUBLIC POLICY DESIGN PROBLEM

How do you design a public policy (or corporate strategy) when you cannot specify the goal?

Public policy makers and corporate decision makers usually assume that they can identify the goals of the entity for which they are responsible, that they have or can acquire the know-how to reach those goals, and that they can therefore design efficient policies and procedures. These assumptions hold for most classes of problems. But what if this model is precisely wrong, that is, what if these assumptions do not hold?

How can you make sensible policy or strategy in a nondeterministic, evolutionary, and highly complex world, that is, a world where the most desirable outcomes are unknown but there may be many possible acceptable outcomes, where change is characterized by both path dependence and unpredictability, and where there are many diverse components, interaction, and feedback among components and multiple dimensions to each problem? This is the design problem with respect to public policy.

For example, can you design an innovation system or industrial cluster such as that in Silicon Valley? The literature suggests that there are few, if any, examples of successful clusters having been initiated by public policy, but also that public policy can play a supportive role once a cluster gets started

Bo Carlsson, *Weatherhead School of Management, Case Western Reserve University.*

260   (see, e.g., Bresnahan, Gambardella, and Saxenian, 2001). Silicon Valley is a good example. The factors that gave rise to the cluster (a favorable climate for entrepreneurship, suitable corporate culture, a high degree of connectivity among the key players, excellent relations between academia and industry, and so on) became apparent only after the cluster had taken off. To the extent that public policy played a role, it was certainly not by prior design.

Why are some high-tech clusters more successful than others? Why do some regions grow in a particular high-tech field while others don't? What is the role of public policy, and what are the design features of successful policies?

THE EXPERIMENTALLY ORGANIZED ECONOMY

Standard (neoclassical) economic theory is not well suited to dynamic problems of this nature. Instead, what is needed is a different kind of theory.

Schumpeter (1911) argued that economic growth is a result of new combinations of products, processes, markets, sources of supply, and organizations. It is essentially a matter of experimental creation of a variety of ideas, some of which result in new technologies that are confronted with potential buyers (customers) in dynamic markets and hierarchies. Thus, economic growth results from the interaction between a variety of actors who create and use technology and demanding customers.

Greater connectivity among actors and ideas creates more possible combinations. The economy is a system consisting of elements and connections. "When connections change, so too does the structure of the system. When structure changes, the dynamic properties of the system change also. This changes the conditions under which connections exist; new ones may form, existing ones may fail or may even become strengthened" (Potts, 2001, p. 2). Technological change occurs when the relationships among elements change or when new connections are established. Densely connected systems give rise to a large set of technical possibilities (a large state space) whereas more sparsely connected systems create fewer possibilities.

This understanding of the modern economy is quite similar to the Eliasson concept of an experimentally organized economy, EOE (Eliasson and Eliasson, 1996). In contrast to standard economic theory, EOE incorporates a virtually unlimited set of technical possibilities as well as bounded cognition and rationality. This combination makes it impossible to identify *all* possibilities (i.e., optimization is not possible); mistakes are common; and more experiments lead to a larger number of technical possibilities.

Certain environments are more supportive of experimentation than others. What are the features of such environments? Can they be designed?

It is useful to think of the environment as an innovation system. Although several types of innovation systems have been examined in the literature, the notion of a technological system (Carlsson and Stankiewicz, 1991; Carlsson, 1995, 1997, 2002) has the advantage that it focuses on a particular technology or set of technologies and incorporates all the actors (not just those in the market), the networks through which they interact, and the institutional infrastructure. Thus, technological systems constitute frameworks that support the supply of innovations that give rise to new business opportunities. One of the functions of a technological system is to provide connections among various elements of the system.

There are three dimensions to technological systems: (1) a *cognitive dimension* defining the clustering of technologies resulting in a new set of technological possibilities; (2) an *organizational and institutional dimension* capturing the interactions in the network of actors engaged in the creation of these technologies; and (3) an *economic dimension* consisting of the set of actors who convert technological possibilities into business opportunities.

Technology can be interpreted as a set of combinatorial *design spaces* formed by *clusters of complementary technical capabilities* (Stankiewicz, 2002). Design spaces undergo constant evolution. There are three modes of technological growth (accumulation) in the design spaces: (1) expansion of the space through the *addition of new capabilities*; (2) progressive *integration and structuring* of the design spaces through the coevolution of its various elements; and (3) *accumulation of application-specific know-how* linked to the evolutionary trajectories of particular artifacts, such as, for instance, aircraft.

When the design space changes, the elements of the organizational and institutional dimension also change: individual actors, networks, organizations such as universities, research institutes, public agencies, and institutions in the form of regulations, standards, and so on. Some elements are no longer relevant, some change, and new ones are added. As a result, the connections among the elements also change.

THE DEMAND SIDE: COMPETENCE BLOC

The greater the connectivity (density) of the design space (in both the cognitive and organizational dimension), the greater is the possibility of identification of technical possibilities (innovation) that can be converted into business opportunities. The role of entrepreneurs is to identify profitable innovations among all the technical possibilities and convert them into business opportunities. In order to do so, entrepreneurs need support in the form of finance,

262   especially venture capital. To facilitate redeployment of resources and ownership changes, well-functioning exit markets (such as an IPO market) are needed. Collectively, competent customers, innovators, entrepreneurs, venture capitalists, exit markets, and industrialists who take successful innovations to large-scale production may be referred to as a competence bloc (Eliasson and Eliasson, 1996). Whereas the technological system is defined from the technology supply side, the competence bloc constitutes the demand or market side. Both are elements of the EOE.

The conversion of new possibilities into profitable business opportunities is by no means automatic. Only when the actors in the technological systems and competence blocs interact with each other closely and frequently enough do the new technical possibilities result in economic growth. The greater the number and variety of actors with different beliefs and expectations, the greater are the chances that new ideas will result in economic growth. Institutions (such as markets and technological systems) reduce the costs of certain transactions by establishing powerful connections (Loasby, 2001, p. 407).

DESIGN OF POLICY

What, then, are the conditions that are conducive to the creation of a variety of new ideas? How can policies be designed that are both necessary and sufficient for effective and efficient selection and retention of winners?

Previous research suggests some basic features of technological systems that are successful in generating new ideas. Sometimes the first and most important policy objective is to remove obstacles to creativity and to foster entrepreneurship rather than to take new initiatives. The formation of new clusters can be facilitated but not directed. Planning cannot replace the imaginative spark that creates innovation. However, once clusters form, a comprehensive set of facilitating policies, from information provision and networking to revision of existing tax codes, regulations, labor laws, and so forth may be necessary.

Three types of facilitating policies stand out. One consists of measures designed to *increase absorptive capacity or receiver competence.* Absorptive capacity refers to the ability of actors within the system to identify new technical possibilities and convert them into business opportunities. This capacity is increased on the part of private actors through research and development, hiring of competent personnel, training of personnel, and accumulation of experience. Clearly, public policy can play a supportive role here. The concern of public sector actors lies not only in influencing the educational system and university research and development but also in avoiding "lock-in" to long-established technologies.

National innovation systems and technological specialization of countries change only very gradually and — especially in newer and rapidly evolving sectors — much more slowly than the technological needs of firms (Narula, 2000). Thus, firms need to acquire the best technology from wherever it is available. Public policies that impede this are not conducive to the nurturing of successful clusters. On the other hand, policies that stimulate and support the buildup of absorptive capacity in key technologies on a regional basis can be highly effective.

The second type of facilitating public policy involves *increased connectivity* among the players in the system: increasing the number and intensity of linkages — among businesses, between business and academia, and among these and policy agencies — and stimulating international linkages of all actors. Bridging institutions, including public and semipublic agencies, can play a role here.

The third type of public policy is oriented more to the demand or market side than to the supply side (creation of new technologies). This type of policy *promotes entrepreneurship and encourages variety*, ensuring the completeness of the competence bloc. No chain is stronger than its weakest link. All functions of the competence bloc must be in place (competent customers, innovators, entrepreneurs, venture capitalists, exit markets, and industrialists). Otherwise, new technical possibilities will not be identified as business opportunities, and business opportunities will not be exploited and yield economic growth. Given the risk and uncertainty associated with each link in the chain, the greater the number of players, each with uncertain and divergent beliefs about the chances of success, the greater are the chances of successful outcomes. This is a game of effectiveness, not efficiency. Let the market (or the public), not bureaucrats, select the successful projects.

Thus, an appropriate role of public policy is to create incentives to filling gaps (removing incompleteness) of competence blocs, removing bottlenecks, achieving critical mass, and addressing deficiencies in the entrepreneurial climate. Policy should focus on making entrepreneurship easy. The higher the opportunity cost of entrepreneurship, the lower the quality of entrepreneur because the process becomes driven by adverse selection. In the extreme, the only agents willing to undertake entrepreneurship are those who cannot do anything else. This means that public policy should reduce the costs of failure, for example, by easing the effects of bankruptcy.

Even though national borders may form natural geographic boundaries of technological systems, not all institutions, organizations, and policies within those boundaries are equally relevant for all technological systems. In the policy arena, the appropriate configurations of policy measures differ from one

264   system to another and also vary for each system over time. In the early, formative phase of a technological system there may be a need to create awareness of new opportunities, increase absorptive capacity, and increase connectivity by fostering a sense of community. In a later phase, the greatest need may be to promote entrepreneurship. As the system matures, it may be necessary to encourage variety in order to avoid lock-in to incumbent firms and stagnant technologies. Thus, one policy does not fit all needs, and the policy makers must be flexible and sensitive to varied and changing requirements: a light touch rather than a heavy hand. Otherwise, following Keynes's dictum, the policy is likely to be precisely wrong.

REFERENCES

Bresnahan, T., A. Gambardella, and A. Saxenian. 2001. "Old economy" inputs for "new economy" outcomes: Cluster formation in the new Silicon Valleys. *Industrial and Corporate Change*, 10(4): 835–60.

Carlsson, B., ed. 1995. *Technological systems and economic performance: The case of factory automation.* Boston/Dordrecht/London: Kluwer Academic Publishers.

———. 1997. *Technological systems and industrial dynamics.* Boston/Dordrecht/London: Kluwer Academic Publishers.

———. 2002. *New technological systems in the bio industries—An international study.* Boston/Dordrecht/London: Kluwer Academic Publishers.

Carlsson, B., and R. Stankiewicz. 1991. On the nature, function, and composition of technological systems. *Journal of Evolutionary Economics*, 1(2): 93–118.

Eliasson, G., and Å. Eliasson. 1996. The biotechnological competence bloc. *Revue d'Economie Industrielle*, 78 (4), Trimestre, 7–26.

Loasby, B. 2001. Time, knowledge and evolutionary dynamics: Why connections matter. *Journal of Evolutionary Economics*, 11(4): 393–412.

Narula, R. 2000. Explaining "inertia" in R&D internationalization: Norwegian firms and the role of home-country effects. Working paper, Centre for Technology, Innovation and Culture, University of Oslo.

Potts, J. 2001. *The new evolutionary microeconomics: Complexity, competence and adaptive behaviour.* Cheltenham, UK: Edward Elgar.

Schumpeter, J. 1911. (English edition 1934). *The theory of economic development.* Harvard Economic Studies. Vol. XLVI. Cambridge, MA: Harvard University Press.

Stankiewicz, R. 2002. The cognitive dynamics of biotechnology and the evolution of its technological system. In *New technological systems in the bio industries—An international study*, edited by B. Carlsson. Boston/Dordrecht/London: Kluwer Academic Publishers, 35–52.

37

Toward a Design Vocabulary
for Management

Richard J. Boland Jr. and Fred Collopy

NOBEL LAUREATE Herbert Simon and the many contributed chapters in this book give us an appreciation of the following:

Design is one of the three required competencies for being an effective manager.

We do not take design seriously enough in our teaching of or research on management.

Design is the giving of form to ideas and the shaping of alternative courses of action in a problem space.

Our language shapes the problem spaces we deal with by naming them. A name frames the situation being faced as being of a familiar type and thereby both enables and constrains our thinking about it.

We use language with either a design or a decision attitude during problem-solving episodes.

The problem spaces we name contain the solutions we will find by enabling and constraining our search for answers.

The problem attitude we use limits the set of the possible solutions in a problem space that we will develop as a solution.

Taken together, these mean that our language is crucial in constructing the situations we face, the ways we deal with them, and the kinds of solutions we can expect to achieve. In short, language matters.

A cursory view of current conditions shows us that for fifty years, manage-

Richard J. Boland Jr., *Weatherhead School of Management, Case Western Reserve University, and Judge Institute of Management, University of Cambridge.* Fred Collopy, *Weatherhead School of Management, Case Western Reserve University.*

266 ment education and management practice have promoted a decision attitude and a decision vocabulary that has, to a great extent, marginalized the design attitude and suppressed the emergence of a design vocabulary in the language of management.

Ironically, it was Herbert Simon who was one of the key inspirations for the development of the decision attitude and decision vocabulary that predominates today. We have taken just a part of his message seriously, reflecting our own "bounded rationality," which was Simon's way of characterizing the limited rational capacity of the human mind. He was awarded the Nobel Prize for showing how bounded rationality operates in all human activity, especially in the economic realm. It is time to correct the long-term effects of having marginalized design thinking in management

The language of management was powerfully depicted in the writings of Sir Geoffrey Vickers, who served for many years as director of the British Coal Board. He wrote beautifully about *The Art of Judgment* as it is exercised by managers and policy makers in their decision making. Like Simon, he focused on the importance of language and, in particular, how managers use a language that equates progress with growth and expansion. He argued that the relentless search for increase as a measure of betterment was misguided because all management decisions are always a question of balancing multiple, conflicting priorities and goals. He wrote from his own experience how a language of balance, tension, and mutual achievement was more productive, humane, and moral than one of progress, growth, and increase. In essence, if we strive for balance among valid competing tensions through the art of judgment, growth and progress will follow. But if we strive for growth and increase, we will undoubtedly create unbalanced, unsustainable organizational futures. We propose that a design attitude is the best way to accomplish Vickers's call for appreciative judgment in management.

One cannot separate values from language and language use. The language of decision and increase, which dominates in business and politics today, is inherently antagonistic to the language of design and balance. What is seen to be good by the one is seen to be bad by the other. Speed and decisiveness in approaching a problem are prized by a decision attitude, but they are carefully avoided by a design attitude. Sweeping in as many influences as possible in seeking a balanced design is seen as a good thing but is a tragic mistake for an efficient decision.

We believe, as our colleague David Cooperrider has often said, that "words are fateful—words make worlds." This is an enduring theme of the sociological movement of the late twentieth century known as *The Social Construction of Reality*, from the classic book written by Peter Berger and Thomas Luckmann. At the same time, we know from the work of Ludwig Wittgenstein, perhaps the greatest modern philosopher, that words do not simply point to things, but are used by people to accomplish things in their everyday activity, or their forms of life. He referred to the process of using language in our forms of life as *language games*, and showed how words always have multiple meanings, which are always only found in their actual use. So we do not foolishly propose that adopting a few new words into the vocabulary of management will change behaviors, meanings, and outcomes by itself. Words must be used in action of a certain sort in order to be a part of change, and that is why we emphasize the importance of a design attitude to guide management problem solving.

A new vocabulary plus a new attitude in use can exert a force for change, and that is what we hope to achieve with this book. The words we offer below are an initial design vocabulary for management. They highlight words that are in the chapters of this book, as well as words that were discussed during the workshop. Some words are familiar to the decision attitude, which prevails in management education and practice, but take a new meaning and use with a design attitude. Where that is the case, we show the different uses employed by the different attitudes.

AN INITIAL DESIGN VOCABULARY FOR MANAGEMENT

Agonize

To agonize is to be more than just worried or concerned about an issue. It is an emotional struggle with the competing forces and demands of the situation and indicates an intense level of care about the right course of action. One agonizes about a problem because one knows that there are multiple, conflicting criteria and no identifiably "true" answer. One must act, even though one does not have a sense of comfort that the alternative chosen is the best that could have been achieved. It also connotes an emotional, visceral commitment to find the best solution, an enduring uncertainty as to whether it has been achieved, and the feeling that one's reputation is on the line to achieve it. Problems that one agonizes about are fundamental to a professional identity and a sense of responsibility for living up to one's own standards.

Artifact

The tangible result from a design process is an artifact—a product, process, communication, or technique that we have designed. Appropriate use of the term helps us to realize how much of the organizational world is designed by managers, either consciously or unconsciously. Managers are responsible for their artifacts and should consider whether they are well designed or not.

Balance

A good design solution always reflects a balance of competing demands among user needs, the environment, future generations, resource capacities, real costs, and the unique historical tensions of the situation. Human judgment is the only way to achieve balance, and human judgment is an art developed over time by one who takes a designer's responsibility for shaping the world that others must live in.

Borrow

To borrow ideas and approaches in design work is commonplace. And an awareness of those elements of a design that are being taken from another project, another colleague, or another sphere of human activity is helpful in creating good design solutions. Designs almost always display borrowing because the slate is never blank at the beginning of a project, and all ideas and design elements are ultimately related to others. The important thing is to recognize what one is borrowing from other designs and situations, so that one can reflect on the appropriateness of using it, rather than inventing a new approach for this situation.

Boundary Object

A boundary object is an artifact (for example, prototype, report, pictorial representation, model) that serves as an intermediary in communication between two or more persons or groups who are collaborating in work. The phrase connotes that the object is a symbolic carrier of multiple meanings, which the parties to the interaction can use as a basis for productive interaction. A boundary object allows parties with diverse interests to raise the possible meanings it has for them in a conversation of discovery. It serves as a stimulus to a sense-making process rather than a message in a communicative exchange.

Circulation (also Path)

People experience organizations, systems, and policies as paths through the social and economic landscape. They affect human interaction by encouraging the use of certain actions and inhibiting others. People interact with each other as they follow paths through the systems in which they live and work and experience those systems as the paths they follow, not as the grand logic that a system designer may have had for them, whether it is a building, a software system, a reward and promotion system, a logistics system, or a departmental structure.

Client

A designer always has a client and is always producing a product or service for that client. A client is indispensable to the statement of the design project and the setting of the design problem. Every manager and every worker in an organization has a client who should be taken into account in defining what projects and what purposes are being or should be served.

Collaboration

A path-creating design will necessarily involve collaboration among partners who each bring unique expertise and talents to the project. Without collaboration across boundaries of disciplines, organizations, and perspectives, a design project has limited possibilities for invention of new solutions.

Constraint

Every project has constraints that serve to give boundaries to a problem. In a decision attitude, constraints are seen as undesirable, but to a design attitude, constraints are the elements of challenge in the problem situation. They can serve as stimuli to the invention of new approaches and to the creative adaptation of materials, techniques, and practices from other domains. When one identifies the constraints of a design problem, one is defining the problem.

Crystallize

A design project becomes crystallized when the basic structure and form of the solution, as well as the materials, technologies, and processes to be employed in the design, have been decided upon. Once a project is crystallized, the ability to revise elements of the design is greatly reduced, without incurring substantial extra costs. In general, a decision attitude moves toward crystallization too quickly.

Default

The most familiar and expected solution to a design problem is the default solution. It is often the first thing that comes to mind and is related to the logic of path dependency. For instance, the default executive office has a large desk

270   facing the door, with a window behind it and several seats in front of it for visitors. Organizational systems that follow commonly encountered standard operating procedures are default systems. Default solutions are often the safest organizationally, but are usually the least effective in creating an advantage for the firm. Being aware that default ideas will be generated first in a design process can make it easier to reject them and search beyond them for higher payoff, path-creating solutions.

Dialogue

Design problems, which contain multiple, conflicting objectives, cannot usually be solved by the logic of one person alone. To achieve a good solution, dialogue among the actors in the design process is usually required, if not to develop the design ideas, then to explore dimensions of the best alternative.

Drawing (also Sketch)

Drawing is a mode of thinking that is especially appropriate for design work. To draw, freehand and quickly, is to let your ideas take shape in a holistic, intuitive process of thought that flows among elements of the design problem. Drawing can create an especially effective boundary object because a drawing is tentative, evocative and depicts relations of the whole.

Emotion (also Energy, Excitement, and Feeling)

Designing is one managerial activity that openly and enthusiastically includes emotion as a part of its process and as a part of its product. The emotional content of a design brings it a human meaning. It is the basis upon which people experience a design as being truly meaningful in their lives. For an organization design, it is the difference between a mediocre and a high-performing organization. A design without emotional content is dead and will not serve to enhance organizational performance. A design is truly functional only if it includes an emotional reaction by its users. Designers who are emotionally connected to their design process can agonize about certain aspects of the design in a genuine way.

Experiment (also Invention)

Unless one is following a path-dependent, default approach to a design problem, one will necessarily become involved in experiment and invention. Whenever a designer cannot simply draw upon a standard set of elements (materials, technologies, work practices, calculations, and so forth) in a design project, experiment will be necessary. Experiments should be done with a self-reflective awareness of how one is performing as a scientist in drawing on a theory, posing a hypothesis, and testing for the results. If you are not experimenting and inventing new materials, processes, systems, or technologies, you are following a default solution and should be openly aware of that fact.

Fit

The designer senses a better alternative through a sense of fit. Fit refers to the way that the materials, technologies, logics, objectives, timing, scale, and scope of a design work together in harmony to support the overall purpose of the design project. If an element of the design gives the feeling that it does not fit, it is probably inappropriate. A sense of fit, like an aesthetic judgment, is a subjective matter and should not be relinquished to a technique of calculation.

Form

The overall structure of an artifact is its form. A building, organization, technology, or process has a form to which actors within it respond. The form of an artifact can shape the types of activities that take place within it or in interaction with it, by enabling and constraining the sets of actions, expectations, values, and assumptions of its users.

Functional

Functional is the ultimate criterion of success in a design project. It denotes not just that a design is efficient and effective, but that it relates appropriately to human emotion, ecological sustainability, the cultural history of the organization and society at large, and the multiple contexts in which it will interact or that it will affect.

Gesture

A gesture is an organizing element of a design that serves to distinguish it from other possible solutions to the same design problem. A gesture gives a unique feel to the structure of a design and serves as a marker for sensemaking by its users. It also conveys the aesthetic that guides a design and helps to set the vocabulary that will be carried through a design. In an organizational context, a rule that all employees have the same benefit system would be a gesture.

Goal (in relation to Purpose)

A design problem must have a goal or it will not be a viable design project. The goal should be open-ended (as in a purpose) rather than specific, so that it can serve as the basis for posing an ideal that is sought in the design. This allows the design problem to be one that calls for one's best efforts to strive beyond default solutions and, at the same time, gives a ground for making design judgments of fit, balance, and functionality.

Groundlessness

A designer experiences groundlessness in the sense that she is uniquely responsible for a project in which the problem definition, criteria for success, and standards of evaluation are all without an objective reference point. Every aspect of the design project could be other than it is without violating an incontrovertible rule and is radically dependent on the subjectivity of the designer.

Handrail

Any new design will inevitably seem strange to its users at first encounter. A design should explain itself to its users and convey a feeling of comfort and welcome. It should provide a handrail for those engaging it so that the unfamiliar can become familiar without causing undue stress.

Improvise

Using objects, resources, and structures that are readily at hand for a purpose other than that which they are normally intended is improvisation. As in music, it connotes a playful and skillful working with elements in a novel way to achieve a desirable outcome. Avoiding a default solution and achieving a path-creating design solution will almost always require improvisation.

Iteration

Moving through the design process again, after an initial solution has been proposed, is iteration. Iteration can keep a problem open by resisting the tendency to fall in love with the ideas of the solution as developed thus far and by proposing an alternative approach. Or, iteration can begin to crystallize a solution by adding refinement and working out subproblems inherent in the solution being considered.

Liquid

When a design problem is open as to its form, technologies, and materials, it is liquid. During the liquid state, a design problem is open to many possible directions in its solution and serves as a vehicle for wide-ranging explorations and dialogue. Keeping a design problem in a liquid state is difficult but essential if a best design solution is being sought. Without an effort to the contrary, a design problem will too quickly become crystallized, and inquiry into the best solution will be constrained.

Love

The human experience of love is fundamental to the creation and appreciation of designs. We do things because we love to, and we feel that design ideas are good ones because we fall in love with them. Humans often fall in love with the first good idea they develop and can become blinded to other possibilities. A designer has to maintain a constant tension between loving an alternative he is exploring, so that he can approach it with true passion, and resisting falling in love with an alternative until he has explored a sufficient number of them.

Model

A model is a physical or virtual representation of a possible solution to a design problem. A model serves as a boundary object during project work and also allows for a process of thinking with one's hands, both during model construction and also when manipulating the model. Good design does not confuse the model for the thing being designed and treats the model as a vehicle for thinking and exploring ideas. In the early stages of a design project, the expectation should be that the model will be replaced by something quite different and will not be refined into the design solution.

Opportunistic

Designing involves adaptation to or incorporating elements that surface during work on a project. Search for an improvement in one aspect of a design may lead to an awareness of new ideas, technologies, or processes relevant to another aspect of the design. Being opportunistic enables the designer to recognize the possibilities for some aspect of the project of an unexpected discovery. It requires an openness to consider found objects and initially unrelated ideas as being relevant to the project.

Path Creating

Developing a new, generative, and reinforcing set of relationships among elements in a socioeconomic system is path creating activity. Path creation breaks from the expectations of the familiar , "logical" way of proceeding, based on the self-reinforcing patterns of the past. Path creation is the way to establish sustainable innovations as the elements of a system begin to reinforce each other and lead to a shift in their costs, availability, and functionality, thereby shifting the ideas of what is a "logical" choice in a design problem.

Path Dependent

In any business situation, over time, there will emerge one dominant pattern of problem solving because self-reinforcing relationships of expectations, demand, production costs, logistics, and technologies will form. These self-reinforcing relationships are often the result of chance occurrences or unexpected events, but once established they become seen as the rational way to approach a problem solution, often without regard to the true appropriateness of the solution. Path dependence leads to a sense of economy and efficiency in the reinforced relationships that dominate our understanding of a situation, but often at the expense of the effectiveness of unexplored alternative solutions.

Placeholder

When some aspect of a design is unresolved, it need not stop work on the remainder of the project. A placeholder is often used to show that the designer realizes something is missing or needed in some part of the design, but it has not been identified, invented, or determined yet.

Play

An open, liquid design process involves playing with ideas, alternatives, and elements of the design. The design emerges through playful interaction with materials, models, and alternatives being considered. Playing with meanings, implications, and purposes of a design project can lead to the emergence of unexpected insights or discoveries that can be opportunistically included in the project.

Project

The design process is bounded by or contained within projects. A project has a desired outcome, has a client, and has a beginning and an end. A project has stages beginning with an exploratory definition stage, an initial design concept stage, a detailed design stage, and a construction and implementation stage. The stages are not neatly linear, but are recursive and partially concurrent. The project has a manager who is responsible for its successful completion.

Prototype

A model of the design artifact that is made quickly is a prototype. It serves as a boundary object in testing form, fit, and functionality. A prototype is most effective if it is made to be discarded in a multistage process of posing and evaluating possible approaches to a design solution and not merely as a version to be refined as the final design.

Recycle

Aspects of a design that have worked in the past are often drawn upon again in subsequent projects. This can be a good idea but is dependent on the designer having awareness that they are recycling the elements. Without such an awareness, the designer risks producing a default solution or strengthening a path dependency.

Repertoire

The designer's repertoire consists of those different techniques and approaches to design problems in which she has developed fluency. The size of a designer's vocabulary is usually proportional to the size of her repertoire. A repertoire grows with experience and engagement with different design projects over time. Other things being equal, a larger repertoire is associated with greater probabilities of success in a design project.

Space

A design artifact, whether it is a building, a software system, a financial reporting system, or a personnel evaluation system creates a space that is experienced by people who engage with it. People experience being located within the space and being able to move in it. The experience of space and of movement within space is the basis for experiencing time. The space of an organizational system can be experienced as narrow and confining or broad and expansive. It can be comfortable and inviting or off-putting. It can encourage collegiality or isolation.

Study

A model or prototype of a small element of a design solution that is being explored is a study. Design problems have a nested nature in that each step toward a solution to a design problem raises new, unforeseen problems, the possible solutions to which, in turn, pose other unforeseen problems. Because design problems are in that sense a labyrinth, a design project involves many studies.

Tension

A good design problem has multiple tensions between the competing logics, needs, and goals of its many stakeholders. Engaging those tensions openly and creatively is necessary for good design.

Thrownness

A designer is never in a situation without a history. A situation always already has interested actors, cultural norms, path-dependencies, infrastructures, policies, laws, and expectations related to it that will shape the problem space being addressed.

Vocabulary

A designer approaches problems with a set of images, concepts, sensibilities, tastes, preferences, and logic that have been developed through time and experience. These, plus the words, materials, forms, and logics that a designer employs in a particular design project are referred to as the designer's vocabulary. Designers approach a project with an awareness of their own history and the history of others who have worked on similar problems before. A strong design vocabulary both enables and constrains a designer. Being aware of one's own vocabulary and that of previous work in the area is important for being able to maintain a coherence in one's design as it is developed (by maintaining a coherent vocabulary) and for being able to avoid a default solution (by avoiding clichés).

Contributors

RICHARD J. BOLAND JR. is Professor of Management at Case Western Reserve University and a Senior Research Associate at the Judge Institute of Management at the University of Cambridge. He was founding editor of *Information and Organization* and does qualitative studies of individuals as they design and use information. His interest is in how people make meaning as they interpret situations in an organization or as they interpret data in a report. He has studied this hermeneutic process in a wide range of settings and professions, but primarily has focused on how managers and consultants turn an ambiguous situation into a problem statement and declare a particular course of action to be rational. He has approached this in a variety of ways, including symbolic interaction, metaphor, cause mapping, frame shifting, language games, and exegesis. Most recently he is fascinated with narrative and design as modes of cognition that are systematically undervalued, yet dominate our meaning making.

HILARY BRADBURY is an Associate Professor of Organizational Behavior at the Weatherhead School of Management at Case Western Reserve University. Three broad themes are evident in Hilary's research — deep organizational change, action research, and sustainability. Hilary is coeditor with Peter Reason of the *Handbook of Action Research* (Sage, 2000). A forthcoming book by the two will describe in more detail how to engage in action research in the midst of organizational life. In 2000, Hilary was awarded a multiyear NSF grant, along with three colleagues at MIT, to support an action research effort that brings together corporate practitioners, consultants, and researchers interested in speeding up the transition to sustainability of mainstream corporations.

278   RICHARD BUCHANAN is Professor of Design at Carnegie Mellon University where he teaches interaction design, communication planning, and the philosophy and theory of design, with a special interest in the rhetorical thinking that lies behind the human-made world. His research addresses issues of interaction design, verbal and visual communication, communication planning and design, and product development. He is coeditor of *Discovering Design: Explorations in Design Studies, The Idea of Design*, and *Pluralism in Theory and Practice*. He is also editor of the international journal *Design Issues: History, Theory, Criticism*.

BO CARLSSON is the William E. Umstattd Professor of Industrial Economics at the Weatherhead School of Management at Case Western Reserve University. His current research interests include the new economy, entrepreneurship, technology transfer, and the nature and role of innovation systems in economic growth. Since 1987 he has been the director of the research project "Sweden's Technological Systems and Future Development Potential," involving four leading research institutes in Sweden. He has published twenty-two books and numerous articles in industrial economics, small business and entrepreneurship, technological change, and industrial policy. His most recent book, entitled *Technological Systems in the Bio Industries: An International Study*, was published in 2002.

PO CHUNG obtained his BSc from California State University at Humboldt in Fisheries Management in 1968. Upon returning to Hong Kong, he worked with Topper Toys (H.K.) Ltd. as operations manager for two years. In 1972, he cofounded DHL International Limited, together with DHL Airways Inc. of California, which owns and operates DHL services in U.S. territories. These two companies operate the DHL Worldwide Network, which is the world's leading air express company, handling more than 100 million documents, parcels, and freight a year across five continents. He is now Chairman Emeritus of DHL.

FRED COLLOPY is Professor and Chair of the Information Systems department at the Weatherhead School of Management at Case Western Reserve University. He has been designing instruments that enable musicians to play images in the way that musicians play sounds. His Web site at RhythmicLight.com provides illustrations and historical background on the field, whose roots can be traced to 1743 and work inspired by Newton. In 1979, Fred designed *The Desk Organizer*, the first desk management software for personal computers.

In 1989, he designed Rule-Based Forecasting, an approach to business forecasting that used rules derived from forecasting experts to improve upon standard and best forecasting practices. His current research interest is related to how highly interactive instruments are best designed.

NICHOLAS COOK was appointed Professor of Music at the University of Southampton in 1990, becoming a Research Professor in 1999. A musicologist and theorist, he has previously taught at the Universities of Hong Kong (where he was on the foundation staff of the Department of Music) and Sydney, with visiting professorships at Yale University (1994) and Ohio State University (2000). He holds degrees in music and history, and much of his published work has been interdisciplinary in nature. He is editor of the *Journal of the Royal Musical Association*, and his research has appeared in most of the major journals in the field, covering such diverse topics as Beethoven, Liszt, analytical methodology, music in TV commercials, and the aesthetics and psychology of music. His books, most of which are published by Oxford University Press, include *A Guide to Musical Analysis* (1987); *Music, Imagination, and Culture* (1990); *Beethoven: Symphony No. 9* (1993); *Analysis Through Composition* (1996); *Analysing Musical Multimedia* (1998); and *Music: A Very Short Introduction* (1998). Oxford also published *Rethinking Music* (1999), a major collaborative volume coedited with Mark Everist.

PETER COUGHLAN and ILYA PROKOPOFF are coleaders of Transformation by Design, a practice within the IDEO design consultancy that specializes in helping organizations manage complex change using design tools and methods. They are playing a leading role in developing techniques for helping cross-functional teams to rethink their organizational mission, envision new services and practices, and redesign organizational structures to deliver them. They have taken on clients as diverse as Internet start-ups, Native American tribes, chemical manufacturers, governmental funding agencies, multinational food companies, and healthcare organizations. Peter holds a PhD in Applied Linguistics from UCLA, and Ilya holds a PhD from the Media Lab at MIT.

BARBARA CZARNIAWSKA is Professor of Management Studies at the Gothenburg Research Institute. Barbara is currently involved in two major research efforts. The first is a study entitled "Managing Big Cities" and the other is a study of management as the construction and re-construction of action-nets. She has recently been elected to the Swedish Royal Academy of Sciences and

280   in 2000 was awarded the Lily and Sven Thuréus Technical-Economic Award
for internationally renowned research in organization theory. Her books include *A Tale of Three Cities, or the Glocalization of City Management*, Oxford
University Press (2002); *Writing Management: Organization Theory as a Literary Genre*, Oxford University Press (1999); *A Narrative Approach in Organization Studies*, SAGE (1998); and *Narrating the Organization: Dramas of Institutional Identity*, University of Chicago Press (1997).

NIELS DECHOW is on the faculty of the Said School of Business at the University of Oxford. Prior to that, he was Assistant Professor at the Weatherhead
School at Case Western Reserve University. In his teaching, Niels focuses
on modern management control techniques and their organizational implications. His research interests cover interorganizational relationships, the integration of information systems and accounting, and novel approaches to
management education. Prior to receiving his PhD from the Copenhagen
Business School, Niels worked in the consulting industry with base in his native Denmark.

PAUL EICKMANN recently retired as Provost and Vice President for Academic
Affairs at the Cleveland Institute of Art. Prior to that, he served as Vice President for Student Affairs at Syracuse University for nine years, while at the same
time maintaining his teaching at Syracuse University in its Schools of Music,
Education, Management, and Nursing (music as healing).

YRJÖ ENGESTRÖM is Professor of Adult Education and Director of the Center
for Activity Theory and Developmental Work Research at the University of
Helsinki. He is also Professor of Communication at the University of California, San Diego. Yrjö is known for his theory of expansive learning and studies
transformations in work and organizations, combining microlevel analysis of
discourse and interaction with historical analysis and modeling of organizations as activity systems. His research groups use intervention tools such as the
Change Laboratory, inspired by Vygotsky's method of dual stimulation, to facilitate and analyze the redesign of activity systems by practitioners. Yrjö's recent books include *Cognition and Communication at Work* (edited with David
Middleton, 1996) and *Collaborative Expertise: Expansive Learning in Medical
Work*, Cambridge University Press.

JURGEN FAUST is Professor and Chair of Technology and Integrated Media
(T.I.M.E.) at the Cleveland Institute of Art. Jurgen teaches digital arts and design and 2D/3D design. As a practicing artist and designer, he shows his work

widely in Europe and the United States. In 1983, he cofounded a private art school in Germany (Freie Hochschule Metzingen), where he was the co-director for sixteen years and was responsible for the development of several programs. Between 1996 and 1999, he was the acting Dean of New Media. In this position, he designed a new digital art and design program. For many years, he has been working on a theory of sculpture. He applies this theory also in the area of managing organizations.

KEVIN GALLAGHER is a recent PhD from the Weatherhead School who studied under Betty Vandenbosch. He is currently at the University of South Florida.

FRANK O. GEHRY is one of the most highly renowned architects of our day, and Case is proud to have one of his greatest buildings as the home of its Weatherhead School of Management. In an article published in the *New York Times* in November 1989, noted architecture critic Paul Goldberger wrote that Mr. Gehry's "buildings are powerful essays in primal geometric form and . . . materials, and from an aesthetic standpoint they are among the most profound and brilliant works of architecture of our time." Hallmarks of his work include a particular concern that people exist comfortably within the spaces that he creates and an insistence that his buildings address the context and culture of their sites. Frank has won numerous awards for his work, including the Pritzker Architecture Prize in 1989, perhaps the premiere accolade of the field, honoring "significant contributions to humanity and the built environment through the art of architecture."

JOSEPH A. GOGUEN has been a Professor in the Department of Computer Science and Engineering at the University of California, San Diego, since January 1996. He is Director of the Meaning and Computation Lab and was previously Director of the Program in Advanced Manufacturing. Prior to that, he was at SRI International holding the positions of Senior Staff Scientist and Senior Member of the Center for the Study of Language and Information at Stanford University. Joseph's research interests include: software engineering; database integration and ontologies; user interface design; theorem proving; discourse analysis; sociology of technology and science; object-oriented, relational, and functional programming and their combinations; semiotics; and fuzzy logic.

JULIA GRANT is Associate Professor of Accountancy at the Weatherhead School of Management, Case Western Reserve University. She was on the fac-

282   ulty of The Ohio State University prior to joining Weatherhead in 1991. Her research interests include developing a greater understanding of how to effectively use financial information about a firm. These interests have led to several research projects examining the reports of financial analysts and the disclosure policies of corporations. She also has published several papers applying game theoretic social dilemma settings and their effects on group and policy outcomes. Julia has been interviewed concerning various accounting scandals and their aftermath and cited in many national media outlets, including the *Wall Street Journal*, the *New York Times*, National Public Radio, Bloomberg News, *News Hour with Jim Lehrer*, and *Business Week*.

KEITH HOSKIN is Professor of Strategy and Accounting at the Warwick Business School. He has studied classics, modern languages, educational psychology, and history and was previously in the field of educational history. There, his major interest was in learning and why we know so little about it and usually fail to talk about it. His interest in how we learn to learn led to an interest in how practices such as writing and examining shape our learning to learn and therefore our categories of "real learning." His major research interests now are in the relation among accounting, accountability, and management practices. This work also leads him into such areas as the nature of sign systems, modes of valuing, and translation. His major current area of work is in the invention of modern management as manifestation of our modern forms of disciplinary practice and is being developed as a book with Richard Macve, *Powerful Knowledge*.

MARIANN JELINEK is at the College of William and Mary in Williamsburg, Virginia, where she has been Richard C. Kraemer Professor of Business since 1989. She recently completed service as Director of the Innovation and Organizational Change Program at the National Science Foundation, on loan from her regular duties. Her career interests include innovation, technology, and their strategic implications; organization learning; and administrative systems and organization design, which are topics on which she has written extensively. Prior academic appointments include the Weatherhead School of Management at Case Western Reserve University, where she held the Lewis-Progressive Chair; the State University of New York at Albany; McGill University; and Dartmouth College. She is author or coauthor of five books, including *Innovation Marathon* with C. B. Schoonhoven, and forty papers, including the 1995 "Best Paper of the Year" in Entrepreneurship: Theory and Practice.

STEN JÖNSSON is Professor and Director of the Göteborg Research Institute and is studying communication in multicultural management teams. His research covers a broad spectrum — development and strategy issues (organizational crises, myths as management tools, budget processes) and regulation of good accounting practice; the use of economic information in the management of operations and the interaction between local and central units in large organizations; and most recently, management style and competitiveness and the evaluation of the decentralization reform in the city of Gothenburg. Sten has written more than ten books and published twenty-five articles in leading scientific journals.

PAUL KAISER is a digital artist whose work has been exhibited at Lincoln Center, MASS MoCA, the Barbican Center (London), the Pompidou Center, SIGGRAPH, the Wexner Center for the Arts, and many other venues. He has received numerous awards. Kaiser's early art (1975–81) was in experimental filmmaking and voice audiotapes. He then spent ten years teaching students with severe learning disabilities, with whom he collaborated on making multimedia depictions of their own minds. He later applied this approach to an interactive documentary on Robert Wilson's early work entitled *Visionary of Theater* (1994–97). Recently Kaiser has created the virtual dances *Hand-drawn Spaces* (1998) and *BIPED* (1999), both with Merce Cunningham and Shelley Eshkar, and *Ghostcatching* (1999), with Bill T. Jones and Shelley Eshkar. Recent solo works include *Flicker-track* + *Verge* (both 1999–2000). Kaiser currently teaches a virtual filmmaking class at Wesleyan University and serves as an Osher Fellow at the Exploratorium Museum in San Francisco.

JOHN LESLIE KING is Professor and Dean of the School of Information at the University of Michigan. His research includes the problems of developing high-level requirements for information systems design and implementation in strongly institutionalized production sectors. The goal of this work is to improve the design of information technologies and to inform policy and strategy development at the firm, sectoral, and institutional levels. Recent and current projects focus on the role of technical and institutional forces in the coevolutionary development of intermodal transport and logistics, case management in felony criminal courts, global wireline and wireless telephony, and the transition of the automobile industry from product to service sector. New projects include a study of the institutional forces involved in the development of global electronic commerce and a historical analysis of the evolution of the information disciplines.

284   ALICE KOLB is Vice President of Research and Development, Experience Based Learning Systems and Director of The Ohio Consortium on Artistic Learning's longitudinal outcome study of artistic learning.

DAVID KOLB is Professor of Organizational Behavior at the Weatherhead School of Management, the author of *Experiential Learning*, and the creator of the Learning Style Inventory. His and Alice Kolb's research is focused on development of the theory and practice of experiential learning. Their latest book is *Conversational Learning: An Experiential Approach to Knowledge Creation*.

MIRIAM R. LEVIN is Associate Professor of History at Case Western Reserve University. Her research and teaching interests center on the history of industrial culture, which is a transatlantic phenomenon with global impact. She also works on the history of science education in the United States. She has published several books and articles on this subject. Currently, she is working on a book on the idea of control in the industrial era, as well as editing a collection of essays on that subject by other authors with a foreword by Thomas Hughes.

JEANNE LIEDTKA is Associate Professor of Business Administration at the Darden School. She also serves as Vice President and Chief Learning Officer for United Technologies Corporation, designing and directing its education, training, and development programs. Her current research interests involve the diffusion of strategic thinking capabilities to all organizational levels. Liedtka joined the Darden faculty in 1992. She has also taught at Rutgers University, IESE, and Simmons College. Previously she was affiliated with the Boston Consulting Group, Wang Labs, and Johnson & Johnson, Inc.

KALLE LYYTINEN is Professor of Information Systems at the Weatherhead School of Management at Case Western Reserve University and an adjunct professor at the University of Jyvaskyla in Finland. He teaches advanced degree students and executives on topics related to systems development, risk management, and electronic and mobile commerce. His educational background includes computer science, accounting, statistics, economics, theoretical philosophy, and political theory. He has published eight books, more than fifty journal articles, and more than eighty conference presentations and book chapters. He is well known for his research in computer-supported system design and modeling, system failures and risk assessment, computer-supported cooperative work, and the diffusion of complex technologies. He is

currently researching the development and management of digital services
and the evolution of virtual communities.

WANDA J. ORLIKOWSKI is Professor of Information Technologies and Organization Studies at MIT's Sloan School of Management and the Eaton-Peabody Chair of Communication Sciences at MIT. She received a PhD from the Stern School of Business at New York University. In examining the organizational changes associated with the use of information technology, Wanda investigates the ongoing relationship between information technologies and organizing structures, work practices, communication, culture, and control mechanisms. She has conducted extensive studies on the use of groupware technologies and electronic media in organizations, and she has explored the social and technological aspects of working virtually. She is currently leading a five-year project on the social and economic implications of Internet technology use in organizations.

JOSEPH A. PARADISO joined the MIT Media Laboratory in 1994, where he is now Associate Professor of Media Arts and Sciences, directing the Responsive Environments Group. He is an expert on sensing technology for human-computer interfaces, having developed and fielded a wide variety of systems that track human activity using electric field sensing, microwaves, ultra-low-cost laser ranging, passive and active sonar, piezoelectrics, and resonant electromagnetic tags. His work has found application in areas such as interactive music systems, wearable computers, smart highways, and medical instrumentation. He is also serving as codirector of the Things That Think Consortium. In addition to his physics career, Joe has been designing electronic music synthesizers and composing electronic music since 1975, and he has long been active in the avant-garde music scene as a producer of electronic music programs for noncommercial radio. He has built (and still uses) one of the world's largest modular synthesizers and has designed MIDI systems for internationally known musicians such as Pat Metheny and Lyle Mays.

ALAN PRESTON is the former Second Commissioner of Taxation for the Australian Taxation Office. Following an early career as an academic economist, Alan joined the Australian Public Service in 1979. His commitment to design emerged from his professional responsibilities in relation to the Australian taxation system during the period from 1986 until he retired early in 1992. With Richard Buchanan's assistance as design mentor, Alan focused his tenure as Second Commissioner of Taxation on establishing and consolidating the Integrated Taxation Design Project as the vehicle for implementing the Review's

286   recommendations about tax system design. The objective has been to harness the disciplined creativity of design in the systematic management and delivery of much more satisfying tax system outcomes.

RIKARD STANKIEWICZ is Professor of Science and Technology Governance at the European University Institute in Florence. He studied at Warsaw University and subsequently at Lund University in Sweden where he received a PhD in sociology. In 1998, he became Professor of Science and Technology Policy and the director of Research Policy Institute at Lund University. He has conducted research on the organization and management of research and development in both public and private sectors, university and industry relations, comparative science and technology policy, and technological innovation systems. His most recent research and publications are concerned with the evolutionary models of technological change, science technology-relations, the structure and dynamics of the knowledge base of technology, and the impact of the new biotechnologies on innovation in the healthcare sector.

LUCY SUCHMAN is Professor of Anthropology of Science and Technology at Lancaster University, having come there after twenty years as a researcher at Xerox's Palo Alto Research Center. Her research has centered on relations of ethnographies of everyday practice to new technology design. She draws on ethnomethodological studies of work, science and technology studies, and feminist theorizing, in order to recover the specific, culturally and materially embodied identities, knowledges, and practices that make up technical systems. This involves, among other things, reconstructing technologies from singular objects located at the center of a surrounding social world, to heterogeneous assemblages of socio-material practices. She and her colleagues have engaged in a series of projects sited in particular workplaces (an airport, a large Silicon Valley law firm, a state department of transportation) that combine ethnographic studies of work and technologies-in-use with the in situ development of new prototype information systems.

ALEXANDER TZONIS holds the chair of Architectural Theory and Design Methods at the University of Technology of Delft and is Director of Design Knowledge Systems, a multidisciplinary research center on architectural cognition. He was educated at Yale University and taught at Harvard University between 1967 and 1981. He has held visiting professorships at MIT, Columbia University, the Universities of Montreal, Strasbourg, Singapore, University of Technology Vienna, the Technion, Israel, and the College de France. Among his publications are *The Shape of Community* with Serge Chermayeff and *To-*

wards a Non-oppressive Environment. He has written more than two hundred
articles on architectural theory, history, and design methods.

BETTY VANDENBOSCH is currently Associate Professor of Information Systems at the Weatherhead School of Management. After completing her MBA, Betty spent seven years working for McKinsey and Company in Toronto and Amsterdam, where she consulted with clients on strategic, organizational, operational, and technology issues. Betty then earned a PhD in Management Information Systems from the Ivey School at the University of Western Ontario. Her research investigates how executives use information to learn through mental model development. Betty has just published her first book, *Designing Solutions for Your Business Problems.*

INA WAGNER is Professor of Multidisciplinary Systems Design and Computer-Supported Co-operative Work and Head of the Institute for Technology Assessment and Design at the Technical University of Vienna. Ina's research reflects a methodological commitment to participatory design and to situated experimentation with prototype solutions in different media. She also engages in sociological research related to work and occupations, organizations and technology, and gender studies. One of her main current interests focuses on the multidisciplinary design of computer systems for architectural design and planning. A particular focus of this research is on understanding the role of different kinds of visual artifacts for cooperative work, in particular, how material and digital artifacts can be combined in complex work environments.

KARL E. WEICK is the Rensis Likert Distinguished University Professor of Organizational Behavior and Psychology at the University of Michigan. He is among the first researchers to appreciate the roles of metaphor and sensemaking in organizational life. He has written extensively on organizations, change, and the methods we use to research them. Titles such as "The Head Nurse as Quasi-Hippie" and "The Aesthetics of Imperfection in Orchestras and Organizations" hint at the engaging style he brings to understanding complex systems. His book *The Social Psychology of Organizing*, first published in 1969 and revised in 1979, was designated one of the nine best business books ever written by *Inc. Magazine*. His current research interests include collective sensemaking under pressure, medical errors, handoffs in extreme events, high reliability performance, improvisation, and continuous change.

YOUNGJIN YOO is Associate Professor of Information Systems at the Weatherhead School of Management. He holds a PhD in information systems from

288   the University of Maryland. He received his MBA and BS in Business Administration from Seoul National University in Seoul, Korea. His research interests include knowledge management in global learning organizations, pervasive computing, and the design of socio-technical information environments for large organizations.

Index

Page numbers in italics refer to figures and tables.

Manager / designer + execution

, rather than origin, of
new ideas.   no problem

from specs to prototypes
user needs to enactment (with tech)
(cooperation, iteration prototyping)

.. small projects, planning for cooperation..